# ROUTLEDGE LIBRARY EDITIONS: CHILDREN'S LITERATURE

Volume 2

CW01096078

# EMPIRE BOYS: ADVENTURES IN A MAN'S WORLD

# EMPIRE BOYS: ADVENTURES IN A MAN'S WORLD

JOSEPH BRISTOW

Routledge
Taylor & Francis Group

LONDON AND NEW YORK

First published in 1991 by HarperCollins*Academic*

This edition first published in 2016
by Routledge
2 Park Square, Milton Park, Abingdon, Oxon OX14 4RN

and by Routledge
711 Third Avenue, New York, NY 10017

*Routledge is an imprint of the Taylor & Francis Group, an informa business*

© 1991 Joseph Bristow

All rights reserved. No part of this book may be reprinted or reproduced or utilised
in any form or by any electronic, mechanical, or other means, now known or
hereafter invented, including photocopying and recording, or in any information
storage or retrieval system, without permission in writing from the publishers.

*Trademark notice*: Product or corporate names may be trademarks or registered
trademarks, and are used only for identification and explanation without intent to
infringe.

*British Library Cataloguing in Publication Data*
A catalogue record for this book is available from the British Library

ISBN: 978-1-138-94397-1 (Set)
ISBN: 978-1-315-66992-2 (Set) (ebk)
ISBN: 978-1-138-94429-9 (Volume 2) (hbk)
ISBN: 978-1-138-95314-7 (Volume 2) (pbk)
ISBN: 978-1-315-66993-9 (Volume 2) (ebk)

**Publisher's Note**
The publisher has gone to great lengths to ensure the quality of this reprint but
points out that some imperfections in the original copies may be apparent.

**Disclaimer**
The publisher has made every effort to trace copyright holders and would welcome
correspondence from those they have been unable to trace.

# Reading Popular Fiction

# EMPIRE BOYS: ADVENTURES IN A MAN'S WORLD

## JOSEPH BRISTOW

HarperCollins*Academic*
An imprint of HarperCollins*Publishers*

© Joseph Bristow, 1991
This book is copyright under the Berne Convention. No
reproduction without permission. All rights reserved.

The author asserts the moral right to be
identified as the author of this work.

Published by
**HarperCollins*Academic***
77-85 Fulham Palace Road
Hammersmith
London W6 8JB
UK


First published in 1991


*British Library Cataloguing in Publication Data*

Bristow, Joseph
  Empire boys : adventures in a man's world.
1.  Children's literature in English – Critical studies
I.  Title     II.  Series
820.99282
ISBN 0–04–445630–1

*Library of Congress Cataloging in Publication Data*

Bristow, Joseph
Empire boys : adventures in a man's world / Joseph Bristow.
        p.      cm. — (Reading popular fiction ; 2)
Includes bibliographical references and index.
ISBN 0–04–445630–1 (HB). — ISBN 0–04–445631–X (PB)
1.  Children's stories, English—History and criticism.
2.  Adventure stories, English—History and criticism.
3.  Boys— Great Britain—Books and reading—History.
4.  Imperialism in literature.
5.  Colonies in literature.
I.  Title.     II.  Series.
PR830.A38B75      1991                                    90–21815
823′.809352054—dc20                                        CIP


Typeset in 10 on 11 point Plantin and printed in Great Britain
by Billing and Sons Ltd., London and Worcester

# Contents

OUR YOUNGEST LINE OF DEFENCE.

Boy Scout (*to Mrs Britannia*) "FEAR NOT, GRANDMA; NO DANGER
CAN BEFALL YOU NOW. REMEMBER, I AM WITH YOU."
(*PUNCH*, 1 September 1909, Vol. 137, p. 147)

# Introduction

*Empire Boys* developed out of two related concerns that became increasingly important for me in the 1980s: first, the emerging (and now considerable) body of writing by men on masculinity;[1] and, second, a felt need to expand my knowledge of British imperial history (I come, in part, from an army officer background). Both interests amounted to political obligations. These particular debates gained prominence in Britain, North America, and Australia, for a variety of not unrelated reasons. One was the belated response by men to feminism. These new writings by radical men were investigating the psychic structures and the cultural histories informing dominant types of Western masculinity. It practically goes without saying that dominant, or hegemonic, masculinity is endorsed by a longstanding genealogy of violence. And it is, perhaps, because of the extraordinary power such masculinity holds over men's lives that it has taken so long for men (notably, heterosexual men), usually aligned on the Left, to question their investments in masculinist practices.

The other reason motivating this study, and its concentration on British imperialism, developed out of a new consciousness of post-coloniality within white cultural politics, where the voice of not only Western masculinity, but of the West per se, was being challenged as never before.[2] Since my academic work was mostly focused within Victorian literary studies, it struck me that I could, to a limited degree, engage with both the debates about masculinity and the concerns of post-colonial critique by examining, in the main, fictions of late nineteenth-century boyhood. I wanted to discover the historical and political processes which gave rise to what might readily be called 'boys' own' adventure – of fearless endeavour in a world populated by savage races, dangerous pirates, and related manifestations of the 'other' to be encountered on voyages towards dark and unexplored continents.

Furthermore, I wished to relate literary analysis to a broader field of social and political forces. In a sense, I have attempted to put together connected parts of a cultural history of imperialist boyhood and manhood. Throughout this study, textual analysis, if mostly focused on fiction, extends to other bodies of writing: parliamentary debates, government reports, and periodical criticism. The intention is to accentuate how literary representations of imperialist maleness belonged to wider discussions of the moral and physical well-being of boys, especially in relation to schooling, health, and military recruitment.

This book is not a chronicle. Although the period covered mostly falls within 1860–1920, the chapters do not follow on from one another in historical sequence. Instead, each chapter focuses on particular formations of boyhood and empire. The first looks at culture, literacy, and so-called 'juvenile' literature; the second at public school fiction; the next two examine changes in the direction of the adventure story: first, the Robinsonade, and second, the African romance. The final chapter analyses the type of heroic boy survivor championed by Baden-Powell, Kipling, and Burroughs at the height of empire. The book moves, stage by stage, from the domestic realm into the imaginary depths of the empire's dark continents. The choice of materials, if attempting to be representative, is necessarily selective. The select bibliography should point readers towards major studies in a wide variety of academic fields which touch on the concerns of this book.

Jonathan Dollimore and Alan Sinfield supported my earliest proposals. Derek Longhurst raised numerous helpful questions about the first draft of the manuscript. My thanks to them, and to the librarians at the Mary Badland Library, Sheffield City Polytechnic, who assisted with a great many inter-library loan requests. The Scout Association kindly granted permission to reprint the figures on pp. 192 and 194.

## Notes

1   There is insufficient room here to list all the major monographs and collections of essays on masculinity by men. A representative sample of this writing can be found in Martin Humphries and Andy

Metcalf, eds, *The Sexuality of Men* (London: Pluto Press, 1983). For an extended review of the achievements and limitations of some of this work, see Joseph Bristow, 'How Men Are: Speaking of Masculinity', *New Formations* 9 (1988), pp. 119–31.

2  Two of the most influential post-colonial voices in literary and cultural studies are Gayatri Chakravorty Spivak and Homi K. Bhabha, both of whom published numerous essays on questions of race, class, and gender in the 1980s. See, for example, Spivak, *In Other Worlds: Essays in Cultural Politics* (London: Methuen, 1987), and Homi K. Bhabha, 'Representation and the Colonial Text: A Critical Explanation of Some Forms of Mimeticism' in Frank Gloversmith, ed., *The Theory of Reading* (Brighton: Harvester, 1984), pp. 93–122. For the majority of white academics, the debate about post-coloniality began with Edward W. Said's *Orientalism* (London: Routledge and Kegan Paul, 1978).

# 1

# Reading for the Empire

## Boys, Class, and Culture

PLENTY of people will try to give the masses, as they call them, an intellectual food prepared and adapted in the way they think proper for the actual condition of the masses. The ordinary popular literature is an example of this way of working on the masses. Plenty of people will try to indoctrinate the masses with the set of ideas and judgements constituting the creed of their own profession or party. Our religious and political organizations give an example of this way of working on the masses. I condemn neither; but culture works differently. It does not try to win them for this or that sect of its own, with ready-made judgements and watchwords. It seeks to do away with the classes; to make the best that has been thought and known in the world current everywhere; to make all men live in an atmosphere of sweetness and light, where they may use ideas, as it uses them itself, freely – nourished and not bound by them.
(Matthew Arnold, 1869, *Culture and Anarchy*)[1]

The Working Classes of this country are very generally, and I venture to think very justly, accredited with the possession of 'sound common sense', 'shrewd intelligence', and other the like mental characteristics of a more or less intuitive order. But not even their best friends or warmest admirers can say of them that they are a cultured class.
(Thomas Wright, 'On a Possible Popular Culture')[2]

Culture or Civilization, taken in its wide ethnographic sense, is that complex whole which includes knowledge, belief, art, morals, law, custom, and any other capabilities and habits acquired by man as a member of a society. The condition of culture among the various societies of mankind, in so far as it is capable of being investigated on general principles, is a subject apt for the study of laws of human thought and action.

(Edward B. Tylor, *Primitive Culture*)[3]

Culture: this word, for at least the last 100 years, has been an exceptionally loaded and hotly debated one. In Victorian Britain, the word predominantly came to signify a specific set of values that every civilized individual should possess. As this chapter indicates, debates about culture impinged on attitudes to literacy, especially in relation to the reading matter of working-class children. It was the work of Matthew Arnold and his more conservative heirs that defined the concept of culture as an ennobling form of education. Yet it is important to remember that Arnold himself was strongly criticized in his own time for confining culture to a limited definition of spiritual and moral improvement, which only a select few possessed, and which the middle classes had to emulate. For example, Frederic Harrison, the well-known Victorian positivist, contended Arnold's high-minded notion of culture in the late 1860s. In 'Culture: A Dialogue', Harrison has a sceptical German philosopher ask his English proponent of culture how 'sweetness is to be attained'. The Englishman (the barely disguised Arnold) says: 'I suppose it comes'.[4] Harrison amusingly shows how Arnoldian 'culture' has no rational basis.

There were other Victorian ways of thinking about the meaning and value of culture. As the quotation from Tylor's founding study of comparative anthropology shows, the concept of culture was also seen to represent ideas of community and custom, in all echelons of society. It is these alternatives or counter-definitions of culture that the work of the post-war critic, Raymond Williams, sought to reclaim, and, in many respects, it is Williams's writings – from *Culture and Society 1780–1950* (1958) onwards – that have opened up the space in which a book, like this one, has been able to emerge.

Williams's sustained interest in the competing definitions of culture is, as he says, situated at the convergence between '(i) the anthropological and sociological senses of culture as a distinct "whole way of life" . . . and (ii) the more specialized if also more common sense of culture of "artistic and intellectual activities"'.[5] As Williams observes, the notion that culture is something that has to be looked up to, that harmonizes the human spirit, and that can only be ascribed to, as well as acquired from, the so-called 'fine arts' (those recognizably nineteenth-century categories of 'classical' music and 'English literature') has considerable influence to this day. It is a word that still generates an air of elitism, pitching itself above the everyday and the ordinary. For many working-class people, what is often understood as culture may not appear to belong to them (even though it is clear to anyone involved in the study of this concept that there are identifiable working-class cultures in Williams's first, and primary, sense). Instead, the idea of culture for those who dissociate themselves from the term brings to mind those refined artistic practices that are supposedly the province of the rich. It has taken many years (from the late 1950s onwards) to legitimate the analysis of 'popular culture' – as opposed to the unpopular 'fine arts' – within academic institutions. However, as the epigraph by Thomas Wright indicates, there was a debate about 'popular culture' being conducted in the late Victorian period.

These competing definitions of culture – 'fine arts' versus a 'whole way of life' – are particularly relevant to this study since the need for culture in education, notably in debates about literacy, was frequently discussed in the numerous Victorian periodicals read by the educated classes. This chapter examines how advances in literacy among young working-class people (particularly boys), and the popularity of 'penny dreadfuls' among them, flew in the face of bourgeois (cultured) literary standards. The aim is to provide a detailed account of how and why debates about reading became focused upon the uses and abuses of leisure time, especially among those who were gaining the supposed benefits of literacy. The second section of this discussion investigates the emergence of a new kind of boys' paper that had few pretensions to literary culture but achieved a popular form of improving respectability among both working- and middle-class readers, and which accommodated excesses of violence and imperialist militarism at an acceptable level.

Extraordinary value was placed on the morally improving nature of culture in the nineteenth century. For Arnold and his followers, notably Walter Pater, culture was the finest condition any person could attain. This highly selective version of culture aimed, in part, to supersede the supposed lowering and narrowing of moral and spiritual standards among the Christian churches. Arnold particularly objected to middle-class dissenters, whose church services he felt

were mechanical and uninspiring. (This was a longstanding prejudice among authoritarian liberals hailing from the establishment.)
Described in metaphors of 'sweetness and light', Arnoldian culture
presented itself as an alternative to the dry religious fanaticism of
the baptists, methodists, and other sects which were an alternative
to the Church of England. Culture was, supposedly, the supreme
form of aesthetic perfection. It brought together the finest things ever
achieved by the finest minds; its harmonizing properties guaranteed
restraint; and it could be made available to more and more people
through a developing refinement of the senses. All these points are
raised in Arnold's best-known work, *Culture and Anarchy*, whose title
opposes its two terms. The book is a putatively liberal, and thereby
tolerant, tract that, by virtue of the polemical twists and turns of its
idealism, succumbs to the faults of dogmatic and sectarian thinking
it so eagerly denounces. With his double assault on middle-class
small-mindedness and working-class unruliness, Arnold promulgates
culture as the social heal to the divisive interests of a world where
'doing as one likes' lamentably has full rein.

An example from *Culture and Anarchy* will serve to indicate
the general direction of Arnold's influential thesis, a thesis whose
conservative elements would be appropriated by Henry Newbolt in
the drafting of *The Teaching of English in England* (1921), which set
a culture-oriented agenda for literary education in Britain until at
least the 1970s. In the passage that follows, Arnold is surveying the
contemporary scene of religion and politics. The period is the 1860s.
Bearing in mind that history is necessarily progressive (history is a
process of improvement: a central tenet of liberal ideology), Arnold
looks forward to a future when his particular model of culture has
absorbed what is best from the current state of affairs, and what is
worst has been duly sacrificed to the past:

> Now, culture admits the necessity of the movement towards fortune-
> making and exaggerated industrialism, readily allows that the future
> may derive benefit from it; but insists, at the same time, that the
> passing generations of industrialists – forming, for the most part,
> the stout main body of Philistinism [those driven towards wealth
> and nothing else], – are sacrificed to it. In the same way, the result
> of all the games and sports which occupy the passing generation
> of boys and young men may be the establishment of a better and
> sounder physical type for the future to work with. Culture does not

set itself against the games and sports; it congratulates the future, and hopes it will make a good use of its improved physical basis; but it points out that our passing generation of boys and young is, meantime, sacrificed. Puritanism was perhaps necessary to develop the moral fibre of the English race, Nonconformity to break the yoke of ecclesiastical domination over men's minds and to prepare the way for freedom of thought in the distant future; still, culture points out that the harmonious perfection of generations of Puritans and Nonconformists has been, in consequence, sacrificed. Freedom of speech may be necessary for the society of the future, but the young lions of the *Daily Telegraph* in the meanwhile are sacrificed.[6]

Since culture avoids excess (bad behaviour, like rioting), Arnold's judgements about what should and should not become part of the future are made to look entirely reasonable. Culture, therefore, is destined to appeal to everybody's implicitly flexible and tolerant instincts. It is a state of mind that all people could achieve if only they would stop trying to justify their own beliefs and values. For Arnold, the world is riven by opinionated and inferior loudmouths endlessly jostling for positions of power. Culture is designed to bring an end to these vulgar and divisive attitudes. It is calm, not dynamic; abstract, not tangible; spiritual, not physical; and, above all, natural, not artificial. Outside history, removed from politics, and yet anticipating a time when both shaping forces have been perfected, culture presents itself as non-ideological. It could, then, be thought of as a higher form of commonsense or the very best sort of intuition.

But how might culture of this kind be communicated to Arnold's disharmonious band of Philistines, public-school athletes, Nonconformists, and bigoted *Daily Telegraph* readers? By instinct or education or both? Chris Baldick notes the practical difficulties facing Arnold in this respect:

The inward condition of culture, and the inner restraint encouraged by it, are more valuable to Arnold than a new institution which would in all likelihood be overrun by Philistines. It is more to his habit to foster a habit of intellectual conscience and deference by pointing to England's cultural shortcomings and to the need for a centre, than to create a real centre which might fall short of the ideal. To paraphrase Voltaire's famous remark about God, it could be said of Arnold's intellectual centre that its most important attribute was not its actual existence but an acceptance of the need to invent it.[7]

Arnold's evasiveness about the means to bring about the ends of culture adopts an even more surprising aspect when his day-to-day employment is taken into account. He was one of Her Majesty's Inspectors of Schools. Yet whenever Arnold gestured towards some kind of academy for the promotion of sweetness and light, he frequently turned to Oxford, not the hundreds of schools he visited as a matter of course. Arnold's admiration for this high seat of learning needs to be treated with some caution since, as Baldick observes, 'in private letters and some of his lesser-known educational reports Arnold admitted that Oxford was little more than a glorified finishing school for the Barbarians, with a stagnant intellectual life.'8 But in *Culture and Anarchy*, as in his well-known poem 'The Scholar-Gypsy' (1853), Oxford receives a remarkable tribute in high-flown rhetoric. In spite of all its faults, Oxford has pursued one ideal far more significantly than any other – 'the truth that beauty and sweetness are essential characters of a complete human perfection.'9 It was this perfection that Arnold's interpreters, rather than Arnold himself, sought to disseminate among the populace.

Later in the century, when the Board Schools were established and all working-class children were being drilled in the 3Rs, Thomas Wright, better known as 'The Journeyman Engineer', wrote of 'popular culture' in a manner shaped by Arnold's aesthetic principles. Wright's political suggestions for the improvement of the working classes, however, were at several removes from the idealism of *Culture and Anarchy*. Wright was intervening in a debate about literacy that appeared regularly in journals during the 1880s and 1890s. Discussion concentrated largely on three things: the deficiencies of elementary schooling; the low quality of working-class reading; and the consequent damage both were having on most working people. He begins with one of Arnold's basic assumptions: that culture is founded in 'sound common sense' and 'shrewd intelligence'. Proper use of these faculties of mind, therefore, will give rise to a state of well-being. But rather than make culture the objective for all classes (Arnold's jokily named breeds of Barbarians, Philistines, and Populace; the upper, middle, and working classes, respectively), Wright decides to split culture into two. One kind of culture, of a 'higher, more strictly aesthetic order', is distinguished from another type, one with a 'simpler, more robust sense', namely 'popular culture'. This division of educational interests has persisted in several strands of conservative thinking during the twentieth century.[10] Wright, a radical for his time, turned to this model of different cultures – high culture and popular culture – as a plausible solution to improving the lives of working people.

The culture at the centre of Arnold's human world is placed far too high for the working classes Wright is thinking of, and this is largely because of the marked rise in literacy in the 1860s and 1870s and the astonishing growth of penny fiction. He argues that culture is a relative term, which has different meanings depending on which class of people it refers to. Yet, like many of Arnold's followers, Wright believes it is English literature, when carefully selected and presented to the people, that may act as the central civilizing agent to lead the masses towards bettering themselves. Here is his despairing account of the penny dreadfuls, which appropriate classics should replace:

> Never before was there so little prospect of those given to such reading being driven to more wholesome mental food by a limited supply of garbage. In this respect the working classes were much more fortunately situated a generation ago than they are at this day. True, even the penny dreadfuls were not unknown, but every week did not bring forth its new one. Nor did they appeal so directly to boys as do the existing race of dreadfuls – *The Boy Highwayman*, *The Boy Brigand*, *The Boy Pirate*, *The Boy King of the Outlaws*, &c., are modern inventions. The long drawn out *Mysteries of London* and *Mysteries of the Court*, the leading dreadfuls of the last generation, were happily not meat for babes. Then, as now, also penny serials – which should not be confounded with the penny dreadfuls – were a popular form of reading. But they were very much fewer in number, and decidedly better in quality than those of the present day. Their To-be-continued-in-our-next stories were more robust, and their miscellaneous contents less trashy and frivolous. At that time, moreover, the influence of the lower type of penny serial was largely counteracted by an extensive and effective circulation among the working classes of a much higher style of cheap weekly serial. Of these, *The Penny Magazine*, *Eliza Cook's Journal*, and the still flourishing *Chamber's Journal* may be named as leading examples.[11]

Wright is contemplating a brief period when a more 'robust' (implicitly 'manly', as well as morally sound) kind of writing was

being produced by self-educated working-class poets, critics, and
novelists, particularly those men involved in the Chartist struggles
of the 1840s. These were the writers whose virtues were espoused
by the proponents of muscular Christianity, the Christian Socialists,
Charles Kingsley and F. D. Maurice, who made the church, rather
than the concept of a refined culture, the institution that would
bring an end to class dissension. After the collapse of Chartism in
the late 1840s, it was no longer possible for working-class writers
to produce works with the notoriety of (to give a representative
example) Ebenezer Elliott's *Corn-Law Rhymes* (1830). To early
Victorian men of letters, self-educated writers of this kind proved
that working people could indeed achieve higher cultural status. Fine
phrasing, technical accomplishment, and artistic ambition in the face
of difficult living conditions – all these features were applauded in the
1830s and 1840s. Much of this writing was indeed remarkable but it
was not incorporated into the canons of literature when the study
of English became a subject of academic inquiry. Neither did this
kind of self-educated writing reach anything like the wide audience
that the penny dreadfuls (or 'bloods', as they were known) came to
enjoy in the 1850s.

The origins of the penny dreadfuls – increasingly referred to by
that name in the 1860s – lay in the gothic novel. The tales of Sweeney
Todd and Varney the Vampire count among the celebrated examples
of melodramatic stories constructed in a simple narrative style where
the emphasis is more on incident than character.[12] Bizarre and
fantastic events prevailed in these eight-page publications, usually
made attractive by a sensational engraving on the cover. Some of
these stories sold not by the thousand but the million. They were
the first kind of truly mass reading. By 1870 their market had largely
shifted to a 'juvenile' readership (as it was by then named), and the
majority of self-defined cultured people was, like Wright, appalled
by the content of these works. The well-educated middle classes
were aghast at the unforeseen consequences of teaching working
people how to read.

As early as 1858, Margaret Oliphant, a conservative novelist and
regular contributor to *Blackwood's*, decried the failure of charitable
organizations (such as the Societies for the Diffusion of Knowledge)
whose Penny Magazines and Cyclopaedias packed with 'useful' information were not favoured by the mass reading public. Instead, as

Oliphant said, the working classes preferred to consume despicably low-grade fiction, and their interest in cheaply produced sensational tales where the 'characters may be the merest puppets of invention; the springs of the machinery may betray themselves at every movement; the language may be absurd, the invention miserable' was sustained by the seemingly simple pleasures of 'narrative'. Oliphant accounted for this fascination for technically unaccomplished but none the less stimulating narratives in a revealing analogy: 'What does a child care for the probabilities of fiction, for the wit of dialogue, or the grace of style? It is likely they bore him, detaining him as they do from the current of events'.[13] The middle-class child and the literate adult worker supposedly shared much in common. Both had to be trained to read literature of a more improving kind. An article such as Oliphant's (one of many on this topic) discloses how the increasing emphasis on culture at this time rested upon a much older and well-established idea of moral sustenance promoted by evangelical groups, Sunday schools, and religious publishing houses.

By the 1880s, middle-class denunciations of the penny dreadfuls grew increasingly infuriated. B. G. Johns provided a typical summary of this type of popular fiction in the 1887 volume of the *Edinburgh Review*. Throughout his discussion of 'The Literature of the Streets', Johns made it clear that the penny dreadfuls exploit that all too conspicuous lack of restraint that fundamentally violates culture. According to him, the working classes were presumably as wild, sick, and populous as the 'trash' they read. Sewers of this so-called filth overflowed the streets of Britain's cities, and swarms of poor people were everywhere consuming this dangerous stuff:

> [T]he fountain head of the poisonous stream is in great towns and cities, especially in London itself; and it is with that we now have to deal. Here the readers are to be numbered by hundreds of thousands, and the supply exceeds the wildest demand. There is now before us such a veritable mountain of pernicious trash, mostly in paper covers, and all 'Price One Penny': so-called novelettes, tales, stories of adventure, mystery and crime; pictures of school life hideously unlike reality; exploits of robbers, cut-throats, prostitutes, and rogues, that, but for its actual presence, it would seem incredible. To expect our readers to wade through such a nauseous mass would

be useless, even if the task were possible. All that can be done is to select from the whole heap a few specimens. Widely and carefully chosen, that may serve as types of the mental diet now provided for millions of poor children, who buy and devour it with intense relish. It matters little where we begin, so we take the first –

*'Joanna Polenipper, Female horse-stealer, Footpad, Smuggler, Prison-Beater and Murderer'*, a complete romance in eight quarto pages, four chapters of small print, as a sample of the entire series. For, in point of general style, colour, incident, and character of the *dramatis personae*, all these volumes of trash are as like each other as peas in a single pod. Every sentence fairly bristles with adjectives of tremendous and fiery strength; the characters are of but two kinds, whether angels or demons in mortal guise; fools or sharpers; rogues or the victims on whom they prey. Every page is crammed with incidents of the most astounding kind, which succeed each other as swiftly as the scenes in a transpontine drama. Bombastic rant, high-flown rhodomontade, and the flattest fustian from the lips of all speakers alike; and 'Joanna' is no exception to the rule.[14]

The penny dreadfuls may have excited their readers but the very thought of them being read by the unruly multitude set Johns's prose into an equally violent motion. Since there are many instances of sensational narratives going as far back as the medieval period, it is worth inquiring exactly what it was that Johns objected to. Bad style, cheap format, excesses of expression, implausible plotting – these were the points that violated Johns's and his contemporaries' cultured sensibilities. Yet in his account of these pitched battles between heroes and villains, their unlikely adventures and wickedly perpetrated crimes, Johns was disgusted not only at the thought of the working classes degrading themselves but also – and this is the point – of the degradation of reading itself. In their overwhelming numbers, working people were obviously not reading what was thought best for them by the cultured few. And it was the working classes' consent to consume such 'trash' that threw Johns into such a quandary. Their reading was uncontrollable, in terms of both its extravagant sales figures and overworked plots.

Such 'literature of the streets' was clearly at a far remove from the fairy stories and other acceptable narratives Johns had so highly praised in an earlier article published in 1867, where he claimed:

'Fiction seldom paints life as it truly is, though the stream of life is so chequered that no incident can be devised which has not some counterpart in reality. And yet fiction ought to be, and is, in some sense a picture of life; and so far has the power, and ought, to teach true things'.[15] Johns upheld Mrs Barbauld's moral tales (popular evangelical stories from earlier in the century), as ideal reading matter. Although applied to children's literature, these remarks are entirely consonant with theories of realism concerning fictions for adult readers. Indeed, there is something of a link here between moral prescriptions about the rights and wrongs of books to give to children, and those concepts of narrative which sought, after Henry James, to capture an 'air of reality'. Morally rectitudinous stories would prove increasingly unpopular with children of all classes. Similarly, by the 1880s, adult readers – including middle-class ones – looked more and more to forms of adventure and romance to occupy their leisure.

Until the middle of the century, as Oliphant's remarks point out, working-class reading had been viewed as a means of gaining access to useful knowledge produced by the religious societies. Literacy, it has to be remembered, had been perceived by many members of the middle classes as a special philanthropic gift to working people. By the 1880s, with controversy raging over the penny dreadfuls, the elementary school system, paradoxically enough, was apparently providing working-class children with the tools that would exclude them from culture and thereby turn them into criminals. Edward G. Salmon, a young journalist who researched the question of juvenile literature more intensively than anyone else at the time, was stressing this point when he wrote:

> Taking cognisance of the working classes as a whole, there is one thing which I believe to be indisputable – viz. that the instruction imparted through the Board School has not superinduced any large amount of reading, except in a shape contemptible and worthless. Neither the newspaper nor the novelette contains any element calculated to carry peace and contentment to the working man's door. There is nothing in it to elevate, to ennoble, to inspire with a desire for truth and right-living.[16]

For educators in schools, there was for many years no naturally constituted culture to which the workers, even when endowed with inherent commonsense and state-supported skills in literacy, would accede. Harold Silver quotes one of Her Majesty's Inspectors of Schools who reported, just before the Act of 1870: 'a clergyman had found it impossible in a large East London elementary school to get out of the children "an idea of what was meant by 'betters' in the catechism, 'To order myself lowly and reverently to my betters'. They plainly expressed by their manners that they knew no betters'"'.[17] Class divisions apparently created such an unbreachable gap between workers and the educated minority that the task of raising moral standards at times seemed almost impossible.

With this problem in mind, it became clear to those investing sums in launching new juvenile weeklies that instead of emphasizing the moral, the useful, and the instructive elements of a respectable and dutiful life, the attractive excitement of cheaply produced fiction had to be imitated, if in an appropriately modified form. However, right up until the end of the century, in parallel with the establishment of respectable boys' and girls' weeklies, a veritable battle of the books concerning the degenerate aspects of the penny dreadfuls continued to be waged.

The market for all types of juvenile fiction rapidly gained ground in the 1880s. Patrick A. Dunae points out that of fourteen different categories listed in *Publishers' Circular* in 1882, publications for young people accounted for 19 per cent (the largest share) of the total market.[18] Likewise, records of library borrowings in 1892–93 show that juvenile literature accounted for 18.36 per cent of the total number. Prose fiction (for adults) amounted to 61.2 per cent.[19] Similar figures are assembled in an essay published in 1894 on 'Elementary Education and the Decay of Literature', and these percentages are said to provide 'unanswerable evidence that the sanguine expectations as to the results that would accrue from the Elementary Education Act have not yet been justified'.[20] This parlous situation was regularly offered as evidence for the apparent criminality and recalcitrant behaviour among young working-class men and women.

Johns, in particular, was alarmed about the corruption of working-class children who would be led into a world spoiled by the repeated acts of violence committed by the undesirable types glorified by the dreadfuls. These pernicious publications, he said, were 'to be found anywhere and everywhere, throughout the whole domain of poverty, hunger, and crime'.[21] The fact that these children lived in such abject conditions appeared to make less impact on him than the substance of what they read. Their quality of life seemed to be far less important than the quality of their reading – and yet, he suggested that their lives were, in fact, dependent on what they read. That their reading might, in some crucial respects, be dependent on their living conditions is a thought that eluded him and many other commentators who disdainfully cast an eye on the mass fiction market.

Wright, a working man, went against the current of opinion by arguing that the dreadfuls were harmless:

> Boys who do *not* read dreadfuls sometimes rob tills. As a rule, robberies by errand-boys result either from temptations arising out of thoughtlessness of employers, or a constitutional proclivity to dishonesty upon the part of the employed. There were robberies by errand-boys when penny dreadfuls were not, and there would still be such robberies if the dreadfuls ceased to be. If anything like a general effect of the dreadfuls was to induce their readers to attempt to imitate the criminality which they certainly try to heroize, an honest and not a dishonest boy would become the exception to the rule. The admiration for things criminal of the boy-readers of the dreadfuls is abstract and theoretic, not practical or imitative. There should be no mistake upon this important point. The evil of the supremacy of the modern dreadfuls is not that they criminalize, or even – except in a negative sense – demoralize. The evil, and a most calamitous one it is in its results, is that the dreadfuls have for the time being superseded what we will venture to call the natural reading for boys. They have usurped the place of the only reading by which, practically speaking, the foundations of a cultured taste could be laid, and the means to the end of a new happiness erected.[22]

He added that the majority of these young fans of penny dreadfuls refrained from crime. For him, the problem lay with schooling, not reading. In *Our New Masters* (1883), he echoed many other critics of the elementary schools where, as P. McCann points out, 'the mechanical exercise of memory reduced all subjects to dry technicalities which were soon forgotten by most of the pupils.'[23] It is implicit in his writing that the fierce unruliness of most penny dreadfuls was defined against the strict regimentation of the classroom.

Greater emphasis is given to the point about the lack of any connection between reading and crime by G. K. Chesterton, who extended the argument by identifying striking resemblances between high cultural forms and supposedly low ones:

> It is the modern literature of the educated, not of the uneducated, which is avowedly and aggressively criminal. Books recommending profligacy and pessimism, at which the high-souled errand-boy would shudder, lie upon all our drawing-room tables. If the dirtiest old owner of the dirtiest old bookstall in Whitechapel deemed to display works really recommending polygamy or suicide, his stock would be seized by the police. These things are our luxuries. And with a hypocrisy so ludicrous as to be almost unparalleled in history, we rate the gutter-boys for their immorality at the very time we are discussing (with equivocal German professors) whether morality is valid at all. At the very instant that we curse the Penny Dreadful for encouraging thefts upon property, we canvass the proposition that all property is theft. At the very instant that we accuse it (quite unjustly) of lubricity and indecency, we are cheerfully reading philosophies which glory in lubricity and indecency. At the very instant we charge it with encouraging the young to destroy life, we are placidly discussing whether life is worth preserving.[24]

Nietzschean scepticism and Proudhon's anarchism – with, no doubt, a few Zola-esque novels thrown in for good measure – comprise the luxurious and immoral reading that the leisured classes dignify in their own terms as philosophy. Chesterton articulates his estimation of bourgeois hypocrisy in world-weary tones that reveal a profound dissatisfaction with late Victorian life as a whole. All classes, it seems, have spent their energies on 'lubricity and indecency'. The only difference is that members of the educated classes have made their own type of degrading reading respectable by ensuring that the dreadfuls are treated wholly with contempt to become the only site of immorality.

The specific focus of Wright's and Chesterton's working-class readership is the boy whose life was not only wasted on what he chose to read but also in his dead-end employment – a state of affairs not improved by the introduction of compulsory education. (The education of girls is mentioned only in passing, if at all.) In an essay on 'Recreative Evening Schools' in *The Nineteenth Century* for 1886, Freeman Wills despaired at the stultifying effects of school life on working-class pupils, pointing out that elementary education killed off any interest children may have had in learning. 'There is no appetite for books when the crowd of fagged boys escapes from the long daily bondage.'[25] School, he says, is a matter of policing and penal servitude. To provide the working-class boy with the proper education his compulsory schooling omits, Wills suggests the establishment of evening schools to brighten the lives of young men. Such schools would perform the role of culture in the face of ignorance, vulgarity, and the drudgery of learning by rote. Indirectly related to the pedagogy of Friedrich Froebel (of the 1840s 'kindergarten' movement), this project is viewed as a return to a pre-industrial natural world of rural festivity, remote from the urban misery of insanitary housing, poverty, and consequent infirm health:

> To pilot a party of London boys through the forest is a new experience; the world becomes fresh to old eyes from theirs. Wonder inexpressible as a pair of jays dart out before us, chattering down the long avenues; or the wood-pigeons persuade, or the cuckoos are recognized as the original of the cuckoo-clock. The commonest things are gathered as if they were enchanted, until the freight they intended to bring home grows beyond bounds, and the discovery of Nature's prodigality at last makes them throw all away save some little branch or flower, as an evidence that fairyland exists. Then we can have botanical and entomological excursions and open their minds and imaginations by these country dips. Gradually the life of the evening school will become corporate; it will not dissolve at the end of each session; by the grace of the Board we shall keep all that we have gained, and wind refining influences round our young people, and implant a purer taste, which will begin to reflect itself on public amusements.[26]

The prison of the city, then, is to be liberated by the pleasures of the country. Wills's lyrical sentences evoke a romantic sensibility where extraordinary truths may be learned from the most common objects. Nature is cast in the role of a great provider who is also the best of teachers. And a distinctly Victorian interest in the microscopic fascination of the natural world presents itself in the magical and wonderful prospect of 'botanical and entomological excursions'. Nature, a place of pastoral innocence and peace of mind, where the imagination can grow and the spirit is refined, is upheld as the cure-all to the ills of the 1870 Education Act. It is precisely along such lines of thinking that Baden-Powell would base his principles of Scouting.

Wills's essay registers the early, uneasy fears of empire in the face of mass ignorance among young men. Given the extension of the franchise in 1867 and the marked rise in the working-class population, the boy was now identified as a political danger to the nation. He had to be trained not only to read the right things, to turn his mind away from the debasing effects of penny fiction, but he had also to meet the demands of becoming a responsible citizen. Imperialism made the boy into an aggrandized subject – British born and bred – with the future of the world lying upon his shoulders. But the country of his birth was not in itself the guarantee of his ability to participate in ruling a globe with ever-increasing amounts of red on it. It was, time and again, his class affiliation that threatened his imperial superiority:

> These are the future electors who will exercise so much influence on the world's destiny. The constituents of an imperial race, they ought to be educated with a view to the power they will wield. Every Englishman ought to know something about the dependencies of England, as one of the heirs of such a splendid inheritance; he should understand English interests, something about her commerce, her competitors, the productions and trade of other lands. He ought to know his country's historical as well as her geographical position. He cannot, with safety to the empire, be allowed to be so ignorant as to be unfit for his political trust, like loose ballast in a vessel, liable, in any agitation that may arise, to roll from side to side and so to destroy national stability.[27]

In order to discover more about his national, rather than class, origins, two areas of knowledge in particular had to be bequeathed to him – history and geography. From the late 1870s onwards, as Tory designs on the world influenced educational policy, geography earned an increasingly important place among the upper grades of schools. It took until 1900, as Pamela Horn notes, for history – and history of a politically motivated kind – to become a subject to be studied 'as a rule' in elementary education. Before that time, state schooling was preoccupied with teaching basic skills, the 3Rs, and curriculum planning had been largely left in the hands of pragmatic liberals. Horn quotes from a document produced by the Board of Education in 1905 which gives clear reasons for teaching these disciplines:

> from . . . geography lessons the scholars know that Great Britain is only one country among many others. It is, therefore, important that from the history lessons they should learn something of their nationality which distinguishes them from the people of other countries. They cannot understand this . . . unless they are taught how the British nation grew up, and how the mother country in her turn has founded daughter countries beyond the seas.[28]

By the end of the century, then, tenets of imperialism were shaping the ideological dimensions of subjects studied in school. Yet these new rulings on the teaching of history and geography were not imposed by fiat on the world that schoolchildren were learning to appreciate. Instead they reinforced already established imperialist assumptions that had for many years acted as the main precepts guiding the production of adventure fiction for children. Jacqueline Rose has traced the continuity between overtly didactic children's books, such as Thomas Day's *Sandford and Merton* (1783–89), and the realistic narratives of boys' adventure stories (by Captain Marryat, W. H. G. Kingston, and R. M. Ballantyne) which 'are the inheritors of a fully colonialist concept of development, and a highly specific and limited conception of the child.'[29] Gradually, the imperialist knowledge supplied in school lessons would converge with the world-view laid out in what became a canon of children's literature reaching back into the colonial past of the mid-eighteenth century. This trend would be set by Jarrold's *Empire Readers*, published in the 1880s, and adopted by the London School Board. Slightly earlier, between 1865 and 1875 Cassell published adaptations of classics in words of more than one syllable. These were highly popular readers, and included a retelling of Day's eighteenth-century colonial narrative.[30] It would appear that between 1870 and 1900 narratives celebrating empire and techniques in teaching reading and writing gradually converged, although this is not to suggest that schoolchildren were by the turn of the century only interested in stories adapted to imperialist ends. The point is, both inside and outside the classroom, there was more and more emphasis on heroic adventure, and this involved a number of shifts in attitude towards juvenile publishing and curriculum design.

As Britain expressed its needs for stronger bodies and healthier minds among its working-class male population, two related models of educational knowledge came into the world of boyhood, and both of these, at their inception, were defined against what was seen as the mindless inculcation of facts preoccupying elementary education. One was the practical survivalist education of Scouting and the military structure of youth organizations such as the Boys' Brigade which would provide skills not present in the school curriculum. The other was embodied in the adventure story which would take the boy into areas of history and geography that placed him at the top of the racial ladder and at the helm of all the world.

Adventure stories pitched at an acceptably literary level were on the ascendant in the 1880s because of the introduction of respectable boys' weeklies, such as *Boy's Own Paper* in 1879. *B.O.P.*, as it was commonly abbreviated, emerged from a leading Christian organization, the Religious Tract Society. The RTS had a long tradition of publishing books for children. But in order to enter into and succeed in the market of mass reading it was obliged to move away from the blatant didacticism of its already substantial list of juvenile works, many of which were used in Sunday schools. When imperialism came to be known by that name in the late 1880s, the Sunday schools had already contributed greatly to the formation of this type of adventure narrative. A large amount of Sunday reading – reading allowed to take place in the respectable home – significantly related to missionary work. Thomas W. Lacqueur makes this general point about this earlier kind of religious writing:

> Sunday School periodical literature was at its most political when it came to England's world position. It was not a great leap from missionary stories about Cingalese superstition, Chinese mourning practices, or Indian funeral rites to statements of the inferiority of other races. By the 1850s gory descriptions of Hindoo cruelty, accounts of brave missionaries who struggled to combat barbaric practices, and requests that children pray for the soldiers who put down the Indian mutiny had become items for a popular Indian Sunday School anthology [*The New Sunday School Teacher* (1859)]. On the other hand, one must not exaggerate the racism of Sunday School literature. [In 1837] the *Youth's Magazine*, for example,

printed an article 'On Bigotry' which pleaded for racial as well as religious tolerance.[31]

The Sunday schools of the 1850s and earlier may have pleaded for a paternalistic attitude towards other racial and religious groups but it was the zealous ideal of a Christian mission that made a considerable impact on imperial ideology.

Imperialism was from the outset recognized as 'England's Mission', as a significant article in *The Nineteenth Century* of 1878 observed. 'England's Mission' was written not by a Tory, but by the Leader of the Opposition at that time, W. E. Gladstone. His essay lists a number of fundamental distinctions between the aggressive, landgrabbing, and supremacist imperialism of the Tories, and the altogether more even-minded Liberal approach to military power, the healthy growth and extension of trade, and, finally, the respect for limited financial resources on which the economy of a global empire is based. Bearing in mind Disraeli's many fervid speeches of the 1870s, Gladstone claimed that the Tories 'have appealed, under the prostituted name of patriotism, to exaggerated fears, to imaginary interests, and to the acquisitiveness of a race which has surpassed every other known to history in the faculty of appropriating to itself vast spaces of the earth, and establishing its supremacy over men of every race and language.'[32] None the less, the concept of a glorious 'mission' welded together Liberal and Conservative interests in Britain's expanding number of global possessions.

1878 was a crucial year in the history of British imperialism. It marked the beginning of the jingoistic protests that broke up several Liberal rallies throughout the country. Two Sunday demonstrations held at Hyde Park in the name of achieving peace on the Eastern Question were disrupted by a rowdy, beer-swilling, working-class crowd denouncing the pacifists as traitors to their country. These jingoists – named that year after a popular music-hall song – were recruited from the working classes to an empowering Tory patriotism far more reactionary than anything ever witnessed before in the nineteenth century. And this Tory hegemony over national pride is clearly charted in the course and direction taken by juvenile reading during the closing decades of the Victorian period. In a detailed article on competing left- and right-wing claims on patriotism during this time, Hugh Cunningham provides a concise account of the

Tories' imperialism, which would successfully gain an increasing percentage of the working-class vote:

> In an age of imperialism the English were constantly exhorted to be patriotic, and the measuring rod of patriotism was one erected by the Conservatives in the 1870s; the patriot was above class, loyal to institutions of the country, and resolute in defence and honour of its interests. Liberals, radicals and socialists who protested their own patriotism were singularly unsuccessful in wresting the initiative from the right. Patriotism was firmly identified with conservatism, militarism, royalism and racialism.[33]

By the late 1870s, any radical or liberal demands to create a British republic on the basis of a democratic patriotism had lost practically all of their persuasiveness. Disraeli recognized that the working classes could be given a magnificent sense of national pride through a formerly unexploited resource – the monarchy.

Imperialism came to be understood as a right-wing ideology at the moment when Queen Victoria had the title of Empress of India conferred upon her in 1877. This new title was the hard-won outcome of Disraeli's Royal Titles Bill of the previous year. India came under sovereign rule in 1858 with the dissolution of the East India Company. India – now to be regarded as 'the jewel in the crown' (Disraeli's phrase), rather than an economic burden – was the focus of an empire no longer run by self-interested Liberal politicians but which was now claimed to lie under the rule of an almost spiritual being, the Queen, lauded by her natural subjects, the Tories. In his grandiloquent parliamentary speeches, Disraeli compared Queen Victoria to Julius Caesar and Peter the Great. In the course of these improbable comparisons with former tyrants, he claimed that not only Britons but also the much vaster population of India would look up to her as the focal image of the empire. Disraeli certainly distorted the truth when he argued that the title of Empress was 'desired in India'. And, with a telltale parenthesis, he added: 'The princes and natives of India – unless we are deceived, and we have omitted no means by which we could obtain information and form opinions – look to it with utmost interest.'[34] By inventing a consensus of Indian support, Disraeli achieved what was the result of a long-term policy to unite the classes under the banner of Tory monarchism. His strategy for reconciling the working classes to the rule of rich Tory landowners is neatly laid out in his famous Crystal Palace speech of 1872. (This speech was, in large part, a spirited response to Sir Charles Dilke's republican attack on the expense of the royal family delivered earlier in the year.)

> One of the most distinguishing features of the great change of 1832 [First Reform Act, minimally extending the franchise] was that those who brought it about at once abolished all the franchises of the working classes. They were franchises as ancient as those of the Baronage of England; and, while they abolished them, they provided no substitute. The discontent upon the subject of the representation of which has from that time more or less pervaded our society dates from that period, and that discontent, all will admit, has not ceased. It was terminated by the Act of Parliamentary Reform of 1867–68 [the Second Reform Act]. That Act was founded on a confidence that the great body of the people of this country were 'Conservative'. When I say 'Conservative', I use the word in its purest and loftiest sense. I mean that the people of England, and especially the working classes of England, are proud of belonging to a great country, and wish to maintain its greatness – that they are proud of belonging to an Imperial country, and are resolved to maintain, if they can, their empire of England.[35]

Disraeli was prime minister from 1874 to 1880, years which consolidated Tory imperialism, especially through the mechanisms of popular culture. Commenting on the Crystal Palace speech, Bill Schwarz remarks: 'The positive rendering of the concept of Empire, and the diligence with which Disraeli and the Tory leadership attempted to present their party as *the* party of Empire, launched a political project which, despite sometimes dramatic fluctuations, came to define the conservative nation until at least the end of the 1950s'.[36] After Disraeli's death in 1881, the Primrose League – which took its title from what was reputedly his favourite flower – was the first of several propaganda machines to promote the cause of empire through the publication of juvenile literature and the presentation of lantern lectures. John MacKenzie details the rise of this and other imperial societies, remarking that in 1901 the Primrose League had 1.5 million members, of which 1.4 million were claimed to be working class.[37] Although Gladstone (in power by 1880, having toppled the Tories with a majority of over 100 seats), believed that the 'sentiment of empire may be called innate in every Briton', he had lost an irrecuperable amount of working-class support to the imperial ideal enshrined in the ageing queen. Her Golden Jubilee of 1887 may have met with some anti-monarchical feeling, but ten years later, when celebrating her altogether more extravagant Diamond Jubilee, the crowds thronged the streets of London. (In 1837, it needs to be recognized, Queen Victoria ascended the throne to far less notice.) In particular, a new kind of popular Tory press began to emerge. When the *Daily Mail* first went on sale in 1896 it announced itself as 'the embodiment and mouthpiece of the Imperial Idea'.[38] It took, therefore, several decades for Disraeli's brand of imperialism to become overwhelmingly successful, and, even then, it needs to be remembered that the Labour movement was gaining strength and would be in perpetual antagonism with the Tories' manipulation of the education system. (There was, for example, the Socialist Sunday school movement, established in 1892.[39]) Although it is fair to argue that by 1900 Tory ideology finally held sway over conceptions of empire, both on the school curriculum and in leisure-time reading, it should be borne in mind that the Tories did not play a decisive role in instituting state education. That was left to Gladstone's Liberal government with Forster's Act of 1870, the problematic consequences of which are worth considering here.

The debate about the need for greater culture among young working-class people reached its height at the turn of the century when imperialism was at its zenith. This is somewhat ironic since the main proponents of state education were Liberals who had, in theory, a commitment to self-improvement, and thus raising standards of culture. Since its inception, the system of state education seemed to have been failing the working classes abysmally. The narrow concerns of reading, writing, and arithmetic were a continual source of dissatisfaction to people affiliated to sections of both Left and Right. If, to some observers, elementary education did not lead schoolchildren towards the high ideals of self-improvement, then it would appear to have abandoned them to the supposedly corrupting influence of penny fiction. Liberal beliefs in education as a tool that would dissolve class differences found themselves opposed to a loud populist Toryism that could appeal to the adventurous heroism first enacted in the exciting episodes to be found in the penny dreadfuls. This is not to say that the dreadfuls were, inadvertently or otherwise, sources of Tory propaganda. For a start, the dreadfuls dated from an earlier period. Yet there was a close alignment between the fearless tales of boyhood heroism in the dreadfuls, the fighting-fit spirit celebrated in many children's classics, and the narratives of imperial victories that preoccupied the popular press. In theory, Liberals sponsored freedom and independence of mind, rather than nationalism or militarism, which the Tories would increasingly exploit. Yet, set against these high-minded principles, Liberal educationists had no other alternative than to apply a pragmatic attitude towards the nation's needs. There was good reason for this. As the first sponsors of state education for the masses, the Liberals, if concerned with propagating middle-class values, were obliged to keep a close eye on public finances. Education for all obviously came at a cost. It would be left to Scouting (established in 1908) to place Liberal individualism and Tory patriotism into a completely new and strikingly successful combination, and then on a voluntary basis. Baden-Powell's youth movement was in large part initiated because of the perceived inadequacies of state education.

Forster's Act of 1870, passed during Gladstone's Liberal government, was the first of many faltering steps towards comprehensive schooling in Britain. Even the great Liberal theorist of culture, Arnold himself, knew only too well that the day-to-day activities of the elementary school had, for practical reasons, to be organized around a skill-based set of subjects; he wrote in 1867: 'when grammar, geography, English history, and *natur-kunde* [nature study of the type undertaken in Swiss schools] are added, as they ought to be, to reading, writing, and arithmetic, as part of the regular school course, little more can be with advantage asked for from the school children with whom [the teachers] may have to deal'. Citing this passage, Ian Hunter notes the exclusion of literary study from Arnold's list of priorities for the school curriculum, and this is a significant point when subsequent champions of English literature as an academic discipline routinely trace the roots of their convictions to Arnold.[40] Pupils would only discover the high cultural value staked on literary study if they managed to reach the upper grades of their schools or entered higher education. Literacy, instead, was the focus of attention. Stephen Humphries provides this useful overview of the liberalism shaping educational policy at this time:

The liberal educational ideology was the dominant force, at both a national and local level, in the initiating and moulding of school provision, particularly between 1870 and 1902 and during the inter-war period. This ideology was shaped by three central concerns. First, it sought to ameliorate important social problems – principally the demoralization and destitution of some sections of the working class, juvenile crime, street-gang violence, disease and drunkenness – through an infusion of bourgeois values such as hard work, discipline and thrift. Fundamentally, it attributed social deprivation to the ignorance and immorality of working-class culture rather than to capitalist structure and therefore proposed individual as opposed to political solutions to problems of class inequality. The second, related aim of this ideology was the transmission of middle-class culture through the school curriculum in order to encourage the moral development and elevation of the working-class child's personality. Third, the liberal ideology sought to extend the elementary and secondary school systems in order to provide limited opportunities for talented working-class children to achieve social success by climbing the educational ladder. The addition of this meritocratic dimension to the liberal ideology was governed more by economic and political considerations of national efficiency than by any commitment to extend democratic rights and opportunities to the working class.[41]

Schooling, then, was supposed to be a model of efficiency. It left very little room for creative development (except in the playground). In the 1870s, reading for pleasure, therefore, took place in leisure time rather than at school. Fictional narratives that absorbed the adventurous militarism of this new and rising imperial ideology now had a prime opportunity to enter into that comparatively unrestricted world: a world that belonged to the individual boy and not the school he went to. But these adventures would not be excluded from the school curriculum for long. Towards the end of the Victorian period, the type of adventures absorbed outside school would be modified and so make their way into the classroom. If the schoolboy was also a Scout, he would, in Edwardian Britain, find most of his time, both in and out of school, taken up with the ideals of empire.

The restricted concern with literacy in schools had other, far-reaching effects on attitudes to literature. At roughly the same time, educators perceiving themselves as Arnold's heirs were attempting to secure the serious study of literary writing in all areas of education, and, as Reports of the Board of Education bear witness, this initiative played a key role in establishing concepts of Englishness vital to imperialism. Newbolt was Rudyard Kipling's and W. E. Henley's most notable descendant as poet of empire. His poem, 'Vitai Lampada' (1908) contains the famous chant, 'Play up! play up! and play the game!'. Similarly, 'Clifton Chapel' upholds the idea that boys hailing from the public schools embody a superior race.[42] That poetry should be used as a vehicle for patriotism was never very far from the minds of key literary educators. Yet, in the face of educational policies geared towards teaching literacy and numeracy, proponents of 'English' were struggling to have their views accepted as a culturally valuable form of study. Campaigning for the recognition of English literature as an academic discipline in its own right, John Churton Collins set out in 1887 to answer what he saw as a question asked only by Philistines: 'Can English Literature Be Taught?':

> Those whose estimate of the educational value of a subject is not determined by the facility it affords for making marks in competitive examinations are beginning to regard 'English literature' with increasing disfavour. In the examination for the Civil Service of India it has been degraded to a secondary place. From the aarmy examination it has, by a recent order, been entirely eliminated. The council of Holloway College [now part of Royal Holloway and Bedford New College, University of London] have decided to recognize it only in connection with Philology. More than one eminent authority has pronounced that it cannot be taught, that its introduction into our scholastic curricula was an experiment, and an experiment that has failed.[43]

Collins's main objective was to found a School of English at Oxford and its first Chair in the discipline. (He succeeded in establishing the School but failed to be appointed its professor.) Throughout his essay, he urges that English literature can be taught if the public understanding of what it means to study is shifted away from rote-learning and the absorption of dry facts, such as grammatical rules. Reading, he argues, should be a serious (cultured) rather than leisurely activity. Yet surveys of the reading public made striking claims to the contrary.

An article on 'The Reading of the Working Classes' by G. R. Humphrey, published in 1893, assumes that fiction (of any kind) is taken out of public libraries for leisure, not serious reflection: 'It must be kept in mind that novels are *read only*. Scientific books are studied, hence are longer in hand.'[44] Reading, therefore, occupied a contested site where Collins sought to select a canon of works for serious analysis at a time when a mass readership for forms of contemptible, demeaning, and possibly dangerous types of fiction seemed to be overtaking the nation. One consequence of this predicament was to drive 'English' more and more towards analysing, in largely moral terms, a strict canon of respectable works. Moreover, the emerging academic study of English literature in schools and universities increasingly made claims upon two groups wishing to join the educated elite: middle-class men, and women from both the middle and upper classes. Never before had so-called great works of literature (something greater and far more refined than the crudities of the market-place) been placed in such sharp contrast against penny fiction (itself defined by its exceptionally low market value).[45] In the midst of these debates, there remained an open question for publishers, religious bodies, and educationists. At what level might a serious and pleasurable form of juvenile reading be pitched?

Fiction was consumed rapidly and, for many observers, indiscriminately. It would only be with the publication of the Newbolt Report that the educational value of studying set texts was given due recognition by the state. By that time, literary study was being encouraged in schools on a much larger scale than before. Two million copies of works of literature – in other words, acceptable reading – were in circulation among the London schools. The students' favourite books were, in order of popularity, *Tales and Stories from Shakespeare*, *Robinson Crusoe*, *Arthurian Legends*, *Peter Pan*, and *David Copperfield*. There are many other titles listed as well, including *Deeds that Won the Empire*.[46] A title such as the last one could only gain the distinction of becoming a set book on the London Board through a number of decisive changes in patterns of reading and publishing that began in the 1880s. The heroic adventures of the dreadfuls had to find a new mode to make their way on to the school book shelves. In *A Plea for the Revival of Reading*, published in 1906, the well-known journalist, W. T. Stead, invited comments from his readers on good and bad reading for children. His central chapter – on 'A Lads' and Lasses' Library' – focused on the debate about the dreadfuls. Stead claimed that 'the verdict is that boys take penny dreadfuls as children take measles, and they usually recover'. Quoting one of his correspondents, he says:

> In the penny 'blood' a boy gets his money's worth, and that is what he wants. This type of literature is much abused; it is not nearly so harmful as the ordinary newspaper. All the boys I ever knew to read 'dreadfuls' have, after a spell, turned their thoughts to higher forms of literature. You cannot climb the ladder without commencing at the bottom, and the bottom rung must not be despised because of its position.[47]

Stead's aim was to get children consuming as many stories and poems as possible. It does noot, for the moment, really matter what they read, as long as they are reading. And the reading that children enjoy is largely made up of adventure fiction. One woman reader told Stead: 'I didn't want a good book for girls, I wanted to read the books my daddy read.'[48] Thereafter, reading deemed unsuitable for children, and particularly unsuitable for girls, would find its way, in modified form, into school reading schemes.

Surveying the changing markets for juvenile fiction, Dunae writes that the texts 'one generation of critics had denounced as "blood and thunder" came, in a slightly altered form, to be regarded by the next generation as wholesome and patriotic.'[49] The school system, therefore, would gradually take some control over the consumption of fiction by legitimating a range of classic tales of adventure – such as Stevenson's *Treasure Island* (1883) and Kingsley's *Westward Ho!* (1855) – not dissimilar in theme from those to be found on sale as penny publications. For the purpose of study, these books were often abridged and adapted to present what was considered to be a suitable ordering of language. Unnecessary literary idioms were edited from the originals to make them into suitable elementary school readers. Rose has analysed the Report of the 1910 Board of Education, pointing out how it moves in opposed directions where literature for distinct groups of younger and older students is concerned.[50] In the earlier age range (up to fourteen years), the use of 'natural' language – applicable to concrete experience – was favoured in the development of reading skills. Such a policy governed the education of most working-class pupils. The Report states that older, secondary pupils (twelve to sixteen years) are to be offered a distinctly literary approach to language where, implicitly, ideals of Arnoldian culture stand paramount. Students with the middle-class advantage of staying on at school until sixteen had the opportunity to improve their style and to appreciate felicitous phrasing (contact with Chaucer, Shakespeare and Milton was possible). By 1910, then, the only introduction to high culture a working-class child might receive would have been in the form of an instructive adaptation: a good read with practical applications, something, surely, remote, from the world of sweetness and light. A child's (not to be confused with childish) language would be offered to this kind of pupil. It was a utilitarian language stripped of any affectation. Simple and inno-cent, it rendered classic narratives accessible in terms of literacy.

By contrast, most penny dreadfuls were aimed at a working-class readership to provide access to a specific type of literary writing – at a great distance from concrete experience, and, paradoxically, with plenty of aspirations to high culture. To their infuriated critics, these publications debased literary models by making fiction repetitious in style and predictable in plot. In his contribution to the debate on the detrimental effects of popular fiction, Francis Hitchman complained:

> 'Turnpike Dick' is described as the true history of all the celebrated highwaymen, and who appears to be a hash-up of the moral and improving biography of Dick Turpin and his 'gallant companions'. The hero is always in company with a magnificent horse; is always armed with sword and pistols, and always sumptuously dressed; he has a 'rich, mellow voice', in spite of his 'nocturnal rambles' and frequently repeated 'draughts of brandy'; he is of matchless physical strength, and is naturally beloved by the most adorable of women; and he beguiles his leisure with wine and song amidst a select crew of 'Knights of the road', whom he treats in a 'haughty yet affable manner'. The moon is always 'shining merrily' on his gallant exploits, and fortune is ever on the side of the handsome hero, and as constantly unfavourable to the stupid, cowardly, and ill-looking constables and their assistants.[51]

For all his irritation with these penny publications, Hitchman none the less discloses their enduring popularity with the working classes. Narratives of this type fulfil specific expectations – in terms of length (standard format of eight pages); idiom (emphatic use of adjectives and adverbs); and characterization (making heroes out of criminals). Each aspect shows no respect for the refinements of literariness. The text is practically worthless (it costs only one penny); it tries in no respect to be original (authorship is unimportant); and it has no moral sense (it flouts the law). But Turnpike Dick, who outwits the police, carouses with his mates, pulls the women, and thereby plays the role of a notorious Jack-the-Lad, is a complete master of his environment. All these points are represented in language that is easy to understand. Yet the language used to describe Dick's exploits is far from natural, concrete, or literal. The text deploys an antiquated register – glimpsed in that telling reference to the 'Knights of the road' – that is appropriate to an old-fashioned kind of romance. The story uses commonplace literary devices to meet head-on with specific skills in literacy, namely what goes into a good read, and what makes a story different from a piece of text learned by rote.

Recognizing fiction as a far-fetched story that does not have any practical application to the world, the working-class reader of penny dreadfuls made literature appear to possess no value at all. What this young person read was cheap and disposable. Not only was such reading supported by literacy skills acquired at school, it was also flying in the face of those liberal values of good citizenship that were the foundation of elementary schooling. This point preyed on the conscience of many middle-class commentators who felt that they had bequeathed a dangerous gift to the masses. By 1900, statistics show that 97.2 per cent of adult males were literate (the figure for women is 73.2 per cent).[52] Such figures reveal that the 3Rs were certainly having a remarkable effect. The anxious debates about the dreadfuls reveals one thing very clearly indeed – that literacy is a precarious instrument of power. While reading was designed to equip pupils to rise up in a meritocratic society, it simultaneously managed to drag down the standards demanded by the ideologues of culture writing in the periodical press. Literacy, therefore, had led to the corruption of literature, and reading among young working-class people had, by 1890 at least, become an almost criminal pursuit.

A more respectable (but not, in the Arnoldian sense, cultured) variety of fiction for boys began in 1866 with the first of Edwin Brett's many magazines aimed at the juvenile market, *Boys of*

*England; A Young Gentleman's Journal of Sport, Travel, Fun and Instruction*. Louis James outlines the overall design of its earliest numbers, noting in particular how the journal recognized lower middle-class attitudes:

> The main readership . . . was the same as that which George Newnes was to provide for as young adults with *Tit-Bits* (founded 1881) – the upwardly mobile middle classes. 'BOYS OF ENG-LAND', said the editor in his opening 'Address', 'in these days of cheap education, cheap standard literature, of cadet volunteer corps, cricket-clubs, and gymnasia; in these days when even with unaided self-help you may achieve such wonders, it is your own fault if you do not grow up wise and strong men.' Readers are reminded that Bunyan, Telford, Ferguson, Burns, Stephenson, Captain Cook, Milton, and Columbus were all of humble birth – 'with these bright examples before you, brave boys, let your motto ever be "Excelsior!" onwards and upwards!' [*Boys of England*, 1, 27 November 1866, p. 16]. Upward mobility involved continual activity. There were columns for 'The Young Artist', 'The Young Mechanic', and 'The Young Gardener'. Sports pages illustrated 'The Lazy Boy' and 'The Active Boy', with corresponding sketches of 'Decrepit at Fifty' and 'Hearty at Fifty'. The sporting columns were in fact pioneers of their kind – well-written and illustrated, and backed by news of local sporting events. In an early issue readers were offered free instruction at the Endell Street swimming baths.[53]

As James goes on to point out, the ethos of the journal is clearly fashioned by the liberal principles of Samuel Smiles's *Self-Help* (1859), renowned for its championing of independent citizenship, along with those key middle-class values of thrift and hard work. Muscular Christianity, philathleticism, and the Darwinian interest in species, destined to become a doctrine of racial superiority in the hands of Francis Galton – all are conspicuous in the pages of Brett's paper. The resemblances between Brett's publications and Baden-Powell's *Scouting for Boys* (1908) are clear to see (chapter 5 examines these links). Hitchman found 'nothing flagrantly offensive' in this journal which was at that time in its fourteenth volume.[54] But neither did he think there was much to recommend in it. *Boys of England* was no doubt more tolerable than 'Turnpike Dick' because of the lower middle-class orientation of its contents.

One story, from its earliest issue, shows how by the late 1860s the pattern of boys' serial fiction was set for practically every tale that would follow up to and including the time of *Gem* (1907–39) and *Magnet* (1908–40). The tale in question is 'Jack Rushton' by Charles Stevens. Unlike the scurrilous but heroic Turnpike Dick, Jack is an earnest and well-meaning boy who comes from a respectable background. The narrative interest lies not in Jack's heroic status (in fact, his respectability guarantees he is a bore) but instead in the men he meets on his travels. It is Mark Ambrose the pirate who dominates the story. *Boys of England* carefully negotiates the entry of this burly ne'er-do-well into its pages. Murderer, mutineer, and finally a traitor to his country, Ambrose is a man with blood on his hands. And now, via a dazzlingly rapid sequence of events, Jack is in his protection. Will Jack, as Ambrose's captive, live or die? In this continually suspenseful story, the answer to this terrifying dilemma is that young Jack will have neither to resist nor fight but merely listen to Ambrose telling an enthralling tale of why he turned to piracy. A number of features need to be noted here to grasp what this type of narrative is saying about class, boyhood, and, ultimately, masculinity.

The pirate has encouraged Jack to eat some food, promising the lad that he will not let him starve. He then asks the boy to shake hands with him. But Jack will not. Why? '"Because because", stammered Jack, "your hands are stained with the blood of my poor shipmates"' (p. 306).[55] And, bravely, Jack justifies his refusal. 'My mother has taught me . . . that I shall not shake hands with those whom I cannot esteem' (p. 307). The reference to his mother elicits a surprising response from Ambrose. The pirate understands why Jack is reluctant to reconcile himself to a murderer. Honour is at stake. Yet it is important to note the emphasis laid on maternal – rather than paternal – authority here. It signals that Jack is a sensitive, but not necessarily effeminate, young man. The point is, his attachment to his mother's, and not his father's, values indicates the first of several problems about gender identity that irrupt within this morally complex narrative about what it means to be a proper man. At no point must Jack be associated with an aggressive, ruthless masculinity. Jack says: 'I hope my mother is not misunderstood'. This remark gives Ambrose the cue to declare: 'there was a time when I should have refused to have taken a hand stained with blood' (p. 307). At one time, it seems, Ambrose was like Jack. He too has a respectable background. It is this revelation that finally persuades Jack to shake Ambrose's welcoming hand. The narrative, which starts off by defining their differences, now makes a point of insisting how similar they are. From there on, the likenesses between them multiply. The text exploits coincidence to the full. Ambrose and Jack discover they both come from Plymouth. What is more, both knew Marion Leigh, now Lady Varney. Marion, we are told, broke Ambrose's heart. And so, therefore, both man and boy share the same lovelorn world. Ambrose prefaces his sad autobiography, which Jack promptly identifies as that of a wronged and honest man, with these remarks:

> 'Well, then, I will twist the yarn, and you shall judge whether I deserve pity or not. Yet, how can I excuse myself? I am a vile pirate, and those whom I destroy never wronged me; while *he – he* escapes. Oh! shall I never know the joy of wreaking my vengeance on him? Some day I will go to England and seek him out. I will not die till I have had my revenge!'
> ' "Vengeance is mine!" the Creator has said', returned Jack seriously, 'besides, we live but a little while, and there is justice hereafter.'
> 'Your mother taught you that', sneered the pirate. 'She is a woman, and women are less vindictive than men. If she had suffered the same kind of wrong that I have, she would not preach patience, I'll be sworn. I open my heart to you, boy, I know not why; perhaps because you come from my native place, because you are frank, and bold, and loveable; however, you shall hear my story.' (p. 310)

By this point, however, the story is almost splintering apart under the pressure of several contradictions. This adventure has to commit itself to conflicting systems of value so that it can continue. To begin with, the spirit of revenge, which has made Ambrose into a murderer, is tempered by the evangelical moralizing of young Jack. The taking of human life has to be comprehended illogically as both just and unjust. Ambrose's response to Jack is equally ambiguous. He admires Jack's Christian principles but he proceeds to justify why he has had to reject them. Moral values turn out to be a matter of expediency. The story selects whatever will fit its requirements at moments of crisis such as this one. Demonstrating that Christian beliefs in the abstract are correct but unsuitable in the circumstances ensures that a duplicitous moral framework accommodates Ambrose's immoral lifestyle. It is because Ambrose identifies with Jack's respectable values (that he does, indeed, what is right) that makes it appear that he has put together an alternative morality for himself. Consequently, what Ambrose has done has to be viewed as wrong but it is none the less – and this is what clinches it – understandable. Two sets of moral values, therefore, are overlaid on one another here. Ambrose is, on the one hand, immoral but, on the other, moral in his acknowledgement that that indeed is what he is. The excitement of the story to a large degree relies on this contradiction. It is in this manner that the bad man can be transformed into a glamorous hero. By playing on Ambrose's similarity to young Jack Rushton, the story enables its boy readers to relish, without guilt, shame, or indignation, the blood covering Ambrose's hands.

That said, the narrative is still not specific about why Ambrose's story should be told to Jack. The boy's upright Englishness is offered as a possible reason. But there is a problem in enabling the story to proceed along these lines. 'I open my heart to you, I know not why', declares Ambrose (p. 310). Something is not quite right about this self-revelation. This is the mark of a particular kind of late Victorian masculinity where feelings were increasingly taken for signs of weakness in grown-up men. They certainly did not fit with the pugnacious male spirit of adventure represented by piracy. The story is rather unsure about how it might rationalize Ambrose's violent history. In order for Ambrose to be acceptable, he has to be shown to possess emotions that are just as profound and worthy as those of young Jack. But the idea of an exceptionally masculine man opening up his heart contradicts the ritualized account of beatings, mutinies, and treachery that follows. The narrative suggests that this tale should not be told to a young boy like Jack. There is something remiss about it both in terms of its suspect morals and the precarious meaning of what it means to be a man. The respectable boy and the criminal male adult both have a part to play in shaping an ideal masculinity. But they do not fit easily together. *Boys of England* is asking its young male readers to accept two sets of ostensibly incompatible attitudes – where the law, Christianity, and heartfelt emotions are placed on one side, and merciless killing, crime, and treachery on the other – and see them as belonging to the same world-view.

After 1866 the market for boys' penny fiction was driven in two directions, dividing roughly across working-class and middle-class lines. With the astonishing increase in juvenile periodicals, particularly in the late 1860s and 1870s, a split in the readership appeared. Working-class boys were tempted by *The Bad Boy's Paper*, set up in 1875 by Charles Fox, one of the penny dreadful magnates. It was a short-lived enterprise. More extreme was the celebrated *Wild Boys of London*, suppressed by the police in the 1890s. Brett's lower middle-class *Boys of England* lasted longer, running until 1899. It was followed by numerous rival publications under the control of the Emmett brothers. George Emmett's *Young Englishman's Journal* (1869) was matched by Brett's *Young Men of Great Britain* (1868). Both publishers put out a host of other magazines with almost identical titles. Many of them were lucrative. *Boys of England* had a circulation of no less than 250,000 in the 1870s.[56] Recognizing the huge success of boys' papers in a juvenile market in which it had a diminishing share, the RTS reconsidered how it might take hold of the minds of young men by using a similar format that was altogether higher in quality. In 1866 the Rev. J. Erskine Charles had attempted to improve boys' reading with *Chatterbox*. His journal, however, seems to have found favour only in middle-class homes. It ran for only two years. Over a decade later, *Boy's Own Paper* (*B.O.P.*) successfully brought together different classes of reader under the influence of a unifying ideology: imperialism.

*B.O.P.* was the first journal, and the most enduring of its kind, to be welcomed by the critics of penny fiction. Yet, as E. S. Turner writes, it 'may not have been strictly blood-and-thunder, but it was a long way from milk-and-water.'[57] Arnoldian ideals of culture had certainly not found their way to the nation's increasing numbers of young men. Instead, imperialism took on all the attributes of moral and educational improvement. Those virtues so highly praised in culture – sweetness and light – were overshadowed by a more literary middle-class version of those violent narratives that made their bad-mannered working-class readers objects of ridicule, fear, and contempt. The migration of cultural values was, in effect, moving in two directions, up and down. Up towards a more respectable ideology of securing the empire, and down towards a more popular kind of narrative celebrated by the reading of the masses. (This vertical model, of aspiration and degradation, is a persistently Victorian one.) In the context of late Victorian popular boys' reading – whether in Brett's *Boys of England* or the RTS's *B.O.P.* – the rarefied atmosphere of culture no doubt seemed irrelevant to a world governed by adventure, survivalism, and, as the end of the century approached, war.

## A Good Boy's Paper: *B.O.P.*

*Boy's Own Paper* ran from 1879 to 1967. Until the First World War its contents and layout hardly varied from one week to another. Its sister paper *Girl's Own Paper (G.O.P.)* was set up in 1880. Although both were remarkably successful, *G.O.P.* reached a wider audience in terms of class and occupation (young single and married women). Exact records of sales and circulation figures are not available. However, Jack Cox, the historian of *B.O.P.*, reckons 250,000 to be a fair estimate of the number of young readers.[58] Kirsten Drotner notes how juvenile weeklies benefited from technological advances in Linotype printing developed in the 1880s, and adds: 'the general expansion in retail trades created a national network of local tobacconists, sweetstalls, and cornershops to which adolescents swarmed on their way from school or work to get the Wednesday or Saturday weeklies'.[59] Competitively priced at one penny, *B.O.P.* appeared in a sixteen-page octavo format. Every year readers could purchase coloured binders for a substantial volume running to 800 pages. In 1914 the paper changed to a monthly publication. Two years later the price rose sharply to one shilling. In style the journal most closely resembled the *Boy's Own Magazine*, published by Samuel O. Beeton from 1856 to 1874. *B.O.P.* aimed to address Beeton's readership along with young men whose families read the popular RTS weeklies, such as *The Leisure Hour* (1852–94), which managed to combine 'instruction and recreation' on the Sabbath in the lower middle-class Victorian home. What is more, these journals redefined earnest Sunday reading as a form of leisure.

From the late 1860s the RTS had voiced the need for an appropriate journal to counter what was perceived as the criminal influence of the penny dreadfuls. At the annual general meeting of the Society in 1878, serious discussions took place to establish a good boys' weekly. The Society's Annual Report of 1879 revealed the tension the Committee felt existed between boys' reading and religious instruction. Cox cites the following passage:

> Juvenile crime was being largely stimulated by the pernicious literature circulated among our lads. Judges, magistrates, schoolmasters, prison chaplains, and others were deploring the existence of the evil and calling loudly for a remedy, but none seemed to be forthcoming. The Committee, fully admitting the terrible necessity of a publication which might to some extent supplant those of a mischievous tendency, yet hesitated upon the task. To have made it obtrusively or largely religious in its teaching would have been to defeat the object in view. Yet it did not seem to come within the scope of the Society's operations if this were the case. It was therefore hoped that some private publisher would undertake the task of producing a paper that should be sound and healthy in tone, and which the boys would buy and read. But no one would incur the risk of pecuniary loss which such a publication seemed to threaten . . . It was thus forced upon the Committee to attempt an enterprise from which the others shrank.[60]

How, then, would the RTS, one of the country's most respected religious bodies, guarantee its investment against the vagaries of a market of which it had little knowledge? They appointed George Hutchinson, who came to them with twelve years' experience of editing *Night and Day*, a magazine for Dr Barnardo's boys. Yet he found it hard to persuade the Committee that the proposed *B.O.P.* would be appropriate to the work of the RTS. His pilot issue was not acceptable to the Society's governing board. Hutchinson was obliged by them to find a formula which, as Cox says, would be 'a compromise between the kind of paper boys would read, and buy; the kind of paper parents and teachers would approve; and the kind of paper the Society, as responsible Christian publishers, wanted to reproduce.'[61]

When it went out on sale, *B.O.P.* gave pride of place to fiction – more than half of its contents, in fact. It usually ran three serials concurrently. Up to thirty instalments of 2,000–3,000 words took turns to feature on the front page. The opening paragraphs were laid out next to a large illustration detailing the high points from that week's thrilling episode. Inside, printed text dominated, although high quality engravings were sometimes given a full-page spread. Visual materials were scattered here and there. Yet they were supplementary to the three-ruled columns of adventure, short essays, and correspondence. B.O.P. was clearly not to be looked at; it demanded to be read. It carried some advertisements, notably for books in the B.O.P. library. Occasional and rather lavish fold-out colour plates were issued to be bound into the page opposite specific articles on general knowledge. Poems, songs (including the scores), a regular brainteaser on chess, and shorter pieces on field sports stood alongside essays providing all sorts of information about hobbies, the military, and 'strange but true' stories. Competitions, ranging from music to carving, were set each week, and subsequent winners were duly listed. A short column entitled 'Doings for the Month' provided useful tips on a variety of topics. Caring for animals was frequently one of them. These materials were understandably geared towards young men. But it is striking how exclusively male the contents are. Women rarely appear in B.O.P.. (There was, however, a proportion of women authors. The paper advertised for such things as perambulators, so it seems that mothers were expected to cast an approving eye on its pages.) If the stories and features are not concerned with boys and men, they depict a 'Jungle Book' of predatory creatures – foxes, bears, tigers – along with domestic cats and dogs. These beasts were, then, both fierce and friendly, exciting and sentimental at once, in a domain based on emotional extremes of protecting and fighting.

   Here nothing presents itself as overtly political. No news is in evidence. Most of the paper, however, is devoted to information directly connected with the world (the expanding empire). But this is a world defined according to a highly selective version of history and geography. Ancient culture and far-off places are particular sources of interest. Remote in time and place, they (rather than present-day events) are shaped by the contemporary imperial context. Such a world appropriately excited but did not threaten the boy. And this is simply because this world was bounded by his leisure: hobbies, adventures, sports and games. In fact, *B.O.P.* had no explicit ties with time spent at either school or work. (The public-school story, which ran in practically every issue, may seem aberrant here. Yet, as chapter 2 shows, adventure rather than education is the focus of the schoolboy narrative.) Instead, the paper brings together selected aspects of imperialist ideology – aggressive, competitive, and yet gentlemanly behaviour – to make the most of the boy's free time. This is not to say that the paper is jingoistic. Rather, it appears respectably patriotic. Yet its patriotism celebrates not just the empire but also the boy himself. One of its many rollicking songs, 'Boys of England', makes this point in its title. Singing the praises of his country, the boy was idealizing a quality he himself enshrined. Empire and boyhood, then, were mutually supportive. Everywhere the nation's young hero encountered texts and illustrations that made him the subject of his reading. Here the boy was both the reader and the focus of what he read.

One notable item was the back-page 'Correspondence'. There the editor listed brief (often incisive) replies to a wide range of readers' enquiries. (The column gained some notoriety for its invigorating recommendation for curing 'secret vices'. A cold tub was thought best to bring an end to compulsive masturbation.) Readers' letters were not printed. Instead, the editor signalled his replies by sometimes using either code words or acronyms. On other occasions initials and surnames appeared. There was a frequent use of nicknames and words pertaining to the nature of each enquiry. A sample from the tenth volume (1887–88) gives a fair indication of readers' needs, anxieties, and obsessions:

PENSEROSO – It is not our custom or intention in these pages to encourage boys to waste their time in dabbling in party politics.

SLOGGER – Mr A.W. Fenner of 10, Seymour Street, Euston Square, charges ten shillings for fitting a new blade to an old handle, and six shillings and sixpence for fitting a new handle to an old blade. Binding a bat handle costs ninepence.

C. E. BROWNE – Finish the cleaning of the brass with a rag made slightly greasy with vaseline or paraffin. Any other oil will do harm.

MANCUNIENSIS – There is nothing illegal in your omitting to sign yourself with all your Christian names or initials; but in official documents it is as well to give them, so as to secure identification.

A. C. JANES – John Gibson, the sculptor, measured the Queen for a statue, and according to him she was then exactly five feet high. What her height is now we do not know, but it is probably less than that.

CHARLIE – Too many questions. It matters not which balls you use for juggling, but they are best of the same weight as brass ones. The easiest way of identifying stamps is by the illustrated catalogue. Glass tanks are the best for aquariums.

ZEALANDIA – 1. The three islands in the Straits of Corea forming Port Hamilton are Sodo, a mile broad and three and a half miles long; Sunhodo half as big; and Observatory Island, which is very small. 2. Labuan has a population of 6000; Singapore has 150,000; Hong Kong has 180,000; Socotra has 4000. 3. There is only one railway across the Panama at present.[62]

This sundry list of replies was one of the few places where boys could feel they were explicitly acknowledged as individual participants in their paper. This rather quirky – and secretly coded – 'Correspondence' was designed to entertain and, above all, help each and every one of its readers. Yet these editorial ripostes, often opening with a forceful imperative, adopted an authoritarian tone that kept their near-anonymous readers at a distance. Boys were expected to look up to the editor – a veritable fount of knowledge. No one enquiry was more meritorious than another. Trivial curiosities were offered to all young correspondents as matters of interest. Knowing the height of the Queen was just as valid as obtaining the best materials to build an aquarium. Similarly, the most appropriate weight for juggling-balls was shown, by virtue of juxtaposition, to be as significant as the size, location, and population of various South-East Asian islands. In nearly every case, boys were asking for highly detailed information. Whatever the theme, editorial replies provided exact amounts and laid out correct procedures. Readers were clearly obsessed with getting things – indeed, any things – right. But it was easy for a boy to stray from making acceptable enquiries. 'Penseroso', too thoughtful by half, probably asked which was the best political party. To this line of questioning, there was no practical answer. He should find a hobby instead.

Useful knowledge, therefore, was held within the narrow confines of measurable facts that enabled the boy to imagine he could size up and control his world. Illusory power – the power of what it meant to be a boy – was granted to him in his own repository of carefully remembered details. Each reader listed above clearly wanted to add to a collection of things he knew. (In some respects, this fetishistic, if random, fact-learning seems to be a reaction to the rigorous drills rehearsed in the elementary schools. At least the boy could learn facts that were, for him, his own, not the school's.) The content of such collections – whether concerning geography, history, weaponry, or whatever – may not necessarily have had any immediate application but the skill at remembering details that were in themselves useless was one of the major defining features of imperial boyhood. Boys would, of course, pick up tips, like how to clean brass, from the 'Correspondence' of *B.O.P.*. But not all the boys would be doing all the things listed week in, week out. The overall message ran as follows: whatever you choose to do, master it well (selection and coercion at one and the same time). And, in order to get it right, ask the editor. Similar to rote-learning in structure, it is rote-learning by request. The boy (with the editor's unfailing assistance), and not the curriculum, could dictate what mattered to him.

Many adventure stories in *B.O.P.* were historical romances that aimed to tame the British past by the principles of Victorian imperialism. Understandably, the past would not always make sense of the contemporary context. One story from the 1887 volume reveals how the invention of a patriotic tradition runs into difficulties with a historical moment (the interminable Anglo–French wars of the 1790s) that is, simultaneously, less developed than an imperial age of progress and yet a source of validation for military prowess in the 1880s. Patriotism depends, to a large degree, on nostalgia. But there are certain aspects of history that must be either modified or censored for patriotism to exist. The twenty-six part serial in question is entitled, somewhat typically, 'For England, Home, and Beauty: A Tale of the Navy Ninety Years Ago' by Gordon Stables

C.M., M.D., R.N. (the letters after his name clearly underline his social standing). Stables had served for many years as a naval surgeon. In 1899 he was voted favourite author by readers of *B.O.P.*. (He came top of a list of 121 names.)[63] Stables's story follows the rise of a young man from the gentry through the ranks of the navy until, in the closing pages, he becomes captain of his own ship. The sequence of events is desultory, to say the least. (Its shaping generic influence is the picaresque.) And it contains many violent episodes. Throughout, Stables uses an intrusive narrative voice that frequently interjects to guide the boy carefully through the tale. Stables is eager to demonstrate why some practices that were a part of life in the past may seem morally disreputable in 1887. The trouble is, his story thrives on such unjust practices as press-ganging.

The press-gang, one of the most 'exciting' features of the navy's bygone days, proves the hardest thing to handle. Stables fills up one episode with a bizarre account of how a midshipman dresses up as a woman (singing in his sweet counter-tenor voice) to seduce twelve men who are lured by his siren song only to be promptly pressed into service. Stables frames this highly implausible story in humorous terms (the cross-dressing is supposed to be funny) because he recognizes that press-ganging is to most minds immoral. But the perverse jokes cannot alone wholly justify his glorification of those gangs of men obtaining involuntary recruits. Since the 1790s are presented as an age of heroic Englishmen, some continuity between past and present must be found. It is at this point that Stables's mental acrobatics begin:

> When, in those old times, the number of men in the King's Navy had suddenly to be raised by many thousands, sometimes even doubled, it was to our merchant service our admirals had to look. We hear a great deal about the press-gang in those times. Well, there *was* a press-gang, but it must not be supposed that all our men were impressed. No, far from it. There was a bounty, and that bounty enticed volunteers; but there was something better even than a bounty, there was a genuine love of adventure, and you may add to this a genuine love of country – that patriotism which has made for hundreds of years the men of these islands brothers at heart, and brothers to go hand-in-hand whenever danger threatened their hearths and homes.

A time may come again –may be nigh at hand, alas! – when the number of our ships and the number of our gallant sailors will have to be largely supplemented. Where shall we find our recruits? From the merchant service? Shall we fill up with the scum of the earth? Heaven forbid, for what bond would or could knit men like these together? (p. 578)[64]

Such idealized history was certainly not as patriotic as it might have been. In the 1790s the state had to make men serve their country against their will. And yet this golden age of adventure has to be offered up as proof that Englishmen were and always have been inspired by nationalistic fervour.

Here Stables is more polemical, and thereby explicitly political, than anywhere else in 'For England, Home, and Beauty.' Yet his outspoken words seem neither incongruous nor intrusive in the broader context of *B.O.P.*. On the page opposite the eighth episode are the words and music to 'Old England's Heroes' by one of the paper's most popular songwriters, the Rev. W. J. Foxell, B.D., B.Mus. (Lond.). The lyrics to the first verse and chorus are as follows:

> Come, boys, let us tell of the heroes
>     Who have fought and dar'd to die,
> For St. George and merry England,
>     In the brave days long gone by,
> Who have swell'd their country's glory,
>     And made the foeman flee,
> The patriot, prince, and soldier,
>     The mariner bold and free.
>
> Tell how England won her glory,
>     Tell how England won her fame,
> We'll sing aloud for we are proud,
>     Proud of our English name. (p. 552)

Both Stables's story and Foxell's song oblige boys to consider their duty to fight for their country. In the world of *B.O.P.*, because boys are identified not so much with but rather as the nation, they are in effect being entreated to fight for themselves. That is, they are the England they should be fighting for. Yet the finger in the famous First World War poster ('Your country needs you', spoken by the fine mustachioed figure of General Kitchener) is not pointing as directly at boy readers as might be imagined. Stables's narrative reveals a further problem in the representation of war where heroic deeds can lead to murder. Moreover, Stables labours under another moral obligation – to avoid the kinds of gratuitous violence that characterized the penny dreadfuls.

The next extract demonstrates all these issues. In this passage, the boy hero Dick Trelawney, who comes from 'one of the finest and old fighting families in Cornwall' (p. 435) bravely boards a French frigate:

> Armed with a ship's cutlass which he had snatched from the grasp of a dead sailor who had fallen on his face near a gun, Dick took the shortest road on board, and let himself down actually in the centre of a group of Frenchmen. Did he slash about him with cutlass and fell the Frenchman right and left? He did nothing of the kind. Boys of Dick's age often work wonders, but they cannot perform miracles except in the pages of a penny dreadful or on the boards of twopenny theatre. He would not have been a Trelawney, however, if he had not at once attacked the enemy. That is, he made a lunge at a fat round-faced Frenchee; a big fellow he was too, and as his stomach stuck out considerably in advance of him, Dick made a prod at that. And such a determined and skilful prod was it, that, had it entered where it might have entered, it would have spoiled the fellow's appetite considerably. (p. 553)

Dick is, for all to see, certainly not a murderer. But the story, by sleight of hand, allows the boy reader to imagine that young Dick is trying as best he can to lay the Frenchman low. The emphasis falls on Dick's fearlessness rather than the feat he wishes to accomplish. Yet the fact that Stables so vehemently dissociates his story from the penny dreadfuls suggests there were worrying similarities between both types of narrative. A further quotation makes the resemblance far greater than he is able to disavow: 'The carnage on board the enemy's ships was revolting to think of, the scupper-holes literally ran blood, reddening the water around them, and so many were wounded that hundreds of them bled to death for lack of surgical attention' (p. 610). Even if such a scheme is to be found 'revolting', it grants the reader the permission to imagine it in all its gory detail. The dreadfuls were not so discerning but they let the same quantities of blood.

In 1901 Helen Bosanquet wrote with considerable distaste about 'Cheap Literature', commenting at length on the manner in which it represented violence:

> It is not merely the amount of unnecessary bloodshed which is objectionable. There is far more actual killing in *King Solomon's Mines* [1885] and *Treasure Island*, but no one objects to it there. It must be the want of skill and imagination which leaves us absolutely indifferent as to whom is killed or how . . . Perhaps it is in this mechanical and unconvincing·treatment of the horrors of violent death that we may find some justification for the view that they suggest brutalities to our London 'Hooligans'.[65]

Bosanquet assumes that it is the literary merit of H. Rider Haggard and Robert Louis Stevenson that justifies their many murderous episodes. In its own adventure series, *B.O.P.* thought much the same. Violence had to be taken away from the recently named hooligan and restyled for the respectable boy. It was an aesthetics of a new kind of militaristic masculinity, one hardly tempered by the cultured refinements of sweetness and light. Here was a distinctive imperial spirit of rebellion that turned its back on the strictures of the schoolroom and looked across the world for the imaginative escape to be enjoyed in adventure and romance. Understandably, then, boys of all classes gravitated towards the serials published in *B.O.P.*, and *B.O.P.* paved the way for the rather more scurrilous escapades to be found in *Gem* and *Magnet*.

Both of these papers were deplored by George Orwell, who in a well-known essay pointed to their class snobbery, their racism, and their irrepressibly conservative tone, while noting their powerful appeal to the likes of a young miner avidly turning the pages in his breaks between work. Towards the close of his essay on 'Boys' Weeklies', published in 1939, Orwell asked 'why is there no such thing as a left-wing boys' paper?' And he went on to state:

> At first glance such an idea merely makes one slightly sick. It is so horribly easy to imagine what a left-wing boys' paper would be like, if it existed. I remember in 1920 or 1921 some optimistic person

handing round Communist tracts among a crowd of public-school boys. The tract I received was of the question-and-answer kind:

Q. 'Can a Boy Communist be a Boy Scout, Comrade?'
A. 'No, Comrade'.
Q. 'Why, Comrade?'
A. 'Because, Comrade, a Boy Scout must salute the Union Jack, which is the symbol of tyranny and oppression'. Etc. etc.

Now, suppose that at this moment somebody started a left-wing paper deliberately aimed at boys of twelve to fourteen. I do not suggest that the whole of its contents would be exactly like the tract I have quoted above, but does anybody doubt that they would be *something* like it?[66]

Orwell's remarks are important because they indicate that by the 1930s popular representations of masculinity were completely governed by those right-wing ideologies of nationalism and supremacism that shaped expectations of what it meant to be a boy. Radical opposition could only be conceived of in the didactic moral terms of the Victorian Sunday school. Instead, those forms of reading – the penny dreadfuls and the shilling shockers – which were consumed by the growing numbers of literate working people in the late nineteenth century had been exploited by the Religious Tract Society to make a new generation of young men feel that they were the central social actors of their day. Boyhood may have only been a story (something seemingly outside the political realm) but its narrative dimensions clearly bore close relations (admittedly complex ones) with the way men would learn to live their lives – *as men*.

## Notes

1  Matthew Arnold, *Culture and Anarchy*, (ed.), J. Dover Wilson ([1869]; Cambridge: Cambridge University Press, 1935), p. 70.
2  Thomas Wright, 'On a Possible Popular Culture', *Contemporary Review*, 40 (1881), p. 25.
3  Edward B. Tylor, *Primitive Culture: Researches into the Development of Mythology, Philosophy, Religion, Language, Art, and Custom*, fourth edition ([1871] London: John Murray, 1903), p. 1.

4   Frederic Harrison, 'Culture: A Dialogue', *Fortnightly Review*, NS 2 (1867), pp. 604–5.
5   Raymond Williams, *Culture* (London: Fontana, 1981), p. 13.
6   Arnold, *Culture and Anarchy*, p. 61.
7   Chris Baldick, *The Social Mission of English Criticism 1848–1932* (Oxford: Oxford University Press, 1983), pp. 45–6.
8   ibid., p. 46.
9   Arnold, *Culture and Anarchy*, p. 61.
10  On this point, James Donald remarks: 'The differentiation through standardization strategy has been around as long as popular education. Look closely at any of the more thoughtful conservative educationists and usually you will find that this is what they are on about . . . G. H. Bantock, drawing on the cultural thinking of T. S. Eliot [in many ways, Arnold's heir], has been insisting for more than thirty years that the health of a culture, understood ethnographically as a way of life, depends on both the differentiation of the classes and also their shared membership of the same (national) community . . . Bantock has therefore proposed two different curricula, with the "bottom fifty per cent of pupils" being freed from the demands of academic culture and instead being offered a "popular culture"': 'Beyond Our Ken: English, Englishness, and the National Curriculum' in Peter Brooker and Peter Humm (eds), *Dialogue and Difference: English into the Nineties* (London: Routledge, 1989), pp. 18–19.
11  Wright, 'On a Possible Popular Culture', p. 37.
12  Extracts from Thomas Peckett Prest, 'Sweeney Todd' (1846) and James Malcolm Rymer, 'Varney the Vampire' (1840s) can be found in Peter Haining, (ed.), *The Penny Dreadful: Or, Strange, Horrid and Sensational Tales!* (London: Gollancz, 1975), pp. 95–133.
13  Margaret Oliphant, 'The Byways of Literature: Reading for the Million', *Blackwood's Edinburgh Magazine*, 84 (1858), p. 205.
14  B. G. Johns, 'The Literature of the Streets', *Edinburgh Review*, 165 (1887), pp. 42–3.
15  B. G. Johns, 'Books of Fiction for Children', *Quarterly Review*, 122 (1867), pp. 60, 80–1.
16  Edward G. Salmon, 'What the Working Classes Read', *The Nineteenth Century*, 20 (1886), p. 117.
17  Harold Silver, *Education as History* (London: Methuen, 1983), p. 88.
18  Patrick A. Dunae, *British Juvenile Literature in an Age of Empire: 1880–1914*, unpublished Ph.D dissertation, University of Manchester 1975, p. 10.
19  George H. Elliott, 'Our Readers and What They Read', *The Library*, 7 (1895), pp. 277–8.

20   Joseph Ackland, 'Elementary Education and the Decay of Literature', *The Nineteenth Century*, 35 (1894), p. 419.
21   Johns, 'The Literature of the Streets', p. 42.
22   Wright, 'On a Possible Popular Culture', pp. 35–6.
23   Wright, *Our New Masters* (1873) cited by P. McCann, 'Trade Unions, Artisans and the 1870s Education Act' in Roger Dale *et al.*, (eds), *Education and the State*, Vol. One, *Schooling and the National Interest* (Lewes, Sussex: The Falmer Press, 1981).
24   G. K. Chesterton, 'A Defence of Penny Dreadfuls' (1901) in *Chesteron Essays*, (ed.), K. E. Whitehorn (London: Methuen, 1953), p. 66.
25   Freeman Wills, 'Recreative Evening Schools', *The Nineteenth Century*, 20 (1886), p. 137. On the restrictive nature of rote-learning in elementary education, see Sydney C. Buxton, 'Over-Pressure', *The Nineteenth Century*, 16 (1884), pp. 806–25. Detailed information about the relations between elementary schooling and literacy is to be found in David Vincent, *Literacy and Popular Culture: England 1750–1914* (Cambridge: Cambridge University Press, 1989), pp. 86–94. Vincent cites one school inspector who remarked in 1872–73 that schoolchildren had 'words without ideas, and ideas without words' (p. 92).
26   ibid., p. 137.
27   ibid., p. 133.
28   *Suggestions for the Consideration of Teachers and Others Concerned in the Work of Public Elementary Schools* (London: HMSO, 1905) cited in Pamela Horn, 'English Elementary Education and the Growth of the Imperial Ideal: 1880–1914' in J. A. Mangan, (ed.), *Benefits Bestowed? Education and British Imperialism* (Manchester: Manchester University Press, 1988), p. 42.
29   Jacqueline Rose, *The Case of Peter Pan or The Impossibility of Children's Fiction* (London: Macmillan, 1984), p. 57.
30   A brief overview of elementary school readers can be found in Alec Ellis, *Books in Victorian Elementary Schools*, Library Association Pamphlet, no. 34 (London: The Library Association, 1971); see, in particular, pp. 21–36.
31   Thomas W. Lacqueur, *Religion and Respectability: Sunday Schools and Working-Class Culture 1780–1850* (New Haven, Conn.: Yale University Press, 1976), p. 209.
32   W. E. Gladstone, 'England's Mission', *The Nineteenth Century*, 4 (1878), p. 569.
33   Hugh Cunningham, 'The Language of Patriotism 1750–1914', *History Workshop Journal*, 12 (1981), p. 24.

34 Benjamin Disraeli, Speech on the Royal Titles Bill, *Parliamentary Debates*, third series, 227 (1876), col. 1727.

35 Disraeli, *Selected Speeches of the Late Right Hon. Earl of Beaconsfield*, Vol. Two, (ed.), T. E. Kibbel (London: Longmans, Green, 1882), pp. 527–8.

36 Bill Schwarz, 'Conservatism, Nationalism and Imperialism' in James Donald and Stuart Hall, (eds), *Politics and Ideology* (Milton Keynes: Open University Press, 1986), p. 164.

37 John M. MacKenzie, *Propaganda and Empire: The Manipulation of British Public Opinion, 1880–1960* (Manchester: Manchester University Press, 1984), p. 150.

38 Cited in Alan Sandison, *The Wheel of Empire: A Study of the Imperial Idea in Some Late Nineteenth- and Early Twentieth-Century Fiction* (London: Macmillan, 1967), p. 10.

39 For discussion of opposition to empire by radical educationists, see Brian Simon, *Education and the Labour Movement* (London: Lawrence and Wishart, 1965), pp. 49–96.

40 Quoted from Arnold's School Report of 1876 in Ian Hunter, *Culture and Government: The Emergence of Literary Education* (London: Macmillan, 1988), p. 114.

41 Stephen Humphries, *Hooligans or Rebels? An Oral History of Working-Class Childhood and Youth, 1889–1939* (Oxford: Basil Blackwell, 1981), p. 31.

42 Henry Newbolt, *Poems: New and Old* (London: John Murray, 1912), pp. 76–9.

43 J. Churton Collins, 'Can English Literature Be Taught?', *The Nineteenth Century*, 22 (1887), p. 643.

44 G. R. Humphrey, 'The Reading of the Working Classes', *The Nineteenth Century*, 33 (1893), p. 694.

45 Brian Doyle traces the complicated relations between the study of English and questions of gender and nationalism. He states: 'English was elevated through being imbued with the kind of cultural authority previously invested in classics, but now with the addition of a powerful national dimension that yet somehow transcended nationality', observing how, by the early decades of the twentieth century, the 'sense of "Englishness" that English came to signify was apparently so free of any narrow patriotism or overtly nationalist or imperialist politics that any debate about the meaning of the term itself was deemed unnecessary until quite recently': *English and Englishness* (London: Routledge, 1989), pp. 27, 40.

46 Newbolt *et al.*, *The Teaching of English in England* (London: HMSO, 1921), p. 375.

47  W. T. Stead, *A Plea for the Revival of Reading* (London: Stead's Publishing House, 1906), pp. 75–6.
48  ibid., p. 73.
49  Dunae, 'Penny Dreadfuls: Late Nineteenth-Century Boys' Literature and Crime', *Victorian Studies*, 22 (1979), p. 150.
50  Rose, *The Case of Peter Pan*, pp. 119–25.
51  Francis Hitchman, 'Penny Fiction', *Quarterly Review*, 171 (1890), p. 153.
52  Richard D. Altick, *The English Common Reader: A Social History of the Mass-Reading Public, 1800–1900* (Chicago: University of Chicago Press, 1957), p. 171.
53  Louis James, 'Tom Brown's Imperialist Sons', *Victorian Studies*, 17 (1973), pp. 90–1.
54  Francis Hitchman, 'Penny Fiction', pp. 155–6.
55  Charles Stevens, 'Jack Rushton: Or, Alone in the Pirates' Lair' in Peter Haining, (ed.), *The Penny Dreadfuls: Or, Strange, Horrid & Sensational Tales* (London: Gollancz, 1975). All references to this edition are included in the text.
56  This figure is quoted by MacKenzie, *Propaganda and Empire*, p. 203.
57  E. S. Turner, *Boys Will Be Boys: The Story of Sweeney Todd, Deadwood Dick, Sexton Blake, Dick Barton, et al.* (London: Michael Joseph, 1948), p. 94.
58  Jack Cox, *Take a Cold Tub, Sir! The Story of the Boy's Own Paper* (Guildford, Surrey: Lutterworth Press, 1982), p. 18.
59  Kirsten Drotner, *English Children and their Magazines 1751–1945* (New Haven, Conn.: Yale University Press, 1988), p. 124.
60  Cited in Cox, *Take a Cold Tub, Sir!* p. 18.
61  ibid., p. 20.
62  *Boy's Own Paper*, 10 (1887–88), p. 240.
63  This poll of favourite authors among readers of *B.O.P.* is discussed in Jeffrey Richards, *Happiest Days: The Public Schools in English Fiction* (Manchester: Manchester University Press, 1988), p. 116.
64  Gordon Stables, 'For England, Home, and Beauty: A Tale of the Navy Ninety Years Ago', *Boy's Own Paper*, 10 (1887–88). All references to this work are included in the text.
65  Helen Bosanquet, 'Cheap Literature', *Contemporary Review*, 79 (1901), pp. 678–9.
66  George Orwell, 'Boys' Weeklies' (1939) reprinted in *Collected Essays* (London: Secker and Warburg, 1961), p. 115.

# 2

# Schoolboys

## Manly Boys and Young Gentlemen

ON THE front page of the first issue of the *Boy's Own Paper* there appeared a brief sketch of public school life. 'My First Football Match' was a fictional memoir by a writer destined to become one of the magazines's most successful authors, Talbot Baines Reed. This short story was followed by six others brought together in a hardback edition by the RTS in 1907. His best-known serial, *The Fifth Form at St. Dominic's*, was similarly collected in 1905 and ranked in the top ten of best-ever books for boys run by *The Captain*, a paper styled on *B.O.P.*, in 1908. Pointing to Reed's great popularity among Edwardian boys across the classes, Jeffrey Richards underlines the fact that *St. Dominic's* perfected the public-school story as a genre.[1] The key ingredients of this type of serial – noted by Isabel Quigly as regularly involving 'the stolen exam paper, the innocent wrongly accused', and other remarkable reversals of fate – are shaped by a philosophy of Christian manliness that has its origins in *Tom Brown's Schooldays* by Thomas Hughes.[2] The heroic schoolboy career of Tom Brown was first published anonymously in 1857 and went into five editions alone in that year. By 1862 an impressive 28,000 copies had been sold. (The 1908 survey in *The Captain* placed Hughes as its readers' first choice.) Clearly, by the time Reed set to work on his other schoolboy epic, *Parkhurst Boys*, Hughes's celebrated account of the public school was a classic of its kind.

Hughes's novel is significant because it stands as the first school story that places a special value on education away from home. The narrative stresses the characteristics of the manly boy. From the moment it went into circulation, *Tom Brown* was recognized as a unique work of fiction. As the reviewer in *Blackwood's* noted, in this novel the 'British schoolboy has become a hero', adding that it had achieved a rather surprising impact on some of its readers: 'Talk which would have made our respectable grandmothers' very china rattle with horror at its "vulgarity", is quoted unrebuked by the lips of very correct young ladies'.[3] Representing a new variety of morally responsible and physically strong manliness, Hughes's novel was attempting to raise a longstanding tradition of disreputable tales of unruly schoolboys up to an acceptable level. Hughes was modifying, for political ends, one of the most notorious aspects of the public schools: namely, that these were places where boys had to learn to stand their own ground. Stories such as Maria Edgeworth's *Frank: A Sequel* (1822) – that depict public schools as places where innocent boys learn to be roughed up into experienced men – are in some respects prototypes for highly masculine young men who populate *Tom Brown*. Bearing these early nineteenth-century school fictions in mind, Raymond Williams has this to say about the remarkable change in Victorian perceptions of established institutions such as Eton and Harrow:

> One interesting factor, obviously related to a continuing general attitude in the period, is that schools, almost without exception, are shown as terrible . . . This is probably the last period in which a majority of English public opinion believed that home education was the ideal. From the sixteenth century this belief had been gaining ground, and its complete reversal, with the new public-school ethos after [Thomas] Arnold [of Rugby], is of considerable general importance. But the new attitude does not appear in fiction until *Tom Brown's Schooldays* in 1857.[4]

Taking Arnold's Rugby as its starting point, this chapter investigates the often conflicting masculinities (including the question of homosexual desire) that shape public-school fiction from the 1850s to the First World War. In particular it examines how boyhood is often founded on the idea of honourably flouting the laws of small and inward-looking communities. Institutions that demand obedience rarely achieve it.

Norman Vance claims that the conspicuous turnabout in nineteenth-century attitudes towards education relates to the increasing
influence of bourgeois ideals of masculinity: 'Sturdy manliness needed
more defence as the unregenerate aristocratic Corinthianism of the
Regency fell under the shadow of more domestic values, an easy
victim of middle-class morality.'[5] The raffish, upper-class Corinthian
(as he was known), who turns up most noticeably in Thackeray's
writing, and whose gaming, swearing, and pugilism were the main
features of Regency masculinity, was certainly no longer respectable
by the 1850s. Hughes's infamous bully Flashman finds his roots
in this earlier, aristocratic style of man. The mid-Victorian manly
schoolboy hero, who is physically strong and morally incorruptible,
is the complete antithesis to the swaggering bullies of a former age who
feel it is their birthright to hold power over men deemed to be their
inferiors. Middle-class morality, however, cannot entirely account
for the dramatic changes in upper-class male behaviour and revised
opinions about public schooling that took place at this time.

The public schools were, of course, training-grounds for a special
elite, and their pupils were largely drawn, until the third quarter of
the nineteenth century, from the wealthy landed classes. Until the
1860s, most boys from dissenting backgrounds would have been
either tutored at home or sent to local day schools. The influence of
respectable middle-class families – whose values were often shaped,
on the one hand, by varieties of liberal (occasionally radical) politics
and, on the other, by evangelical moral strictness – did not apply
direct pressure for entry to the established schools such as Eton,
Harrow, and Winchester. Rather, the middle classes presented an
increasingly oppositional voice, backed by material wealth, that
frequently asserted a staunchly republican spirit – the driving force
behind policies of *laissez-faire* – in the face of aristocratic privilege.
The middle classes were conspicuously productive. They made
money. (The aristocracy and gentry, by and large, inherited it.)
It is a fact that the landed classes in the mid-nineteenth-century
often felt they were in danger of being taken over by the increasing
numbers of would-be entrepreneurs. The public schools provide an
important insight into how the concerns of the different classes might
work together.

This particular struggle between competing classes of men was
a longstanding one reaching far back to the growth of powerful

tradespeople in the Renaissance. As D. C. Coleman indicates in his well-known essay, 'Gentlemen and Players', the second half of the nineteenth century witnessed the intensification of the rivalry between those men labelled by their betters as 'players' – that is, men deemed fit for training and the application of practical skills – and those 'gentlemen' who still enjoyed the leisured benefits of a classical education.[6] The last thing proper gentlemen would have wished to associate themselves with was labour. Rupert Wilkinson emphasizes the great importance attached to leisure in the gentlemanly ideal: 'the gentleman's premium on leisure was closely bound up with the amateur tradition, so faithfully perpetuated by the public schools. Pursuits that were unremunerative – classical study, voluntary service as a magistrate – conferred prestige by the very token that they *were* unremunerative.'[7] It followed that the gentleman could quite happily accommodate the post of Member of Parliament within his everyday paternalistic duties towards his parish. However, men whose wealth was based upon the work ethic and its entrepreneurial aspirations were entering the higher echelons of society, even if they were debarred (as they are still today) from many of its highest reaches. ('Trade' retains much of its stigma among some of the oldest landed British families.) The gathering success of businessmen entering their sons into the world of gentlemen's clubs, sporting societies, and party politics made an indirect contribution to the reform of public-school syllabuses in the 1860s and 1870s. These self-made men fostered a culture of science and engineering, to which some of the newer schools would turn. But, as many major educational documents of the day demonstrate, conservative resistance to the increasingly influential, liberal-minded, and practical sort of man was considerable.

In this context, it is useful to turn for a moment, not to a public-school story, but to Alfred Tennyson's 'monodrama' *Maud* (1855), which must count as the most ambitious poetic exploration of these competing sets of values – ones in crisis at the time of the Crimean War (1854–56). In this poem a son of the landed gentry goes through a maddening series of emotional and financial difficulties in the wake of his father's suicide, a death brought about by huge losses incurred by a mid-century railway speculation. Implicitly, the hero's father has foolishly been misled by the wicked, money-grabbing entrepreneurial values of the ambitious bourgeoisie, and so he takes his own life for having sinfully gambled away his estate. The young man's pride, indeed his whole identity, can only be restored by going forward to fight for his country in the Crimea. But the frequently maniacal, wildly syncopated rhythms of the poem (offset by the contradictory and soothing lyricism of its best-known sections) draw his patriotic resolution into question. This 'monodrama' – wherein upper-class masculinity is painfully emasculated by the self-interested money-making of liberal and radical politics – went on sale two years before *Tom Brown*. The circumstances surrounding the war – where dissenting groups (like the Quaker 'Manchester School' of Richard Cobden and John Bright) campaigned for peace and the maintenance of good trade figures, while the aristocracy went furiously into battle and drained the economy with their needs for munitions – mark one of the central divisions in Victorian politics between Conservative and Liberal ideals.

Such was the importance of this war in shaping imperialism that its effects can be felt in Reed's first Parkhurst sketch in *B.O.P.* some twenty-five years later:

> An officer of the Crimean War once described his sensation in some of the battles there as precisely similar to those he had experienced when a boy on the football field at Rugby. I can appreciate the comparison, for one. Certainly never soldier went into action with a more solemn do-or-die feeling than that with which I took my place on the field that afternoon.
>
> 'They've won the choice of sides', said somebody, 'are you going to play with the wind?'
>
> 'Take your places, Parkhurst!' shouted our captain.[8]

The passage makes one connection clear: the school playing field is like a battleground where heroic deeds are done.

Reed's fiction acknowledges that the mid-1850s established the beginning of a new type of public-school ideology, one connected with war, honour, and, above all, doing well on the playing field. It is often (rightly) claimed that the Crimean War was exploited by the Tories to validate the existence of a class of men who no longer had any visible social function other than commanding the armed forces. The war turned into a valiant display of aristocratic might that aimed to widen the appeal of a kind of Tory patriotism that would by the late 1870s emerge in the bellicose form of jingoism.

Such patriotism was designed to challenge the individualism of the liberal-minded middle classes who were to be viewed as traitors to their country by putting their hands in their pockets and vouching for peace. (Pacifist men, like the Quakers, were sometimes made out to be effeminate in Tory propaganda at this time. Illustrations from *Punch* provide excellent examples.)

The male hero who emerged from the Crimea was not only the wounded warrior dutifully tended by nurses but also the chivalric male astride his charger. Appealing to a romanticized tradition of medieval knights in shining armour, aristocratic masculinity became the major shaping force in British imperialism. Such an ideal would feed down to the middle classes as they entered the newly-founded public schools opened in the 1860s and 1870s in increasing numbers. Most of these new institutions were modelled on the older, venerated schools. As the century reached its close, middle-class aspirations shifted from industrial, republican enterprise (producing wealth and keeping careful accounts) – which competed against the landed classes – to ones that wished to join the gentry and aristocracy on their own terms (namely, Queen and country).

The fictions in question in this chapter indicate only too well that the public school had to reorganize itself in the mid-Victorian period so that it was able to accommodate a dynamic exchange of values between both classes: to cultivate, on the one hand, the virtues of the proper gentleman (fair play, team spirit, decorum), and to embrace, on the other, the values of competition, independence, and a wilful strength of mind. As the upper classes devised strategies for maintaining their military prowess, new middle-class liberal demands for education fed into the public schools, particularly where practical forms of training were concerned. Both worked together to open up an institutional space where a different kind of masculinity could emerge. From *Tom Brown* onwards, the educated male turned into a much more admirable and moral hero – the kind of man all boys (regardless of class) could try to be. He still had the traits of his raffish forebears, in terms of 'grit' and 'pluck'. But he now tried to combine the fighting spirit with the even older, more honourable ideal of the polite gentleman who based his very being in what the middle classes most admired: respect.

The manly, strong-minded boy, then, was also to be the young lord of the manor. The public schools would monitor as they say fit the exercise of his body while keeping a watchful eye on him to guarantee moral control. It is important to stress this division of interests because it has been argued that the competitive spirit of the middle classes was assimilated, and ultimately erased, by the public schools. This is the case presented by Martin Wiener in *English Culture and the Decline of the Industrial Spirit, 1850–1980*:

> The educated young men who did go into business took their antibusiness values with them. As businessmen sought to act like educated gentlemen, and as educated gentlemen (or would-be gentlemen) entered business, economic behaviour altered. The dedication to work, the drive for profit, and the readiness to strike out on new paths in its pursuit waned.[9]

On the basis of this view, Wiener claims that the public schools were instrumental in thwarting the bourgeoisie's entrepreneurial drive. Most boys attending these schools, it would seem, conformed to the traditional pattern, and held enterprise in contempt. Yet, as John Baxendale observes, the late Victorian schoolboy belonged to an entirely different generation of young men, with new demands placed upon his mind and body:

> The Arnoldian ideal of the Christian gentleman was no mere putting together of middle-class moral earnestness with gentry style: it was a new synthesis in which neither hereditary right nor competitive individualism guaranteed fitness to rule. Character training along Christian lines, the mental rigours of the classics and the inculcation of the collective spirit, for all the absence of technical education, represented in their time a decisive shift towards meritocracy in the selection and training of future rulers, and as much a challenge to the culture of the landed gentry as to that of the industrialists.[10]

Although the teaching of classics still predominated in most public schools until the First World War, boys none the less studied and played in an environment that staked an increasingly high value on competition (winning prizes, either on the sports field or in Latin recitation). J. A. Mangan has noted the tension between these – at times – incompatible class values in slightly different terms: 'A curious educational paradox in the nineteenth- and early twentieth-century public schools was the co-existence of two apparently irreconcilable systems of belief – Christian gentility and social

Darwinism: uncomfortable but actual bedfellows'.[11] The schools –
even though they were not identical in their structures and traditions
– generally found it hard to bring these contending qualities into
line. In fact, ideal boyhood veered precariously between violence
and virtue.

It is where this system of potentially antagonistic demands fails to
work that generates most critical interest in public-school fictions.
Indeed, it is the transgressions that take place that produce most
of the narrative pleasure. Much the same could be said of any
fictional narrative, since stories depend on transgression and crisis
as organizing principles. But here it is specifically the Draconian
authority imposed by the schools on their members that writers
endlessly reveal as a system that can be successfully challenged, even
if loyalty to that school is required at the end of the day. Breaking
rules, cheating, sneaking, straying out of bounds, defying masters'
orders – all these ways of testing the limits of the closed societies in
which they occur are not only thwarted, often by ingenious means,
by the hierarchies of the school but also by the necessities of plot.
These stories frequently witness the boy's repeated refusal to stay in
his allotted place, whether on the playing field or in the classroom,
only to bring the school's rules and regulations down upon his head.
Defiance is one thing; obedience is another. But the point is, both
transgression and conformity are insistently defined against each
other in the public school. As many of these novels demonstrate,
the public schools had considerable difficulty in maintaining control
over their headstrong charges. And it is with particular reference to
the problem of school discipline that Thomas Arnold stands out as
a significant educator.

*Tom Brown's Schooldays* presented itself as something of a pro-
spectus for Arnold's Rugby when it first appeared. It made a point
of explaining the principles governing Arnold's most important
innovation: the hierarchy of 'praepostors', whereby older boys were
entrusted with the care of younger ones. Complaints of bullying
and other misdeeds were to be reported first to the praepostors
(or prefects) who would then have to decide upon the appropriate
course of action. Whatever the circumstances, younger boys were
expected not to approach masters in the first instance. As reviews
of *Tom Brown* observe, the novel was, in 1857, of interest not
just to boy readers but also to parents intending to send their

children to schools away from home. Given the detailed amount of information included in the novel, Hughes was addressing an audience (both parents and children) that had a limited knowledge of public-school life. Moreover, Rugby was shown to be a place where a better, stronger kind of man could and indeed deserved to be produced. Chapters filled with adventure were tempered by passages upholding the moral purpose of a Rugby education. For all the fights and floggings, Rugby is a Christian foundation, as Hughes's enthusiastic rhetoric declared:

> But what was it after all which seized and held these three hundred boys, dragging them out of themselves, willing or unwilling, for twenty minutes, on Sunday afternoons? . . . What was it that moved and held us, the rest of the three hundred reckless childish boys, who feared the Doctor with all our hearts, and very little besides in heaven or earth; who thought more of our sets in the School than of the Church of Christ, and put the traditions of Rugby and the public opinion of boys in our daily life above the laws of God? We couldn't enter into half of what we heard; we hadn't the knowledge of one another; and little enough of the faith, hope, and love needed to that end. But we listened, as all boys in their better moods will listen (aye and men too for the matter of that), to a man whom we felt to be with all his heart and soul and strength striving against whatever was mean and unmanly and unrighteous in our little world. (p. 116)[12]

Hughes was saying that moral integrity is unlikely to be gained by understanding the sermon word-for-word. Instead the boy must comprehend what drives a man like Arnold to stand so nobly by his convictions. But what exactly were Arnold's distinctive principles? Hughes explained: 'He who roused this consciousness in them, showed them at the same time, by every word he spoke in the pulpit and by his whole daily life, how that battle was to be fought; and he stood there before them, their fellow-soldier and the captain of their band' (pp. 116–17). In this mimetic invocation of Arnold's sermon, Hughes is placing his former headmaster's educational beliefs within the Christian Socialism (or 'muscular Christianity', as it was popularly known) that brings fighting fitness and moral fibre together, and which is celebrated in Kingsley's novels, such as *Alton Locke* (1850). In some ways, this is a distortion of the truth. Vance

emphasizes that Arnold did not sponsor this type of religious belli-
cosity. Nor did he give a high priority to gymnastics: 'He could pay
lip-service to the rugged British tradition of physical hardihood in a
whimsical note on the surprising use of cushions by tender-skinned
Athenian oarsmen, but he was appalled by the "lawless tyranny of
physical strength" at school.'[13] Consequently, a number of Hughes's
earliest readers found his depiction of Arnold rather odd, in spite
of the extraordinary respect the Doctor commanded. One reviewer
claimed that the novel, if graced with a judiciously generous portrait
of Arnold, none the less depicted what were emphatically '*old* days
at Rugby'.[14] This reviewer also noted how Arnold's Rugby laid too
much stress on forms of knowledge of little use or interest to the
young male mind. Hughes, then, was pitching Rugby on his own
ideological battleground where the school figured as an 'army', and
Arnold stood, implausibly, as its 'captain' (p. 119). School discipline
was a prerequisite to Rugby but it had no military orientation during
the years of Arnold's headmastership.

With this brief in mind, Hughes advocated boxing as a substitute
for the scraps young men are all too likely to end up in:

> Learn to box then, as you learn to play cricket and football. Not
> one of you will be the worse, but very much the better for learning
> to box well. Should you never have to use it in earnest, there's no
> exercise in the world so good for the temper, and for the muscles
> of the back and legs.
>
> As to fighting, keep out of it if you can, by all means. When the
> time comes, if ever it should, that you have to say 'Yes' or 'No' to
> a challenge to fight, say 'No' if you can – only take care to make it
> clear to yourself why you say 'No'. It's a proof of the highest courage,
> if done from true Christian motives. It's quite right and justifiable, if
> done from a simple aversion to physical pain and danger. But don't
> say 'No' because you fear a licking, and say or think it's because
> you fear God, for that's neither Christian nor honest. And if you
> do fight, fight it out; and don't give in while you can stand and
> see. (p. 232)

The passage is remarkable for its moral equivocations. In theory,
boxing in the ring is healthy while venting anger outside in fisticuffs is unmanly. Yet boxing has to be recognized as an excellent
preparation for self-defence. The sport, therefore, possesses a double

purpose: to channel the boy's energies away from fighting but, at the same time, to make him ready to fight 'in earnest'. Again, for a boy to say 'No' to the challenge to fight reveals the highest courage; while to say 'Yes' means staying his ground until the bitter end. Either way, physical abuse is taken for granted as a key component in this kind of masculinity. Christian Socialism devised means for ennobling violent acts.

That said, not all boys in *Tom Brown* are born fighters. One of them, George Arthur, is consumptive. This boy, who embodies a distinctly angelic type of Christian virtue, presents a challenge to the riotously male behaviour of Tom and his closest ally, East. On arrival at Rugby, Arthur is found by his bed at prayer. He is ridiculed by 'two or three boys' who 'laughed and sneered' (p. 176). To protect the new boy, Tom swiftly responds by lobbing a boot at one of the bullies, a sign that Tom is both tough and responsible. But he is not, for all that, as morally respectable as Arthur who knows for sure it is his duty to pray every night:

> There were many boys in the room by whom that little scene was taken to heart before they slept. But sleep seemed to have deserted the pillow of poor Tom. For some time his excitement, and the flood of memories which chased one another through his brain, kept him from thinking or resolving. His head throbbed, his heart leapt, and he could hardly keep himself from springing out of bed and rushing about the room. Then the thought of his own mother came across him, and the promise he had made at her knee, years ago, never to forget to kneel by his bedside, and give himself up to his Father, before he laid his head on the pillow, from which it might never rise; and he lay down gently and cried as if his heart would break. He was only fourteen years old. (p. 177)

Arthur is not strong enough to see his way to the end of the story. Hughes introduces him as a 'mother's boy' – ' "his father's dead", says the matron, "and he's got no brothers" ' (p. 171). Closeness to women has nurtured his love of God. Arthur, then, is hardly a proper young man. In the company of Tom and East – who turn into 'great strapping boys' by the fifth form – Arthur 'has learned to swim, and run, and play cricket' but, for all that, he remains 'frail and delicate, with more spirit than body'

p. 233). He is to all his peers a model of piety. Although Arthur cannot become manly, his Christian fortitude, enshrined in a weak 'feminine' body, gives spiritual purpose to his schoolfellows' physical strength. Christianity, therefore, figures as a type of feminine restraint on the innate aggression that characterizes manliness. The trouble is, the novel finds it impossible to sustain Arthur's spiritual presence. (Since his spirituality is 'weak', it must die.) Better at prayer than football, the boy succumbs to a terrible fever that produces experiences analogous to Christ's agony in the garden. He tells Tom: 'You, who are brave and bright and strong, can have no idea of that agony. Pray to God you never may' (p. 243). In one respect, Arthur is more courageous than the healthy boys who survive him. But their survival, as manly Christians, depends on his sacrifice. The pure spirit of God belongs to higher things, and not the world of Rugby.

Establishing the manly ideal was undoubtedly problematic for Hughes since it could not encompass what he perceived to be the weakening femininity of Christian duty. Hughes's contemporaries often voiced scepticism about the distinctly new emphasis on physical robustness. For them it distracted from the idea of the classically educated gentleman – a refined sort of fellow. An essay in the *Edinburgh Review* of 1868, for example, detects a lowering of human instincts in public-school sports. To its author athleticism has brought about 'the low animal estimate of power, the callous unreceptive condition of mind, the coarse moral fibre, and semi-barbarous adulation of all that resembles physical force in man's dealings with his fellow-creatures, which generations of Englishmen are thus annually carrying forward with them from the little world of school into the great school of the world.'[15] Especially noticeable here is the direct connection between the school and professional life – a world where the school ethos is maintained among an educated elite. That world was necessarily growing in size as more and more administrative posts and positions in the armed forces were put in place to control the empire. Increasing contact would be made with peoples who seemed to be 'semi-barbarous', notably in Africa. Within this fretful logic, the civilized imperial mind had to be dissociated from the potential savagery and worrying sexuality of the human body. To counter such associations between physical recreation and barbarism, the public-school athlete had to change the meaning of the male body. To prove the boy was not a beast largely meant desexualizing him.

One school, Loretto in Edinburgh, was headed by a champion at the philathletic movement, H. H. Almond, who took the doctrine of manliness to extremes. According to Mangan in *The Games Ethic and Imperialism*, Almond 'wallowed in a vocabulary of violence, strength, struggle, sacrifice, heroics and hardiness. His language comprised a conscious attempt to paint in words an image of a neo-Spartan imperial warrior, untroubled by doubt, firm in conviction, strong in mind and muscle. It was a Darwinian rhetoric.'[16] Loretto boys donned a distinctive uniform of open-necked shirts and short trousers to give freedom of movement to the manly body. Almond's school was perhaps the most exaggerated outgrowth of the public-school athletic movement. Yet it needs to be borne in mind that the commitment to sports at Loretto formed part of a much wider concern in the 1860s and 1870s with recreation among all classes. G. J. Romanes's article on this topic, published in the *Nineteenth Century*, makes its social Darwinism clear at the start:

> In all places of the civilized world, and in all classes of the civilized community, the struggle for existence is now more keen than ever it has been during the history of our race. Everywhere men, and women, and children are living at a pressure positively frightful to contemplate. Amid the swarming bustle of our smoke-smothered towns surrounded by their zone of poisoned trees, amid the whirling of machinery, the scorching blast of furnaces, and in the tallow-lighted blackness of our mines – everywhere, over the length and breadth of this teeming land, men, and women, and children, in no metaphor, are struggling for life . . . In such a world and at such a time, when more truly than ever it may be said that the whole creation groans in pain and travail, I do not know that for the purposes of health and happiness there is any subject which it is more desirable that persons of all classes should understand than the philosophical theory and the rational practice of recreation.[17]

In his rousing rhetoric, Romanes was promoting the widely upheld ideal of 'rational recreation' – something more than just amusement or relaxation. Recreation of this kind required mental as well as physical energy. It was a profitable use of time, adding mind and muscle to every human faculty, and thus benefiting the whole of society. Fitness, above all, would strengthen the empire. It would, implicitly, build up the physique and intellect of every 'civilized' Briton, thereby surmounting differences of class.

In this respect, Loretto may not seem so exceptional. In fact, Almond's school stood at the vanguard of an athleticism to some extent initiated at Rugby. Loretto's sports-led curriculum paid little heed to the classics. Much the same could be said of Tom Brown's education. 'I know I'd sooner win two school-house matches running than get the Balliol scholarship any day', says Tom's team captain (p. 101). The Latin *vulgus* – one of the few textbooks mentioned in the novel – is a particular source of comedy. Notorious cribbing occurs, and boys consequently have to risk facing their masters with copy-books marred by identical mistakes. The narrative thrills lie in seeing whether such plots aiming to undermine the school system will meet with due punishment. Little recognition is given to learning. It is better by far to box.

In 1897 S. H. Jeyes despaired at the 'gentlemanly failures' who poured out in manly quantities from the by then numerous public schools: 'Grown and growing up, we see them everywhere: bright-eyed, clean-limbed, high-minded, ready for anything, and fit for nothing – unemployed or wearing out their best years in third-rate situations.' This type did not possess the 'essentials of success in the City of London.'[18] Earlier, between 1861 and 1864, the Clarendon Commission examined the state of education in six boarding schools (Eton, Harrow, Rugby, Winchester, Shrewsbury, and Westminster) and two day schools (St. Paul's and Merchant Taylors). Among its many worrying findings was the telling fact that a Harrow boy might spend an average of fifteen hours a week playing cricket in the summer term. The commission led to the Public Schools Act of 1868 which stipulated changes in the school curriculum, with particular reference to the teaching of natural sciences. The House of Lords voiced objections to the introduction of such novel sciences into school life because they were not considered gentlemanly. Science none the less found its place, taking some of the burden of school teaching away from the classics. In 1862 the Head of Eton told the commissioners that Latin and Greek 'were in themselves distasteful to boys'.[19]

The commissioners' report stated one fact plainly: the majority of public schoolboys were badly educated:

If a youth, after four or five years spent at school, quits it at 19, unable to construe an easy bit of Latin or Greek without the help of a dictionary or to write Latin grammatically, almost ignorant of geography and of the history of his own country, unacquainted with any modern language but his own, and hardly competent to write English correctly, to do a simple sum or stumble through an easy proposition of Euclid, a total stranger to the laws that govern the physical world, and to its structure, with an eye and hand unpractised in drawing and without knowing a note of music, with an uncultivated mind, his intellectual education must certainly be accounted a failure, though there may be no fault to find with his principles, character, or manners.

The report went on to emphasize that this kind of boy was not the 'ordinary product' but a 'type much more common than it ought to be.'[20] Since these scornful remarks had far-reaching implications about the competence of the ruling classes, the report laboured under an obligation to balance its severe judgements with a generous commentary celebrating the public schools as those distinguished institutions from which great statesmen had emerged. Such schools may have been responsible for breeding ignorance but, the report insisted, they had also done the fine deed of turning out gentlemen:

Among the services which they [the public schools] have rendered is undoubtedly to be reckoned the maintenance of classical literature as the staple of English education, a service which far outweighs the error of having clung to these studies too exclusively. A second, and a greater still, is the creation of a system of government and discipline for boys, the excellence of which has been universally recognized, and which is admitted to have been most important in its effects on national character and social life. It is not easy to estimate the degree in which the English people are indebted to these schools for the qualities on which they pique themselves most – for their capacity to govern others and control themselves, their aptitude for combining freedom with order, their public spirit, their vigour and manliness of character, their strong but not slavish respect for public opinion, their love of healthy sports and exercise. These schools have been the chief nurseries of our statesmen; in them, and in schools modelled after them, men of all the various classes that make up English society, destined for every profession and career, have been brought up on a footing of social equality, and have contracted the

most enduring friendships, and some of the ruling habits of their
lives; and they have had perhaps the largest share in moulding the
character of an English gentleman.[21]

The commissioners devote far more space here to congratulating
the schools for fostering manly qualities rather than scholarly ones.
Although classical education is defended in this document, albeit
very weakly, it is curious to think that while the schools are supposed
to have made classics the 'staple' of the curriculum, they have none
the less not 'clung to' them 'too exclusively'. The gentleman is
praised for his physical strength, his exercise of power, and, above
all, his rigorous sense of discipline. All these attributes come together
in a bold assertion of his independence. He is not party to public
opinion, and so he will not defer to the masses. But what, the report
ventures to ask, does he actually know?

Aversion to the public-school ideology that produced more and
more of this new breed of competitive gentlemen found its voice
most forcefully in 1902 with J. A. Hobson's liberal attack on empire,
*Imperialism*. Patriotism is Hobson's target:

> To capture the childhood of the country, to mechanize its free play
> into the routine of military drill, to cultivate the savage surviv-
> als of combativeness, to poison its early understanding of history
> by false ideals and pseudo-heroes, and by a consequent dispar-
> agement and neglect of the really vital and elevating lessons of
> the past, to establish a 'geocentric' view of the moral universe
> in which the interests of humanity are subordinate to that of the
> 'country'. . . to feed the always overweening pride of race at an
> age when self-confidence most commonly prevails, and by neces-
> sary implication to disparage other nations, so starting children
> in the world with false measures of value and an unwillingness
> to learn from foreign sources – to fasten this base insularity of
> mind and morals upon the little children of a nation and to call
> it patriotism is as foul an abuse of education as it is possible to
> conceive.[22]

E. M. Forster would have agreed with this view. *The Longest
Journey* (1907), a novel about public-school life shaped by an anti-
imperialist liberalism, depicts a house master winning the complete
attention of his boys with a rousing speech accompanied by illustrations taken from 'portraits of empire builders' that 'hung on the

walls'.[23] Passing on from this gallery of illustrious forefathers, he proceeds to quote from 'imperial poets' (implicitly, the likes of W. E. Henley), and concludes by appropriating a passage from *Henry V*. Shakespeare by this time was certainly embedded in the national consciousness as a patriotic genius. Yet Forster, unlike Hobson, saw that minor public schools (such as the imaginary Sawston of his novel) contained boys whose class background did not square with those upper-class expectations – based on landed wealth and distinguished family lineages – that motivated this imperialist rhetoric: 'It seemed that only a short ladder lay between the preparation-room and the Anglo-Saxon hegemony of the globe. Then he [the house master] paused, and in the silence came "Sob, sob, sob", from a little boy, who was regretting a villa in Guildford and his mother's half acre of garden' (p. 158). In most major public schools, far greater in status than Sawston, that dignified silence was not broken but filled with awe and respect. (Nor was it upset by the pointed cries of an effeminate young man who hailed from the suburbs.) By the last quarter of the century, patriotism was the greatest instrument of disciplinary control in the public schools. It stood at the apex of a hierarchy of interconnected loyalties – to one's house, one's school, and one's country. Each was, on a scale of increasing dimensions, a model of the other.

In this context, Hobson's polemic aimed to show that social differences – between an elite and the 'interests of humanity' (the liberal idea of a common good) – were concealed by imperial supremacism. At a time when the working classes were so conspicuously unsanitary, deficient in growth, and unruly, the public schoolboy appeared healthier, both in mind and body, than he had ever been. He was certainly a breed apart. It took only a decade after the publication of *Tom Brown*, as the Clarendon Report reveals, to establish the manly young man as the proper gentleman. But this type of boy, bringing together the best of Christian honour and the Darwinian instinct to survive, often found authority a problem hard to deal with. Tom Brown for one did not always do as he was told. And he could not do so because his manliness militated against the dutiful behaviour expected from him. If held in high esteem, duty had a weaker, 'feminine' servility about it. Were he to be entirely dutiful, he would not be independent. Although the school was designed to keep the boy's every move under surveillance, it also instilled in him the importance of being his own man. If the boy could escape the eye of his prefects and masters unnoticed, he had triumphed. And if not, he would face a condign punishment for being so daring. At its most exuberant, imperial boyhood took the risk of asserting its strength out of bounds.

## Out of Bounds

Before 1850 the children's literature published by the RTS and SPCK (Society for the Promotion of Christian Knowledge) kept boys and girls not under the secure authority of the school system but beneath the watchful eye of an altogether higher power. J. S. Bratton, examining the tireless evangelicalism of many of these narratives, demonstrates how the children in these rather morbid stories were always instructively punished by an avenging God for their every moral transgression. In one particularly repulsive example a child suffers an appalling disease of the eye for his improper behaviour.[24] Such tales clearly went hand-in-hand with the religious strictures imposed on children by the Sunday schools.

One early public-school fiction that owed much to this strongly moralistic tradition, F. W. Farrar's *Eric, or Little by Little* (1858), placed the iron rod of the Almighty over and above the disciplinary measures of the school, and that was subsequently derided by a new readership with different tastes.[25] The novel has been vilified by numerous commentators, most of whom are in agreement with one of its earliest reviewers who declared: 'Seldom has a book been written with such an excellent intention, by a scholar and a gentleman, which is so painful to read.'[26] Turgid moralizing may be understandable but the lengths to which Farrar indulges in scenes of extravagant violence are not. Drawing a comparison with Samuel Richardson, Bruce Haley states: '*Eric* is the *Clarissa* of juvenile fiction, denouncing the very sins whose portrayal gives it piquancy.'[27] Evangelical children's literature thrives on depictions of physical torment and sustained crises of conscience. *Eric* clings tenaciously to such narrow-minded moral principles by reaching the only conclusion possible for the boy who has so dramatically sinned against his Maker. The novel hurtles towards tragedy. Young Eric's death is held up as a just act. Yet it is also glorified as a heroic moment of redemption.

Clumsily manipulating the genre, the novel points out how the boy has come to recognize why he must die. Only God, not his school, can save him.

Published one year after *Tom Brown*, *Eric* reveals life at the fictional Roslyn School to be in many ways similar to that at Hughes's Rugby. Eric encounters the usual schoolboy rituals of cribbing and flogging. But where Tom maintains his honour and learns to respect his peers and masters, Eric grows increasingly disobedient. The structure of both schools is roughly the same. The boy heroes' behaviour, however, could not be more antithetical. In *Eric* one episode after another involves a cycle of violation, retribution, and reconciliation that adds up not to moral integrity and the strengthening of a fighting fit character, but to ever-multiplying vices – smoking, blaspheming, and even breaking a cane over the head of a sixth-former. The text is interspersed with Eric's declarations of guilt. After his brother Vernon falls 300 feet to his death in a birdnesting accident on a cliff (an incident which, of course, forebodes Eric's own fate), he cries out: 'Oh how my whole soul yearns towards him [Vernon]. I *must* be a better boy. I *will* be better than I have been, in the hope of meeting him again' (p. 326). But his resolve does not last long. With his vicious turn of mind, Eric has by this point in the story managed to snub his formerly beloved brother, a truly wicked action that makes Vernon the first victim of Eric's irrepressible sinning.

Nothing at Roslyn can alter the fatal course of events. The school cannot reform him. Although Farrar celebrates close friendship – 'the two boys squeezed each other's hands, and looked into each other's faces, and silently promised that they would be loving friends forever' (p. 49) – such comradeship seems to promote only rivalry and opposition between the boys rather than heartfelt solidarity. An older boy 'cursed with a degraded and corrupting mind' is placed in Eric's dormitory. And so the hero learns to swear. Farrar feels obliged to censor 'indecent words' (p. 94) – thus making them seem all the more temptingly salacious. In fact the novel runs across the whole gamut of schoolboy vices until the most hideous of them all emerges within the first 100 pages. Unnamed, this sin above all sins – 'the most fatal curse which could ever become rife in a public school', as one boy puts it, quoting the authority of his father (p. 94) – is generally taken to be masturbation. (It could, even more worryingly, be sodomy.) Once this horror has been mentioned, Farrar promptly moves to a biblical parable from the Book of Numbers – Kibbroth-Hattavah, the burial-ground of those found guilty of sexual indulgence. This 'early grave' from the Old Testament anticipates Eric's premature demise.

Life at Roslyn becomes so impossibly bad for Eric that he finally has to escape its clutches. He moves from one vicious scenario, the public school, to another already well-established in boys' fiction: the ship full of burly, ungentlemanly sailors. On board the *Stormy Petrel* (which 'dashes its way gallantly through the blue sea'), Eric finds 'the captain . . . a drunken, blaspheming, and cruel vagabond' (p. 358). He gets sea-sick, is roughed up by the sailors, and cannot get to sleep in the hammocks. The best man among the crew ('Softy Bob') helps him to jump ship to return to Fairholm, the paradise (in 'The Vale of Ayrton') from where he had set out before he learned to be a man at Roslyn. Once safely returned to the society of his guardian, he receives a note in his father's hand stating that his mother is ill and may well die. Eric, having survived the rigours of a public school and seafaring adventure, implausibly expires from shock. Guilt alone has made him perish. And for that, in the end, he is 'forgiven' (p. 386).

With its unrelenting pessimism, *Eric* may well appear to have been written by a dissenting middle-class author exceptionally critical of public-school education. For one thing, Farrar associates the type of manliness so highly valued by Hughes with smoking, drinking, and fighting, and not in the least with athletics. Yet for many years (1871–76) Farrar was headmaster of Marlborough, later taking a similar post at Harrow. However, he was noted in the Victorian period not so much for his academic work but for his popular preaching. Richards brings together a number of Farrar's writings on education with biographical materials to demonstrate that the author had his own brand of 'Christian manliness, which required sober-mindedness, constant self-examination and a passionate commitment to the faith.'[28] Worldly institutions took a secondary role to the church in supporting this asceticism. It was hard for Farrar to find anything of note at Roslyn. Like the Clarendon Commissioners, however, he was obliged to remark on the general esteem that distinguished this kind of education. At one point, Eric writes to Vernon: 'Many have drawn exaggerated pictures of the lowness of public-school morality; the best answer is to point to the good and splendid men that have been trained in public schools, and who lose no opportunity of recurring to them with affection. It is quite possible to be *in* the little world of school-life, and yet not *of* it' (p. 196). In the most thorough survey of debates concerning the reform of the public schools during this period, E. C. Mack writes:

> Unquestionably the chief reason why to Farrar the world of school seemed so evil and the preservation of virtue so difficult was that, like [Thomas] Arnold, he set his moral standard impossibly high and took it too seriously. Tom Brown was a sturdy, manly boy who was never essentially different from those around him. Farrar's ideal boys were so spotless, saintly, and puritanical that they might have given even Arnold pause.[29]

Conforming to the discipline of the schools depends on innate characteristics that are in themselves unchangeable. There are striking similarities between Farrar's view of irreconcilable species of virtuous and vicious boys and his other well-known work, 'Aptitude of Races' presented to the Ethnological Society in 1867: 'Believing that all men are children of a common Father, and partakers of a common Redemption, I do not require the notion of a physical or genetic unity as a motive to philanthropy.' That is, some 'savage' races should not receive the charity of white people because Blacks are an entirely separate species. He adds that he does 'not believe that all races are equally gifted, or all descended from a common pair'.[30] (He was holding on to a polygenetic argument that would be rendered irrelevant by Darwin's *Descent of Man* [1871]. Douglas Lorimer counts Farrar's views among those of 'the professional intellegentsia of the 1860s' who rejected earlier evangelical and philanthropic beliefs in the redeemable 'noble savage'.[31]) Whether Farrar is thinking of the public school or the various races of the world, he instantly categorizes human beings into hierarchic groups. What Farrar has to say in his ethnological researches about the deleterious influence of Caucasian man on the disappearing numbers of native Australians, Caribs, Maoris, and Eskimos could be extended – with a slight adjustment of terms – to Eric's school career: 'The savage *might* have learned many great and glorious lessons; he *has* learnt only what is vicious and degrading.'[32] Eric, of course, comes from a 'higher race' but the education he receives only serves to debase him. A boy like Eric is fatally susceptible to the corrupt influence of others. He is a savage in the midst of a civilized institution, and it is his own preordained weakness that leads him into trouble. Farrar thought much the same about the exploited and hopeless Blacks – it was their own fault, by virtue of being so 'primitive', that they succumbed to the moral and physical corruption of the whites. But the analogy is a strictly limited one. It helps to explain a consistent structure of thought appealing to innate characteristics as a solution to political and cultural differences.

*Eric* was understood by most of its readers (mostly the anxious parents of potentially rebellious children) as a cautionary tale, and that is precisely how the novel is represented in Kipling's scurrilous public-school story, *Stalky & Co.* (1899).[33] Here Stalky and his schoolfellows Beetle and M'Turk jointly deride Farrar's fictions:

> It was a maiden aunt of Stalky who sent him both books, with the inscription, 'To dearest Artie, on his sixteenth birthday'; it was M'Turk who ordered their hypothecation; and it was Beetle, returned from Bideford, who flung them on the window-sill of Number Five study with news that Bastable would advannce but ninepence on the two; *Eric, or Little by Little*, being almost as great a drug as [Farrar's later school novel] *St. Winifred's* [1862]. 'An' I don't think much of your aunt. We're nearly out of cartridges, too – Artie, dear.'
>
> Whereupon Stalky rose up to grapple with him, but M'Turk sat on Stalky's head, calling him a 'pure-minded boy' till peace was declared. As they were grievously in arrears with a Latin prose, as it was a blazing July afternoon, and as they ought to have been at a house cricket-match, they began to renew their acquaintance, intimate and unholy with the volumes.
>
> 'Here we are!' said M'Turk. '"Corporal punishment produced on Eric the worst effects. He burned *not* with remorse or regret" – make a note o' that, Beetle – "but with shame and violent indignation. He glared" – oh, naughty Eric! Let's get to the bit where he goes in for drink.'
>
> 'Hold on half a shake. Here's another sample. "The sixth", he says, "is the palladium of all public schools", but this lot' – Stalky rapped the gilded book – 'can't prevent fellows drinkin' and stealin', an' lettin' fags out of window at night, an' – an' doin' what they please. Golly what we've missed – not going to St. Winifred's!' . . . (p. 49)

*Stalky & Co.* are ostensibly as disrespectful towards authority as *Eric* is. But where Farrar turns to doctrinal outpourings insisting on atonement and redemption, Kipling celebrates the assertive individualism of his boys. For Stalky, Beetle, and M'Turk are found on the very first page of the novel, out of bounds, secretly smoking in the furze that surrounds the United Services College (USC) at Westward Ho!, North Devon (Kipling's former school). *Stalky & Co.*, which repeatedly mocks *Eric* and its two sequels, deeply upset the ageing Farrar whose novels had, by the close of the century, become the laughing-stock of the genre. In *Stalky & Co.*, Kipling took the figure of Eric and made his uncontrollable nature into a positive thing. Rather than be saved by God, Stalky & Co. are saved by their own strong wills and keen intelligence. They are constantly escaping from United Services College, and then, even when caught, manage to produce alibis far more ingenious than anything their incompetent masters are capable of conjuring up. The most prominent feature of Kipling's novel is the fact that the boys are altogether smarter than the men who struggle to educate them. As in *Eric*, the school seems inevitably bad, and yet it has to be held in high esteem for the type of education it provides.

Kipling dedicated his novel to Cormell Price who had in his charge hundreds of boys from service families. The prefatory poem lauding the school opens with the well-known phrase, 'Let us now praise famous men.' Masters such as Price are to be praised because, in the words of the poem, things were surely 'learned' at such a school but their 'uses' were not 'discerned' at the time. The value of such an education, then, may only be recognized in retrospect. Given this proviso, Kipling is able to portray USC as a place where education – mostly classics and cricket – has barely any significance. School provides the framework which Kipling's boys stand outside. Its laws are there to be disobeyed because the likes of Stalky & Co. tower above them.

The first section of the novel 'In the Ambush' introduces a pattern of fooling the masters with the quick-witted prankishness to be found in every chapter that follows. (*Stalky & Co.* has an episodic structure; there is no overall plot to it.) The book reads like a series of instalments in one of the boys' penny papers. The popularity of *B.O.P.*, to take the best-known example, clearly has some bearing on the organization of each of Stalky & Co.'s adventures. 'In the Ambush' finds the three boys trespassing into what they call the 'wuzzy' – the furze covered estate adjoining the school. The estate owner, an

Irishman, Colonel G. M. Dabney, J.P., catches up with them. But rather than allow themselves to be sent packing to the school, the boys resist the colonel's intimidating behaviour and pluck up the courage to communicate with him on his own terms. Accused of birdnesting, M'Turk quotes 'confusedly from his father': 'It's worse than murder, because there's no legal remedy.' Dabney initiates the following tense exchange:

> 'Do you know who I am?' he gurgled at last; Stalky and Beetle quaking.
> 'No, sorr, nor do I care if ye belonged to the Castle itself. Answer me now, as one gentleman to another. Do ye shoot foxes or do ye not?'
> And four years before Stalky and Beetle had carefully kicked M'Turk out of his Irish dialect! Assuredly he had gone mad or taken sunstroke, and as assuredly he would be slain – once by an old gentleman and once by the Head. A public licking of the three was the least they could expect. Yet – if their eyes and ears were to be trusted – the old gentleman had collapsed. It might be a lull before the storm, but –
> 'I do not.' He was still gurgling.
> 'Then you must sack your keeper. He's not fit to live in the same country with a God-fearin' fox. An' a vixen, too – at this time o' year!'
> 'Did ye come up on purpose to tell me this?'
> 'Of course I did, ye silly man', with a stamp of the foot. 'Would you not have done as much for me if you'd seen that thing happen on my land, now?'
> Forgotten – forgotten was the college and the decency due to elders! M'Turk was treading again the barren purple mountains of the rainy West Coast, where in his holidays he was viceroy of four thousand naked acres, only son of a three-hundred-years-old house, lord of a crazy fishing-boat, and the idol of his father's shiftless tenantry. It was the landed man speaking to his equal – deep calling to deep – and the old gentleman acknowledged the cry. (p. 10)

Surely, this is a remarkable incident? At least that is the response this extract is supposed to elicit.

M'Turk may be lying but he comes up with a virtuoso performance that places his credentials as a gentleman above those of a mere schoolboy. A member of the landed classes, M'Turk presumes he can without question vilify the gamekeeper in the course of making Dabney rise to the occasion with a heartfelt acknowledgement that conservative farming values are the most significant things in the world. These values are so resonant that they have the force of an almost primordial 'cry', and they allow for the astonishing reversal where the younger man commands the respect of his elder. The whole passage is made all the more enchanting by the evocation of the Irish brogue which has an unaccustomed and rather quaint appearance here. M'Turk can manipulate his voice to suit his circumstances, and it has the desired effect. A few paragraphs later the bond between M'Turk and the colonel is confirmed. 'Dabney was talking as one man to another. "This comes from promoting a fisherman – a fisherman – from his lobster-pots"' (p. 17). Even if M'Turk has somewhat distorted the facts to get his chums out of an awkward scrape, this encounter demonstrates a point emphasized in many places in the novel – Stalky & Co. are by rights members of a class that is, with or without a public-school education, naturally suited to managing the employment of others. They alone possess 'the Law' which rules society, whether in the British empire or the fictional territories of *The Jungle Books* (1894–95). Guardians of the law, these boys can roam where they like. The fact that other people – such as the unfortunate gamekeeper – might suffer for their right to do so is simply a source of comedy. Those whose destiny it is to live beneath the law are often the butt of the boys' hilarious practical jokes.

Their masters are made to look particularly inept. Scrambling among the furze, one of them (Prout) finds himself trespassing on Dabney's grounds only to end up in an embarrassing face-to-face confrontation with the colonel himself. Dabney's wrath, once reserved for the boys before he discovered their class origins, is unleashed upon the protesting masters who are comically out of breath in search of their charges:

'I stand *in loco parentis.*' Prout's deep voice was added to the discussion. They could hear him pant.

'F'what?' Colonel Dabney was growing more and more Irish.

'Ye are are ye? Then all I can say is that ye set them a very bad example – a dam' bad example if I may say so. I do not own your boys, an' I tell you that if there was a boy grinnin' in every bush on the place *still* you've no shadow of a right here, comin' up from the combe that way, an' frightening everything in it. Don't attempt to deny it. Ye did. Ye should have come to the lodge an' seen me like Christians, instead of chasin' your dam' boys through the length and breadth of my covers. *In loco parentis* ye are? Well, I've not forgotten

my Latin either, an' I'll say to you: "*Quis custodiet ipsos custodes?*" If
the masters trespass, how can we blame the boys?' (p. 24)

Wrongly assuming they can do as they wish in their pursuit of
boys who have strayed out of bounds, the masters fail to live up
to their own standards. The flagrant irony of this situation suggests
that the public schools (particularly minor ones, like USC) have
an altogether trumped up idea of their own authority. Dabney's
infuriated mockery of Prout's Latin implies that school education
amounts to little more than the parroting of bits and pieces of
grammar. Moreover, Dabney is making a slightingly pompous use
of a classical language that has little or no function in everyday life
on the estate. The gentleman can, then, also be the scholar while
the master is only able – for what little it is worth – to teach the
language.

Back at school, the headmaster has the wisdom (and this is the
compliment Kipling pays to Cormell Price) to see that the masters
have made a bosh of reclaiming the boys, and that Stalky & Co.
have brilliantly engineered a scenario in which Prout and another
colleague have been brutally humiliated. The head knows he cannot
prove without doubt that Stalky, Beetle, and M'Turk committed a
crime against the school, and he admits as much: 'There is not a
flaw in any of your characters.' But he quickly adds: 'And that is
why I am going to perpetrate a howling injustice . . . Well, *now* I
am going to lick you.' Beaten ('six apiece'), the boys are then kindly
offered a 'pile of paper-back books'. Reading is an honourable reward
for withstanding physical abuse. Such a conclusion accomplished by
the 'amazing head' settles all differences without, as M'Turk puts
it, 'beastly questions' (p. 31). Between the boys and their head is
the silent acknowledgement that the masters are a bunch of dolts.
Indeed, as one of Kipling's reviewers noted, the ideal public school
boy 'is always a great statesman. It is his statesmanship, coupled with
the plethora of unemployed teachers, that resolves many schools into
a battlefield of diplomacy, in which the boys and the Head are pitted
against the under-masters'.[34]

In 'The Voice of the Hooligan' – one of the most impatient attacks
on Kipling's fiction – Robert Buchanan was appalled by Stalky and
Co.'s irreverent language and behaviour. For him they brought
together all the worst possible features of the lowest social types

with the privileges of public-school education. (This was a form of small-minded middle-class attack on the rich often made in the 1890s.)

> The vulgarity, the brutality, the savagery, reeks on every page. It may be noted as a minor peculiarity that everything, according to our young Hooligans, is 'beastly', or 'giddy', or 'blooming'; adjectives of this sort cropping up everywhere in their conversation, as in that of the savages of London slums. And the moral of the book – for, of course, like all brutalities, it professes to have a moral – is that out of materials like these is fashioned the humanity which is to ennoble and preserve our Anglo-Saxon empire! 'India's full of Stalkies', says the Beetle, 'Cheltenham and Haileybury and Marlborough chaps – that we don't know anything about, and *the surprises will begin when there is really a big row on!*'[35]

Significantly (if to some degree incorrectly), Buchanan observes how these boys use a vocabulary shared by workers in the East End. ('Blooming' is in fact the one that most plausibly connects these two classes.) The point is, Stalky & Co. have the prerogative to mimic whom they like. Although their impersonation of these lower-class voices is a mark of the boys' snobbishness, it also indicates how their identities as gentlemen are based on the appropriation of certain working-class expressions. The hooligans' wilful breaches of the peace bear some resemblances to the boys' eagerness to wander out of bounds. Although their economic and social status is so obviously different from one another, neither group pays heed to an authoritarian state. Rather, both pay respect not to central government but to a much higher, almost mystical, power – the empire. But it needs to be added that the simplicities of populist jingoism had no part in Kipling's writing because he related it to middle-class vulgarity and poor education. In *Stalky & Co.*, one incident exposes the fatuity of rousing patriotism. A visiting Member of Parliament addresses the boys with a speech filled with platitudes. 'Life is not all marbles', he tells them. Lacking grace and sensitivity, he concludes his address by unfurling a cheap calico Union Jack, a gesture that fails to receive the expected 'thunder of applause that should crown his effort' (p. 138).

For the boys of USC the flag was a symbol to be seen 'at a coastguard station, or through a telescope . . .; above the roof of the Golf Club.' What it represented was for them 'a matter shut up, sacred and apart'. Patriotism is, then, to be experienced almost like prayer, certainly never cheapened by a tawdry exhibition such as this one. For Sergeant 'Foxy', the MP had delivered 'a fine speech' – a sign of his craven middle-class jingoism. The boys, however, had different views:

> They discussed the speech in the dormitories. There was not one dissentient voice. Mr Raymond Martin, beyond question, was born in a gutter, and bred in a Board-school, where they played marbles. He was further (I give the barest handful from great store) a Flopshus Cad, an Outrageous Stinker, a Jelly-bellied Flag-flapper (this was Stalky's contribution), and several other things which it is not seemly to put down. (p. 139)

The whole episode is designed to bring one idea forcefully home. Even MPs, belonging to one of the country's most venerated institutions, can debase what it means to be British. These boys, who came largely from families based overseas in the armed forces, had learned to recognize that patriotism is perpetuated by the fine deeds of the army and navy, not by subjects out of uniform. *Stalky & Co.* carries forward into the twentieth century a minority Conservative belief that holds that the true patriot is the soldier (not the parliamentarian), and that the empire's proper governors are its commanding officers (not members of the cabinet). In the army, the likes of Stalky's company and Tommy Atkins (the working-class hero of *Barrack-Room Ballads* [1892]) entirely comprehend each other's language and sentiments. (And, as Kipling's novel illustrates, they actually share a similar vocabulary.) Any other order of authority – whether parliament or school – cannot be treated seriously. In a sense, there was no way in which Stalky's rather militaristic 'company' could be usefully educated. How they acted in their miniature gentlemen's club stemmed from a class security that none of their masters, other than the head, had the strength of mind to understand.

## Passing the Love of Women

Although Kipling's young gentlemen are notable for their extraordinary precocity, there is one area of life so frequently noted in public-school fiction that eludes them completely – sexual attraction. In all the narratives examined so far, women remain marginal to the story, and the infrequent glimpses of women characters are hardly surprising given that these fictions focus on inward-looking all-male communities. Not surprisingly, sexual relations between boys – for all their tabu status – are in evidence, and they become more and more infamous as the century draws to a close. As early as *Tom Brown's Schooldays* homosexuality can be glimpsed. A footnote supplementing a paragraph describes the abuses of fagging. Here Tom and East have refused to be called to fag by a young boy from another house, a 'small friend' in the service of an older student:

> The youth was seized, and dragged struggling out of the quadrangle into the School-house hall. He was one of the miserable little pretty white-handed curly-headed boys, petted and pampered by some of the big fellows, who wrote their verses for them, taught them to drink and use bad language and did all they could to spoil them for everything* in this world and the next. One of the avocations in which these young gentlemen took particular delight, was in going about and getting fags for their protectors, when those heroes were playing any game. They carried about pencil and paper with them, putting down the names of all the boys they sent, always sending five times as many as were wanted, and getting all those thrashed who didn't go.

The most obvious gloss to put on Hughes's remarks is that the monitorial system at Rugby was far from foolproof. Taken lightly, the corruption at stake here could be read as favouritism. But it is Hughes's willingness not to 'strike out the passage' and then provide a discreet marginal commentary that in spite of itself draws attention to the unstated reason 'why it is left in'. The young boy with his pretty feminine attributes is very much the darling of those who protect him. That he provides the older students with sexual favours is implicit in the sentence where the asterisk is inserted. Such a boy would be spoiled for 'everything'.

---

* A kind and wise critic, an old Rugbeian, notes here in the margin: The 'small friend system was not so utterly bad from 1841–47.' Before that, too, there were many noble friendships between big and little boys, but I can't strike out the passage; many boys will know why it is left in. (p. 182)

Increased commitment to manly athleticism in the public school developed alongside intensified fears of homosexual relations between boys. J. R. de S. Honey observes how 'close associations between boys of different ages in different houses were suspect' by the end of the century; 'indeed, in some schools by 1900 if such boys were even seen speaking, "immorality would be taken for granted"'.[36] Honey traces the passage of close friendships between boys from the 1850s through to the decadent 1890s when the trials of Oscar Wilde brought the word homosexual into common circulation. Before the 1890s there was, in Britain, no conception of the homosexual as a type of person. Sexual relations between men were defined in terms of activity – buggery or sodomy – which were punishable by death until 1836. Sexological research had by the last two decades of the nineteenth century produced various accounts of the sexual deviant who was in all respects genetically and psychologically distinct from the norm. He or she was the pervert from whom much early psychoanalysis took its cue to comprehend the vicissitudes of sexual desire. Jeffrey Weeks – who has written extensively on the making of modern conceptions of homosexuality – comments that 'the perverse adult was the public schoolboy grown up, the infraction of the norm whose existence re-established it.'[37]

Public schools, those places where the finest men were prepared for the best positions in life, created the conditions where strictly forbidden desires became strong enough to risk expulsion. Unlike smoking, cribbing, and straying out of bounds, homosexuality was not an open secret. Nor was it adventurous and manly. Since it contravened the guiding principles of Judaeo–Christian religious law, homosexuality could only be mentioned obliquely in fiction. Even then, there was not much of a vocabulary to describe forms of same-sex relationships – the feelings they produced, their significance for the boys involved, and, given the fact they were prohibited, their causation. That said, it is clear to see that the manly team spirit advocated by the schools with its stress on hero-worship bore a precarious relation to same-sex desire. Honey points out that in the 1870s 'schoolboys were not afraid to use the word "love" to describe their feelings for their masters, nor undergraduates for their tutors, nor were they ashamed to have these feelings'.[38] But manly love could in later years be easily mistaken for what came to be scandalized – in Alfred Douglas's well-known phrase – as 'the Love that dare not speak its name.' (The phrase comes from Douglas's poem 'Two Loves', cited as evidence against Wilde in 1895.)

Hero-worship comes very close indeed to the expression of homosexual desire in a story in *The Boy's Own Volume of Fact, Fiction, History and Adventure* published in 1865:

> I remember exactly how he looked. His great, honest eyes shone like stars. His light figure – supple as a withy – was balanced on its lofty station with an easy, natural grace . . . I fell prostrate before the idol directly. When he threw off his jacket, and bared his *biceps* to display its strength, I pressed earnestly forward before the others, and felt the great muscle with a reverential awe . . . from that day on which I saw him he became the Jove of my Pantheon.[39]

Timothy d'Arch Smith points to the similarities between this variety of heroic adoration for one boy by another and the kinds of 'Uranian' writing – of a pederastic nature – that drew extensively on classical mythology to express homosexual feelings. Uranian writing obtained a select cult status in the 1890s. (Wilde and Douglas were involved in circles in which poems, fictions, and essays of this type were produced.) In this extract, the narrator identifies his hero as Jove. No doubt he sees himself as Jove's son – Ganymede, a name signalling homosexual prostitution from the Renaissance onwards. Uranian writing typically praises the athletic young man in terms taken from Greek myth. It was, paradoxically, in the literature – notably Plato – so highly valued in these schools that homosexuality had to be explicitly censored. In Forster's *Maurice* (written in 1914 but only published posthumously in 1971) an early scene shows several undergraduates translating from the *Phaedrus* for their tutor who, noticing the scandal about to appear in the text, instructs them to pass over the 'unspeakable vice of the Greeks'.[40] Among these undergraduates are two men in love with one another.

One of the main Uranian writers discussed by Smith is William Johnson Cory, who was dismissed from his post at Eton in 1872 under suspicious circumstances. (He had been in post there since 1845.) One of Cory's students, H. O. Sturgis, produced a remarkable homoerotic story of schoolboy love, *Tim*, in 1891. Opening with an epigraph from the second Book of Samuel – where David says of Jonathan, 'Thy love to me was wonderful, passing the love of women' – *Tim* introduces its eponymous hero and his passionate friendship for the ambiguously named Carol. The prose adopts a refined lyrical tone that characterizes the aesthetic propensities of Uranian writing:

> 'What woman could ever love as I do?' thought Tim, as he looked naturally to the seat where Carol sat. At that moment a sunbeam from some hole high in the roof fell on the golden curly head which seemed transfigured; and as Tim's hungry eyes rested on the face of his friend, he turned towards him and smiled upon him in his place. (pp. 158–9)[41]

The rush of light illuminating Carol's face (as if by divine ordinance) is one of the many baroque touches to be found in the novel. Carol is both an angel (with a 'golden curly head') and akin to Christ (he is 'transfigured'). The effect is heavenly. It is also camp. Here the biblical quotation frames a text that, like many gay writings, interpolates the sacred and profane. Camp – a discourse which thrives on a principle of ironically turning accepted values on their heads – has particular homosexual origins, and may go unnoticed by those who are not intimate with its practices. The word seems to have been borrowed from the French in the late nineteenth century, and originally meant to pose something or someone in a painting.[42] Sturgis takes the theme of adolescent innocence to such extremes that his Uranian readers would have found his camp representation of Tim's intense love a hilarious (since so incongruous) masking of what was named in the law after 1885 as gross indecency. To less knowing readers, this excerpt may appear both solemn and moving:

> All the complications of love and romance, never hitherto included in any of Tim's views of the future, started into threatening being for the first time, the more alarming for their vagueness; they seemed to cast quite a new light upon his favourite text, as he repeated it to himself on his knees after his prayers that night, as his habit was. 'Passing the love of woman.' 'The love of woman'; he had never thought of it that way before. He had supposed it meant mother's love, sister's love, all good things he had ever known, poor child; and could only imagine the love of women generally as being gentler and more loving than men. Would Carol ever be what the books called

'in love'? ever marry? and in this remote and awful contingency could they stay close friends, or had he been assured that day for the first time in words of the friendship he most coveted, only to see it melt from his grasp as he claimed it? In vain he asked these questions of his own heart. (pp. 185–6)

The significance of this passage lies in its modern recognition that sexuality – the choice of objects of desire – lies in the period of adolescence. And adolescence was in itself a new category within the contemporary understanding of human maturation. (G. Stanley Hall's study of 1904 defines and explores the term.) In much twentieth-century writing, homosexuality is seen as an adolescent phase. Sturgis reveals a similar view here. The passage, even if concealing its homoerotic interests, allows for a quite avant-garde fluidity in its representation of desire. In his all-boys' school, Tim cannot comprehend what the love of a woman (neither mother nor sister) might be, and why moreover it should exist when his love for Carol is so strong. Carol is obviously an image of power. Women's love is by contrast likely to be gentler. The implication is whether a woman's love can be love at all. Furthermore, Tim – another cosseted mother's boy, continuously associated with the feminine – see himself as passive. Sturgis is largely working out homosexual desire within a heterosexual framework: a structure of opposites based around man and woman. And yet this point is both supported and confounded by the fact that Tim loves a boy with a sexually ambivalent name: Carol. The novel is, then, going some way towards asking questions about the terms in which homosexual desire might be comprehended.

In Forrest Reid's Uranian novella *The Garden God* (1905), a whole range of homosexual code-words comes into play.[43] Here is one of the first manifestations of something rather 'queer'. At school the young Graham Iddlesleigh encounters Harold Brocklehurst, literally the boy of his dreams:

His [Harold's] skin – contrasting with the broad linen collar he wore – was of that dark, olive-brown hue which the Greeks, in their own boys, believed to be indicative of courage; his eyes were blue and dark and clear, his nose straight, his mouth extraordinarily fine, delicate; his dark hair, soft and silky, falling in a single great wave over his shapely forehead.

> 'Who are you?' Graham faltered.
> The boy began to blush a little – then to smile. 'My name is Brocklehurst – Harold Brocklehurst . . . Why do you look at me so strangely?'
> His question made Graham suddenly conscious of his rudeness, and also of his childishness, the impossibility of the idea that had floated into his mind. 'I did not mean to', he stammered, covered with confusion. 'I beg your pardon.' Then, with his eyes lowered: 'You mind me very much of some one I know . . . It is rather queer . . .'

And slightly later Harold agrees: 'We are both a little queer.' In this dreamy interview between Graham and his object of desire, Harold, the school they attend has no bearing whatsoever on them. In fact the story could be set anywhere except in one significant respect: a public school is a plausible context for this kind of relationship which grows more and more intense. Ten pages later Graham summons up the courage to kiss his friend on the cheek. Their physical closeness is remarked on from time to time until Harold sadly dies, and Graham is comforted by his father. *The Garden God* had a small circulation among the Uranian coterie.

It was possible for fictions representing passionate friendships between boys to reach a wide readership and not incriminate themselves. Horace Annesley Vachell's *The Hill: A Romance of Friendship* was published in 1905 to great acclaim.[44] Rejoicing in the usual rounds of school life (in this case, Harrow), the novel focuses on the love between John Verney and Harry Desmond – who become via their initials Jonathan and David to each other. In fact, Verney is nicknamed Jonathan by his peers. Their romance is never explicitly eroticized (had it been, the book would not have gone out on sale). But one passage where Verney sings at a school concert closely resembles Reid's risky novella. Here Verney gives the performance of his life before the august presence of a distinguished guest, a Field Marshal. And he sings better than ever before because of his love for Desmond:

> He stared, as if hypnotized, straight in the face of the great soldier, who in turn stared as steadily at John; and John was singing like a lark, with a lark's spontaneous delight in singing, with an eerie self-abandonment which charmed eye as much as ear. Higher and

higher rose the clear, sexless notes, till two of them met and mingled
in a triumphant trill. To Desmond, that trill was the answer to the
quavering, troubled cadences of the first verse upwards unfettered
by the flesh – the pure spirit, not released from the pitiful human clay
without a fierce struggle. At that moment Desmond loved the singer
– the singer who called to him out of heaven, who summonded his
friend to join him, to see what he saw – 'the vision splendid.'
   John began the third and last verse. The famous soldier covered
his face with his hand, releasing John's eyes, which ascended, like
his voice, till they met joyfully the eyes of Desmond. At last he was
singing to his friend – *and his friend knew it.* (p. 100)

Converted into a scene of transcendent lyricism where love reaches
spiritual heights, remote from fleshly immorality, the boys' emotional attachment is shown to have a truth and a purity that are
almost unimaginable. But the considerable effort made here to
banish erotic feelings – particularly in that key word of disavowal,
sexless – all too obviously points to the fact that no matter how
'unfettered' from that devilish thing 'the flesh', the boy experiences
a climactic orgasm. Vachell represents homosexual desire as a state
of aesthetic perfection in an entirely derivative vocabulary that owes
much to Walter Pater's *Greek Studies* (1895).
   Equally successful in terms of sales but explicitly defensive about
homosexual relations was Alec Waugh's *The Loom of Youth* (1917),
written at the age of seventeen just after he had been removed from
Sherborne, at the request of the head, for improper behaviour. The
novel generated an exceptional amount of debate about the state
of the public schools in *The Spectator* and *The Nation*. Waugh's
critique of school life followed in the wake of Arnold Lunn's
sceptical treatment of establishment education in *The Harrovians*
(1913), published on the brink of the First World War. Waugh
recognizes that homosexual desire is, ironically enough, enabled
by the public school even though it is actually forbidden there.
In the following extract, the hero Gordon considers his attachment
to a younger boy:

At times he would sit in the big window-sill when the school was
changing class-room, and as he saw the sea of faces of those,
some big, some small, who had drifted with the stream, and had
soon forgotten early resolutions and principles in the conveniently

broadminded atmosphere of a certain side of Public School life, he realized how easily he could slip into that life and be engulfed. No one would mind; his position would be the same; no one would think the worse of him. Unless, of course, he was caught. (p. 245)[45]

In the conspiratorial silence of their desires, boys like Gordon would in decades to come become a threat not only to the moral order of the school but also, more disturbingly, to the foundations of the state. Boys like him would pass in great numbers into the armed forces and diplomatic service where, as the twentieth century wore on, the homosexual was constructed as a potential traitor, one who would betray his country for sexual favours. Same-sex desire could only exist in secret, and it became associated with state secrets. By the 1930s at least, the pervert could in no way be a patriot.

Yet in *The Loom of Youth* Gordon is not identifiable as a different species of boy. Whereas Uranian writings often feminized their heroes, Waugh makes Gordon as manly (if not more so) than any of his peers. But to be manly for Waugh in 1917 was a debased ideal that meant excluding all moral principles in order to win one match after another for the glory of the school:

Gordon went to Fernhurst with the determination to excel, and at once was brought face to face with the fact that success lay in a blind worship at the shrine of the god of Athleticism. Honesty, virtue, moral determination – these mattered not at all. The author of *Eric* and such others who have never faced, really faced, life and seen what it is, talk of the incalculable good one boy can do, who refuses to be led astray by temptations, and remains true to the ideals he learnt in the nursery. If there does into any school, he is merely labelled as 'pi', and taken no notice of. He who wished to get to the front has to strive after success on the field, and success on the field alone. (pp. 126–7)

Even in its proud estimation of manly athletics, the school is hypocritical. Christian gentility could not for Waugh go together with physical assertiveness. (This is the issue sensed but not interrogated by Hughes in *Tom Brown*.) Such a passage, however, leaves open the question about where homosexuality might be placed – as either a vice implicitly encouraged by the schools or a virtue to be aligned with 'honesty' and 'moral determination'. Homosexual desire is compatible with neither the virtuousness of the scholar ('pi') nor the aggressiveness of the schoolboy 'blood', and yet it finds its idols in both classical literature and on the sports field. *The Loom of Youth* suggests that there are temptations and hypocrisies far worse than the one thing the school deems most subversive of (if none the less central to) its values – homosexuality.

Unlike the majority of their Victorian predecessors, twentieth-century British men have often found it impossible to sustain close friendships with each other for fear of being thought homosexual. In *Between Men* Eve Kosofsky Sedgwick puts forward the view that male homosocial relations have an uncomfortably close bearing on homosexual ones, and that forms of male bonding are founded not so much on Freudian concepts of 'sublimated homosexuality' but more on homophobia.[46] Virulent kinds of homophobia have served this century to keep a sense of male team spirit as distinct as possible from sexual attraction between men. In more recent essays Sedgwick explains how 'homosexual panic' can set in when a man feels threatened either by his same-sex desires or another person's suspicion of them – or both.[47] At the time of *Tom Brown* there was a much more wide-ranging continuum of emotions expressible between boys in public schools, but as this chapter has sought to explain, it was the discovery of sexuality – not just male homosexuality – that redefined what could be said, touched, or wished for in the course of school life. In the space of fifty years, this new kind of schoolboy, the competitive young gentleman, was prone to all sort of desires that the institutions that had produced them found hard to explain.

# Notes

1  Jeffrey Richards, *Happiest Days: The Public Schools in English Fiction* (Manchester: Manchester University Press, 1988), pp. 103–19.
2  Isabel Quigly, *The Heirs of Tom Brown: The English School Story* (London: Chatto and Windus, 1982), p. 83.
3  Anonymous, 'School and College Life: Its Romance and Reality', *Blackwood's Edinburgh Magazine*, 89 (1861), p. 132.

4    Raymond Williams, *The Long Revolution* (London: Chatto and Windus, 1961), pp. 81–2.

5    Norman Vance, *The Sinews of the Spirit: The Ideal of Christian Manliness in Victorian Literature and Religious Thought* (Cambridge: Cambridge University Press, 1985), p. 12.

6    D. C. Coleman, 'Gentlemen and Players', *Economic History Review*, 26 (1973), pp. 92–116.

7    Rupert Wilkinson, *The Prefects: British Leadership and the Public School Tradition: A Comparative Study in the Making of Rulers* (London: Oxford University Press, 1964), pp. 14–15.

8    Talbot Baines Reed, 'My First Football Match', *Boy's Own Paper*, 1 (1879), p. 1, reprinted in Philip Warner, (ed.), *The Best of British Pluck: The Boy's Own Paper* (London: Macdonald and Janes, 1976), p. 18.

9    Martin Wiener, *English Culture and the Decline of the Industrial Spirit, 1850–1980* (Cambridge: Cambridge University Press, 1980), p. 24.

10   John Baxendale, 'Anti-Industrialism and British National Culture: A Case Study in the Communication and Exchange of Social Values' in Asher Cashdan and Martin Jordin, (eds), *Studies in Communication* (Oxford: Basil Blackwell, 1987), pp. 228–9.

11   J. A. Mangan, *Athleticism in the Victorian and Edwardian Public School: The Emergence and Consolidation of an Educational Ideology* (Cambridge: Cambridge University Press, 1981), p. 135.

12   Thomas Hughes, *Tom Brown's Schooldays* ([1858]; London: Puffin Books, 1983). All references to this edition are included in the text.

13   Vance, *The Sinews of the Spirit*, pp. 71–2.

14   Anonymous, 'Arnold and his School', *North British Review*, 28 (1858), pp. 137, 139.

15   Anonymous, 'Liberal Education in England', *Edinburgh Review*, 127 (1868), p. 140.

16   Mangan, *The Games Ethic and Imperialism: Aspects of the Diffusion of an Ideal* (Harmondsworth: Viking, 1985), pp. 26–7.

17   G. J. Romanes, 'Recreation', *Nineteenth Century*, 31 (1879), pp. 401–2. For a comprehensive analysis of this debate, see Peter Bailey, *Leisure and Class in Victorian Britain: Rational Recreation and the Contest for Control, 1830–1885*, second edition (London: Methuen, 1987), pp. 47–67 and 133–53.

18   S. H. Jeyes, 'Our Gentlemanly Failures', *Fortnightly Review*, NS 61 (1897), p. 387.

19   Cited in J. R. de S. Honey, *Tom Brown's Universe: the Development of the Public School in the Nineteenth Century* (London: Millington, 1977), p. 129.

20　*Report of Her Majesty's Commissioners Appointed to Inquire into the Revenues and Management of Certain Colleges and Schools, and the Studies Pursued and Instruction Given therein* ['The Clarendon Report'] in J. Stuart Maclure, (ed.), *Educational Documents: England and Wales: 1816 to the Present Day*, fifth edition (London: Methuen, 1986), p. 85.
21　ibid., p. 87–8.
22　J. A. Hobson, *Imperialism: A Study*, third edition ([1938]; London: Unwin Hyman, 1988), p. 217.
23　E. M. Forster, *The Longest Journey*, (ed.), Elizabeth Heine ([1907]; Harmondsworth: Penguin Books, 1988). All references to this edition are included in the text.
24　J. S. Bratton, *The Impact of Victorian Children's Fiction* (London: Croom Helm, 1981), p. 35. Bratton is referring to one of the Religious Tract Society's earliest publications, 'A recent Instance of the Lord's Goodness to Children, Exemplified in the Happy Death of James Steven, Camberwell, Near London, Who Died March 8th, 1806, Aged Eight Years and Eight Months' (1814). Bratton's study provides a very helpful introduction to the gradual gendering of Victorian children's reading; see, in particular, the chapter on 'Books for Boys' (pp. 102–47).
25　F. W. Farrar, *Eric or Little by Little: A Tale of Roslyn School*, twelfth edition ([1858]; Edinburgh: A & C Black, 1870). All references to this edition are included in the text.
26　Anonymous, 'School and College Life: Its Romance and Reality', p. 137.
27　Bruce Haley, *The Healthy Body and Victorian Culture* (Cambridge, Mass.: Harvard University Press, 1978), p. 158.
28　Richards, *Happiest Days*, p. 78.
29　Edward C. Mack, *Public Schools and British Opinion since 1860: The Relationship between Contemporary Ideas and the Evolution of an English Institution* (New York: Columbia University Press, 1941), p. 17.
30　Farrar, 'Aptitude of Races', *Transactions of the Ethnological Society*, 5 (1867), pp. 115–26, reprinted in Michael D. Biddiss, (ed.), *Images of Race* (Leicester: Leicester University Press, 1979), p. 155.
31　Douglas A. Lorimer, *Colour, Class and the Victorians: English Attitudes to the Negro in the Mid-Nineteenth Century* (Leicester: Leicester University Press, 1978), p. 147.
32　Farrar, 'Aptitudes of Races', p. 151.
33　Rudyard Kipling, *Stalky & Co* ([1899]; London: Pan, 1986). All references to this edition are included in the text.
34　Anonymous, 'Boy, Only Boy', *Academy*, 57 (1899), p. 458.

35  Robert Buchanan, 'The Voice of the Hooligan', *Contemporary Review*, 76 (1899), pp. 775–89, reprinted in Roger Lancelyn Greene, (ed.), *Kipling: The Critical Heritage* (London: Routledge and Kegan Paul, 1971), p. 246.
36  Honey, *Tom Brown's Universe*, p. 183. Honey is citing C. E. Raven, *A Wanderer's Way* (London: Martin Hopkinson, 1928).
37  Jeffrey Weeks, *Sex, Politics, and Society: The Regulation of Sexuality since 1800* (London: Longman, 1981), p. 38.
38  Honey, *Tom Brown's Universe*, p. 192.
39  Anonymous, 'King of Trumps', *The Boys' Own Volume of Fact, Fiction, History and Adventure* (Christmas 1865), pp. 72–5, cited in Timothy d'Arch Smith, *Love in Earnest: Some Notes on the Lives and Writings of English 'Uranian' Poets from 1889 to 1930* (London: Routledge and Kegan Paul, 1970), p. 5.
40  Forster, *Maurice* ([1914; 1971], Harmondsworth: Penguin Books, 1972), p. 51.
41  H. O. Sturgis, *Tim* (London: Macmillan, 1891). All references to this edition are included in the text.
42  On the nineteenth-century origins of 'camp', see Neil Bartlett, *Who Was That Man? A Present for Mr Oscar Wilde* (London: Serpent's Tail, 1988), p. 168. This study of gay historiography provides many insights into the carefully coded nature of late Victorian male same-sex desire.
43  Forrest Reid, *The Garden God: A Romance of Friendship* ([1905]; London: Brilliance Books, 1986), pp. 22–3.
44  Horace Annesley Vachell, *The Hill: A Romance of Friendship* ([1905]; London: John Murray, 1950), p. 100.
45  Alec Waugh, *The Loom of Youth* ([1917]; London: The Richard Press, 1955). All references to this edition are included in the text.
46  Eve Kosofsky Sedgwick, *Between Men: English Literature and Male Homosocial Desire* (New York: Columbia University Press, 1985).
47  See Sedgwick, 'The Beast in the Closet: James and the Writing of Homosexual Panic' in Ruth Bernard Yeazell, (ed.), *Sex, Politics and Science in the Nineteenth-Century Novel*, Selected Papers from the English Institute 1983–84, New Series No. 10 (Baltimore: The Johns Hopkins University Press, 1986), pp. 147–86, and *Epistemology of the Closet* (Berkeley: University of California Press, 1990).

# 3

# Island Stories

## After Crusoe: The Robinsonade

'Were you ever shipwrecked on a desolate island, like Robinson Crusoe?'

'Yes, Master William, I have been shipwrecked; but I never heard of Robinson Crusoe. So many have been wrecked and undergone great hardships, and so many more have known that one man you speak of, out of so many.'

'Oh! but it's all in a book which I have read. I could tell you all about it – and so I will when the ship is quiet again'.(pp 2–3)[1]

Masterman Ready, the eponymous hero of Captain Marryat's novel, may never have heard of Robinson Crusoe but he clearly knows what Crusoe's story is about. Cast by fate upon deserted island shores, the Crusoes of this world must learn to survive unaided. In this brief exchange of dialogue, Ready reminds young Master William that Defoe's fiction has all the certitude of fact. And so *Masterman Ready* (1841) prepares itself to tell once more a story whose status has for over a hundred years been raised in the European imagination into nothing less than a truth. The fantastic elements of Crusoe's lonely years are supposed to stand adjacent to the life histories of those numerous unfortunate sailors and adventurers washed up on the farthest reaches of the globe. In the Robinsonade, so it seems, it should not be possible to tell fact and fiction apart. Therefore, the story of *Robinson Crusoe* (1719) is indistinguishable from the historical truth that shapes it. In this respect, then, Marryat's novel legitimates its propriety as an adventure story. With or without

*Robinson Crusoe, Masterman Ready* declares that such a story has every right to be told because it has happened time and again. But the haunting suspicion is, right from the outset, that this Robinsonade may be at odds with the historical reality it claims to verify. There is already a noticeable tension between the story that made up Crusoe's history and the particular history – colonialism – that put Crusoe's story into motion in the first place.

This chapter considers the gradual permutations of the Crusoe myth in three island narratives emerging at different points in the nineteenth century, each one marking noticeable changes in the relations between popular fiction, imperialism, and boyhood. Beginning with *Masterman Ready*, passing on to R. M. Ballantyne's *The Coral Island* (1857), and then finally arriving at *Treasure Island* by Robert Louis Stevenson (1883), one development is very clear to see. The island adventure shifts in scope and direction from a didactic tract rooted in eighteenth-century children's literature, designed to provide moral sustenance to the young reader, into a story that unremittingly assumes all the knowledge the earlier novels felt obliged to teach.

The island, from Shakespeare's *The Tempest* onwards, has provided the European imagination with an ideal scene of instruction. On islands – geographically sealed-off units – there is the possibility of representing colonialist dreams and fears in miniature. In children's literature, the island regularly serves as an appropriately diminutive world in which dangers can be experienced within safe boundaries. Boy heroes can act as the natural masters of these controllable environments. Islands provide an appositely 'child-like' space which boys can easily circumnavigate without revealing any lack of manful maturity. Moreover, islands are populated – if populated at all – only by savages. Since savages (even adult ones) are racially inferior, they ultimately prove no threat to the boys who occupy this territory. In the end, they are always surrounded but they will, for narrative purposes, put up a good fight. In the island story, these savage lands are, by implication, underdeveloped because they are so small. Civilization, it would seem, has not had enough room to grow in such a constricted space. It follows then, that white children are superior in strength of body and mind to grown-up islanders. This is the formula to which many nineteenth-century Robinsonades approximate. By the time of *The*

*Coral Island*, it is clear that the enduring Crusoe myth is following a much more forceful imperialist turn of events than before.

*The Coral Island* and *Treasure Island*, therefore, have no difficulty in placing their able and confident boy heroes as the central controlling agents of the plot. In both these books, the boy has little or nothing to learn. Moral wisdom does not come from above, as it would in eighteenth-century children's narratives. Such wisdom is instead a natural resource dwelling within him. Without any trouble at all, Ballantyne's and Stevenson's boys can lead and command. Unlike Marryat's Master William, who has much to discover about adult life, the type of boy elevated to a higher and more powerful status by these later authors can solve most of the problems that beset him. Therefore, moral questions – those concerning Christian belief and ethical choices, that preoccupy a good deal of Marryat's story-telling – dwindle in stature in *The Coral Island* and *Treasure Island*, as frequent violent actions (like bouts of fisticuffs) take pride of place.

During the period that Ballantyne's and Stevenson's highly popular novels appeared, the central character of this type of adventure had conspicuously moved from the ageing and isolated individual associated with Crusoe himself to the boy surrounded by threatening (cannibalistic) natives and ne'er-do-well men (usually pirates). Consequently, as attention is focused more and more closely on the boy's ability to take control of his fate, the issue of moral responsibility almost slips out of sight. There can be more adventure once a boy becomes the master of his fate and the captain of his soul. Likewise, as soon as the boy is put in the position of surveying the size and shape of his island, divisions of class and race deepen to create rifts that only he has the narrative power to overcome. But perhaps, out of all these connected shifts of emphasis, the most interesting change concerns the status of fiction itself, and how the Robinsonade is modified, particularly in Stevenson's hands, into a kind of popular romance highly admired by conservative apologists for the novel. With its boy hero, its ostensibly simple division of moral values, and its perfection of a tried-and-tested genre, *Treasure Island* was praised as a model of romance fiction at a time when imperialism was in the ascendant. In other words, the critical debate about realism and romance, conducted in many periodicals during the 1880s, took place when Britain's own imperial treasures loomed more largely than ever before in the nation's mind. (The 1880s, of course, witnessed intensified European rivalries over Africa.)

*Masterman Ready*, unlike *Treasure Island*, was written in order to teach a specific lesson: to correect the geographical and factual errors made in Jan Wyss's *The Swiss Family Robinson* (1812). A former officer of the Royal Navy, Marryat was irritated by the numerous mistakes that populate Wyss's tale: 'The island is supposed to be far to the southward, near to Van Diemen's Land; yet in these temperate latitudes we have not only plants, but animals introduced, which could only be found in the interior of Africa or the torrid zone, mixed up with those really indigenous to the climate' (pp. xi–xii). However, even if Marryat sets out to rectify the implausible activities of the Swiss Family Robinson, whose initiatives for survival are often astounding (at one point, they eat a flamingo), *Masterman Ready* largely duplicates the strategies of Wyss's novel. Just as the Swiss Family Robinson export their homely values to the tropical extravagance of their new habitat, so too does the Seagrave family in Marryat's story turn their island over into a little world of domestic bliss. Heading for Australia, hit by a storm, and then ruthlessly betrayed by their crew, the Seagraves, along with Ready and their freed slave Juno (a figure who signals the family's right-minded benevolence), are promptly stranded on strange and distant shores. They would not be able to carry on, however, without the able seamanship of the elderly Masterman Ready, the only loyal man among the untrustworthy sailors aboard the fated *Pacific*. Ready, who appropriately lives up to his name (forever willing, readily obliging), occupies a special place in the class relations worked out in the story. Predictably, the other sailors practically mutiny against their captain. Their contemptible actions obviously contrast with those of Ready who untiringly stands out as an admirable example of the working man who knows his place. He never fails to assist his helpless betters.

This juxtaposition of good and bad types from the same class of seafarers has an additional function. Mutinous rebellion is clearly part of the dangerous stuff of adventure upon which this Robinsonade relies. But it belongs to a social code to which the properly behaved and property-owning middle class has no access. Adventure, in the form of transgressing boundaries, is not rightly theirs. Yet the narrative opens up – as narratives tend to – a desire for crisis, difference, and otherness. The start of the novel has already hinted however, that fiction can only be enjoyed when it adheres to historical truth. That is, the romantic impulse to tell (and subsequently rework) Crusoe's tale is counterpointed by a stress on verisimilitude – to minimize, even conceal, the impropriety of fiction. As the debates in the later years about the penny dreadfuls indicate, this tension was related to gathering Victorian concerns about the correct place of fiction in the divided spheres of education and leisure. Fiction should entertain but not divert its readers from useful knowledge and proper conduct.

*Masterman Ready* undertakes to resolve this already articulated conflict of interests: between a puritanical adherence to vraisemblance (almost the negation of fiction itself) and Master William's desire for Crusoe's stimulating story. Mr Seagrave may be returning to his Australian farm – 'several thousand acres of land' – but there is no implication whatsoever that he will risk his life in that colony. Rather, the narrator emphasizes Seagrave's worthy intentions to use to the full 'a variety of articles of every description for its improvement' (p. 4). Farming, unlike a passage across the ocean, promises nothing other than well-rewarded labour. The improving nature of farming hardly possesses the narrative excitement of being shipwrecked and thereby prevented from doing such a good (if earnest) job. Ready enables the Seagraves to make the most of their adventure for several obvious reasons. He has mixed with a bad lot of men and yet not been contaminated by them; he has the expertise to survive in the most adverse conditions; and he attributes any good fortune that falls upon the family not to himself, but to 'Providence' – the beneficent gift from God that noticeably cures Crusoe's many woes. All of Ready's remarkable qualities rest on his association with a seafaring world that wholly contradicts the values he upholds. Lower in class, he is far superior in capability than those whose needs he tends. But he is placed in a position of sustained subservience. In one respect at least, he is an updated version of Defoe's Friday. In another, he represents an idealized figure of working-class compliance. Ready, therefore, provides the structure for an adventure to take place with the least violation of decorum. The story, however, turns out to hold little in the way of action other than the rehearsal of bourgeois pieties.

Once the island is made habitable with Ready's abundant and freely-given labour, and since there is little tension between the Seagraves and their servants, the narrative is left with a limited range of alternatives with which to progress its story. The remainder of the novel follows a pattern that absorbs into its structure the quality so highly praised in Ready: doing one's duty. *Masterman Ready* is designed to provide a useful service to its young readers by filling out its subsequent pages with the kind of information to be found in history and geography textbooks. ("'What is a quagga?'" "A wild ass, partly covered with stripes, but not so much as the zebra; a pretty animal to look at, but the flesh is very bad'" [p. 187] – that is how Ready informs the naturally inquisitive mind of the ideal schoolboy, William Seagrave.) Several chapters are devoted to the many enthralling stories Ready has to tell about his life among the Hottentots. Marryat's novel, then, is gradually filled up with a multitude of inset narratives – all of which are carefully listened to (and doubtless learnt by heart) by Master William. This island story turns out to be an island of stories. But these are all tales about places far away from the island itself. The first of the stories to preoccupy the narrative concerns the political history informing the Seagraves' plight and which, by implication, accounts for Crusoe's abandonment upon his Caribbean island over a century beforehand.

Having placed the Seagraves on an island, Marryat's novel does its own particular duty to its readers by way of a remarkable piece of self-legitimation. It proceeds to explain the rationale of colonialism. The person outlining the expansion of European nations into other continents, this time, is not Ready but Mr Seagrave, who now takes on a new and central function: to teach. While Ready sets about his menial work, Mr Seagrave spends his time answering one of Master William's searching questions: 'Why are England and other nations so anxious to have what you call colonies?' The disquisition that follows is a model of mid-nineteenth-century Sunday school instruction:

Because they tend so much to the prosperity of the mother country. In their infancy they generally are an expense to her, as they require her care; but as they advance, they are able to repay her by taking her manufactures, and returning for them their own produce; an exchange mutually advantageous, but more so to the mother country than to the colony, as the mother country, assuming to herself the right of supplying all the wants of the colony, has a market for the labour of her own people, without any competition. And here, my boy, you may observe what a parallel there is between a colony and the mother country and a child and its parent. In infancy, the mother country assists and supports the colony as an infant; as it advances and becomes vigorous, the colony returns the obligation: but the parallel does not end there. As soon as the colony has grown strong and powerful enough to take care of itself, it throws off the yoke of subjection, and declares itself independent; just as a son, who has grown up to manhood, leaves his father's house, and takes up a business to gain his own livelihood. This is as certain to be the case, as it is that a bird as soon as it can fly will leave its parent's nest. (p. 116)

This is the first of a number of replies to young William's anxious enquiries and exclamations: 'Will England ever fall, and be of no more importance than Portugal is now?' (p. 116) and 'What! the negroes become a great nation?' (p. 117). On each occasion, Mr Seagrave rationalizes the past, present, and future aspects of colonialism, carefully itemizing each of them in wholly naturalized terms. And the structuring of this colonial knowledge explicitly mirrors its content. A father is telling his son that parent empires bring up their outlying lands like children. Economic relations are subsumed into familial ones. Colonial history transforms into a family romance. However, as Master William's questions indicate, the reasons for colonialism are by no means self-evident. Similarly, there is no obvious reason for the Robinsonade in itself, except for the fact that the island story is located in a 'world' where colonial discourse can justify its existence. This Robinsonade, therefore, suggests that it has, simply as a piece of fiction, no self-sustaining value independent from colonialism – the history shaping its moral purpose.

During the course of Ready's extended autobiography, the child–parent relationship is once more given attention, this time with reference to boyhood:

'We certainly are of a perverse nature, as I have often heard the clergy man say, for it appears to me that we always wish to do that which we are not told to do. If my mother had not been always persuading me against going to sea, I really believe I might have stayed at home. Mine was a proud nature when I was a child. I suppose I got it from my father, for my mother, poor thing, was humble enough. I could not bear that any boy should do what I could not; and I often ventured so rashly, that I might do more than other boys dared to do, that it was a wonder, as every one then said, that I had not lost my life a hundred times; and my poor mother was continually hearing of some danger that I was in, and she would first scold and then entreat me not to be so venturesome, and then she would go into her room and weep and pray, for I was her only hope and comfort, and all that bound her to the world. I've often thought since, how selfish I must have been. I was too young to know what pain I was giving her, and how anxiety was preying upon her, all on my account. (p. 135)

This passage makes one point clear. Children are naturally unruly and must learn the error of their ways. These sentiments accentuate the didactic function of the novel. But a second, and more significant, question arises from these moralizing phrases: this extract marks the novel's inbuilt resistance to the puritanism it espouses. According to the narrative – almost in spite of itself – boys are independent at heart, in nature rebellious, and competitive in spirit. They are 'venturesome'. Adventure characterizes boyhood. (This gamesomeness can be glimpsed in the incidental antics of William's naughty little brother, Tommy.) Yet how can there be any adventure when practically all traits of incorrigible boyhood have been eradicated from the story? Only, it seems, by recording their erasure from Ready's formative years. As soon as Ready became 'a supernumerary boy' in the navy, he did his 'duty' and 'was never punished' (p. 197).

Adventure, even if it is the spur to this Robinsonade, remains in the margins of the narrative until the final moment of escape from the island. After the moral lessons, the geographical exploration of Africa in Ready's tale, and many platefuls of turtle soup, the Seagraves and their attendants are attacked by natives wielding spears. These fierce intruders die in considerable numbers. Finally, the family is saved from being overwhelmed by these hostile forces by the providential appearance of a schooner. The narrative, therefore, ends with scenes of the family embattled, frantically trying to protect their lives and their carefully cultivated dominion. Ready himself is speared through the stomach and dies in the closing pages.

(It is certainly not part of his duty to survive the Seagraves.) These crude plot devices show that God is on the colonists' side. But their noticeable deferral in the narrative confirms an important point: only a violent encounter, rather than a vicariously told story (Ready's life) or a lesson in history (Mr Seagrave's theory of colonialism), can end the novel. It is, indeed, this final confrontation with the natives (the repressed 'others' of Marryat's colonized world) that brings the story to a halt. And so *Masterman Ready*, after many moralistic digressions, at last takes the shape of an adventure, something it has resisted nearly all the way through its largely uneventful course.

Yet it is precisely for his adventurous spirit that Marryat is most remembered. Greatly admired by Joseph Conrad, Marryat is often seen as the main precursor of late nineteenth-century juvenile adventure story writers.[2] One mid-Victorian commentator, William Hurton, provided an enthusiastic overview of Marryat's complete works, praising them for their faithful depiction of life above and below deck. Each seafaring tale has proved an inspiration to a whole generation of boys:

> No author, whomsoever, has sent so many young gentlemen to sea as Captain Marryat. We solemnly warn, advise, and conjure all tender and loving mammas, who wisely wish to keep their darlings safely at home, not to permit Marryat's sea-fictions to be read, devoured, gloated over, by their ingenuous boys, until the latter are well on to seventeen, for, by a recent regulation, youths are now allowed to enter even at sixteen years of age. Above all, guard against 'Peter Simple' and 'Mr Midshipman Easy'! for the adventures of these model reefers exercise an irresistible fascination over all lads who have an innate predilection for the sea.[3]

Like his fiction, Marryat's biography reads as a remarkable collection of strangely ordered events – sketching Napoleon on his death bed; deserting his wife after she bore eleven children – many of which are evaluated in a brief and searching essay by Virginia Woolf, 'The Captain's Death Bed', written in 1935. Indeed, his life story appears to be as fantastic as his novels.

In his comprehensive assessment of Marryat's output, particularly of those narratives of young midshipmen at the time of the Napoleonic Wars (such as *Mr Midshipman Easy* [1836]), Patrick

Brantlinger observes a disjunction between the rapidly reported incidents that befall these young men and their lack of characterization: 'Though Marryat's novels express various, mostly adolescent emotions, they are picaresque narrations of one adventure after another which subordinate both emotion and character to action.'⁴ There are close resemblances between Marryat's own ship's log (aboard the *Impérieuse* which took him around the globe) and his fictions. The log records, in a paradoxically brief and dispassionate form, many striking incidents – drownings, shootings, bridge-burnings, and so on. These stories of young midshipmen, initiated into the rigours of manhood, manage to represent acts of violence drily and as a matter of course. The novels, then, were appreciated for remaining faithful to the terrible truths they recorded. Hurton admired the accuracy of Marryat's descriptions too; he quotes a passage from *Frank Mildmay* (1829) outlining the midshipmen's squalid living conditions, and comments: 'A pretty enumeration of the living occupants of a middy's berth, and the furniture and garnishing thereof! One would fancy this description quite enough to knock on the head all romantic notions of a reefer's life, of any enthusiastic boy sighing to write R.N. after his name'.⁵ Both habitual squalor and routine violence – the antitheses of the polite middle-class home – form the substance and the attraction of these unfalteringly realistic stories. These fictions represent, for boys at home, an excitingly different way of life that is none the less safely and respectably governed by a strict adherence to the social order. Where does this fascination for Marryat's truthfulness leave *Masterman Ready*?

It suggests, for one thing, that this Robinsonade was more of a fiction than anything likely to turn up in a ship's log. Wyss's story had taken the Crusoe narrative to awkward extremes, and it was Marryat's project to correct it. But by trying to make the Robinsonade into a plausible succession of events, Marryat was left stranded, so to speak, on his island, having to account for what the Seagraves might, within the terms of the Crusoe myth, be doing there. Once on the island, having dutifully made this strange environment almost identical to their British home, there is nothing else to while away the time but escape from it – into other stories: about Africa, about the rise and fall of empires, and so on. The novel discloses a key double bind within colonial discourse: that the desire for difference has to struggle against an appropriative interest in similitude. The island is made into a place so akin to Britain that it has to be abandoned. In other words, the spirit of adventure that led Marryat there instantly leads him away from it. But to where? Accurate description and moral instruction, it seems. It would be left to Ballantyne, not Marryat, to exploit – in every sense of the word – the 'interest' of the colonized island.

## Going Native: The Coral Island

Writing about the colonial context of *Robinson Crusoe*, Peter Hulme observes that the word 'adventure' contains mutually informing meanings about trade, on the one hand, and fiction, on the other, both of which combine in the concept of risk:

> In one form or another the term has had a continuous existence from the twelfth century to the present day to refer to certain kinds of investor, originally 'merchant adventurer' – anyone investing in overseas trade – more recently 'adventure capitalist', the asset stripper who occupies in contemporary populist demonology the place of the early eighteenth-century stock-jobber. Yet the interest of the word obviously lies in its overlap of the financial worlds of *Lloyd's List* and John Buchan, the common element being risk. It might be said that the 'pure' adventure story, which has to take place outside metropolitan Europe and preferably in as remote an area as possible, reached its apogee as the tentacles of European colonialism were at their greatest reach in the late nineteenth century.[6]

Ballantyne's early career nicely bears out this point. He was apprenticed in his teens as a clerk to the Governor and Company of Adventurers of England, Trading into Hudson's Bay. Out of this experience came *Hudson's Bay Every-day Life in the Wilds of North America* (1847), *Ungava* (1852), and *The Young Fur Traders* (1856). *The Coral Island* follows an established pattern in Ballantyne's work that brings together an interest in developing trade, mixing with the natives, and using the boy as a heroic adventurer.

By turning his attention to Fiji, Ballantyne was able to focus on a number of fears and fascinations encircling this far-flung colony. Although Fiji had been sighted by Tasman, Bligh, and Cook in the seventeenth and eighteenth centuries, it was not until the first half of the nineteenth century that missionaries and traders settled on the islands, spreading Methodism among the tribes and carrying off plentiful supplies of sandalwood to Australia. Fiji, however, was most feared because of cannibalism. *Fiji and the Fijians*, the journals of the Wesleyan missionary, Thomas Williams, were published in 1859, and reported the most astounding accounts of eating human flesh. Williams had left the colony before the arrival of British warships frightened the Fijians into converting to Christianity.[7] The date of their conversion, 1855, roughly coincides with the composition and publication of Ballantyne's adventure.

Fiji was significant to the Victorian mind in another important respect. Its geographical location was notably fraught with danger – many ships had been wrecked upon coral reefs. Coral itself was a source of amazement to natural historians. Apart from being prized as a commodity in its own right, it was viewed as one of the world's most astonishing wonders. Billions of tiny creatures were labouring continuously to create islands. Reviewing Darwin's *The Structure and Distribution of Coral Reefs* (1842) and a later work by James D. Dana, *The Structure and Classification of Zoophytes* (1846), a contributor to *Blackwood's* had this to say about coral:

> These miniature creatures are now entitled to a larger share of consideration than the greatest and most skilful of quadrupeds can claim. All the elephants and lions which have prowled about in its waters – have done much less to affect its physical features, and have left far slighter evidences of their existence, than the zoophytes by whose labours the coral formations have been reared. For the most colossal specimens of industry we are indebted to one of the least promising of animated things.[8]

Indomitable, beautiful, valuable – coral represented a physical as well as an economic risk. But far more alluring was the thought of cannibalism. This practice preyed on the Victorian mind. Eating human flesh was not a part of the Fijians' everyday diet; it contributed to periodic rituals. In Ballantyne's adventure, the islanders' consumption of flesh turns into an insatiable appetite.

Ralph Rover, the narrator, is given this piece of terrifying information from his irascible captor, Bloody Bill the pirate:

'Now, I believe there's thousands o' the people in England are sich born drivellin' *won't-believers* that they think the black fellows hereaway at the worst eat an enemy only now an' then, out o' spite; whereas I know for certain, and many captains of the British and American navies know as well as me, that the Feejee islanders eat not only their enemies but one another; and they do it not for spite, but for pleasure. It's a *fact* that they prefer human flesh to any other. But they don't like white men's flesh so well as black; they say it makes them sick.' (p. 213)[9]

Although Ballantyne's narrative takes many more risks than Marryat's (it moves more rapidly from one event to another; it gives more prominence to pirates and savages), it none the less maintains a strong interest in verifying the crimes perpetrated by these island peoples. By using a pirate as a source of authority, the story enjoys considerable licence when elaborating these horrific facts. Bloody Bill is there, in part, to demonstrate that the lowest type of white man is infinitely more dignified than the Fijian ever could be. "'I never cared for Christianity myself", he continued, in a soliloquizing voice, "and I don't well know what it means; but a man with half an eye can see what it does for these black critters'" (p. 215). Ralph and his mates, Jack Martin and Peterkin Gay, are, naturally enough, good Christian boys, instrumental in guiding the Fijians towards the ways of God. But Ralph, like the boy heroes who follow him into the pages of the penny magazines, possesses virtues not to be found in Marryat's novel. Ralph can move easily between the conflicting worlds of piracy, cannibalism, and missionary zeal.

Like Marryat's family, Ballantyne's boys, once stranded, spend a good deal of time making themselves at home on their coral island. The natives, however, make a quicker entry into the story, and the pirate crew occupies several chapters when, because of a number of unfortunate accidents, Ralph is thrust into their company. Much of the narrative is taken up with the cannibals' treatment of a Samoan woman, Avatea, whom the boys undertake to save from being eaten by a chief she refuses to marry. Avatea is a Christian, Tararo a heathen. The narrative closes with Tararo's providential conversion to Christianity. The teachings of Wesley save the day. And so the boys are free to return home. Survivors, saviours, adventurers – Ralph, Jack, and Peterkin take up a succession of different roles. Ralph acts in particularly ingenious ways which win him universal praise. For example, when seized by the pirates he promptly casts a keg of gunpowder overboard, knowing that it will reach the shores where his mates have been left behind. He proudly defends himself before Bloody Bill, and meets with this unexpected response:

> The captain stepped back and regarded me with a look of amazement.
>
> 'Now', continued I, 'I threw that keg into the sea because the wind and waves will carry it to my friends on the Coral Island, who happen to have a pistol but no powder. I hope that it will reach them soon; and my only regret is that the keg was not a bigger one. Moreover, pirate, you said just now that you thought I was made of better stuff. I don't know what stuff I am made of – I never thought much about that subject – but I'm quite certain of this, that I am made of such stuff as the like of you shall never tame, though you should do your worst.'
>
> To my surprise the captain, instead of flying into a rage, smiled, and thrusting his hand into the voluminous shawl that encircled his waist, turned on his heel and walked aft, while I went below.
>
> Here, instead of being rudely handled, as I had expected, the men received me with a shout of laughter, and one of them, patting me on the back, said, 'Well done, lad! you're a brick, and I have no doubt will turn out a rare cove. Bloody Bill there was just such a fellow as you are, and now he's the biggest cut-throat of all'.
> (p. 197)

This sort of encounter forms part of a familiar story to be found in boys' fiction. Ralph, the model of boyhood, has that strength of mind, that pluckiness of spirit, that defines the best qualities of imperial boyhood; everyone admires it, including the pirates. Moreover, pirates also encapsulate daring adventurousness. Ralph's defiance finds a surprising parallel in Bloody Bill's cut-throat attitude. The only difference between them is that they stand on opposite sides of the ethical divide. *The Coral Island* draws attention to their similarities so that the boy hero can display a wilful, disobedient, and individualistic sense of derring-do while maintaining moral standards. The novel nevertheless betrays the fact that Ralph's intrepid behaviour is defined against the forceful if wayward masculinity of the pirates. It is, indeed, Ralph's likeness to his captors that gives him the strength of mind and body to outwit them.

*The Coral Island* often invites an interpretation that runs against the values it sets out to uphold. The boys are supposedly dissociated from the savages, and the pirates deplore the malevolent cannibalism of Fiji. But these distinctions are broken down when the metonymic relations between small sections of the narrative are taken into account. Contemplating how they might use a cave they have found in times of danger, Ralph remarks: 'Little did we imagine that the first savages who would drive us into it would be white savages, perhaps our own countrymen. We found the coco-nuts in good condition, and the cooked yams, but the bread-fruits were spoiled' (p. 187). It is the idea of the savage that fluctuates so noticeably in this passage. Pirates are those men who have degenerated from Western models of civilized behaviour, and yet, as the previous extract indicates, the boy heroes bear strong resemblances to them. The boys are themselves placed in a predicament where they can relish – amid the incredibly fertile groves of the island – an uncivilized life. Like the Boy Scouts, half a century after them, Ralph and his mates are able to live in many respects like the natives themselves. This island story, therefore, allows the boys to get as close as possible to being both pirates (defiant, daring, individualistic) and savages (survivors taming nature) but without turning into them. Both of these contemptible groups are, metaphorically speaking, the boys' 'countrymen'.

Ralph, Jack, and Peterkin's adventures together are renewed in *The Gorilla Hunters* (1862), which, although set not on an island but in Africa, bears the similar traces of the Crusoe myth: 'I will never forget the powerful sensations of excitement and anxiety that filled our breasts when we came on the first gorilla footprint. We felt as no doubt Robinson Crusoe did when he discovered the footprint of a savage in the sand.' (p. 131)[10] Now young men in their twenties, they meet up again to go on a natural history expedition collecting examples of wildlife for scientific purposes. With this purpose in mind, they do not hesitate to take a passing shot at anything that moves in Africa – 'the land of the slave, the black savage, and the gorilla' (p. 20). But the repetitious killing worries the boys as they journey deeper into the jungle in search of their prey:

'It seems to me', said Jack, breaking silence at the end of a long pause, which had succeeded an animated discussion as to whether it were better to spend one's life in the civilized world or among the wilds of Africa – in which discussion Peterkin, who advocated the wild life, was utterly, though not admittedly, beaten – 'it seems to me that, notwithstanding the short time we stayed in the gorilla country, we have been pretty successful. Haven't we bagged thirty-three altogether?'

'Thirty-six, if you count the babies in arms', responded Peterkin.

'If it were not that we have killed all these creatures in the cause of science', said I, 'I should be perfectly miserable.'

'In the cause of science!' repeated Peterkin. 'Humph! I suspect that a good deal of wickedness is perpetrated under the wing of science.' (p. 169)

This narrative takes the rationale of adventure near to breaking-point, and, in seemingly aberrant moments such as this one, it is led to reassess its ethics. This is not the only occasion when these young heroes express concern at taking the lives of mother and baby animals. Their key target, of course, is the formidable male gorilla. Although Africa, like the coral island, represents a realm of freedom from proper civilized life ('We felt like prisoners set free' [p. 169]), it plunges these hunters into ceaseless acts of troublesome violence, attempting to 'beat' a natural world that poses a continuous threat in terms of both its might and the secrets it holds from Western knowledge. The story raises for itself, parenthetically, questions about what it means to have the licence to kill for its own sake. Here, Ballantyne indicates that there is no moral to this form of hunting. Firearms in hand, the gorilla hunters have nothing to learn other than that Africa can be laid waste.

*The Gorilla Hunters* also brings Ralph, Jack, and Peterkin into closer contact with Black people. This time, the natives are not cannibals but ignorant objects of derision. (Their African servant, Makarooroo, is referred to as an 'ebony junk'; and Peterkin comically abbreviates the servant's name: 'Don't you suppose I'm going to stand on ceremony with you. Your name's too long, by half. Too many rooroos about it, so I'm going to call you Mak in future, d'ye understand?' [p. 68].) When they are not cast in the role of serving the white hunters, the Africans appear as either spear-wielding warriors or men about to be shackled by a wicked Portuguese slave-trader. The Blacks, then, are depicted in three ways: they can be laughed at, lived in fear of, or contemptuously exploited. They must be saved from slavery or savagery. Yet their moral condition can only be improved when the boy heroes have themselves gone native. In *The Coral Island*, the Fijians convert to Christianity after the boys have learned to live like – but not as – savages. Similarly, in *The Gorilla Hunters*, the Africans are saved from their unethical ways once Ralph and his mates have indiscriminately killed elephants, lions, and apes in the name of science. At the close of their travels in Africa, Ralph finds that the destabilized values of savagery and civilization put the hunters in a dilemma:

> On the one hand, we were unwilling to quit the scene of our hunting triumphs and adventures; on the other hand, Makarooroo and his bride were anxious to reach the mission stations on the coast, and get married in the Christian manner.
> 'Our opposing interests are indeed a little perplexing', said Jack.
> (p. 248)

Contact with the gorilla hunters has made willing Christians of the servant and his fiancée. But should the urgent need to reach a mission station for them to marry interfere with the persistent desire for adventure? Which should take precedence? *The Gorilla Hunters*, finally, has to admit that once the native has become a Christian the hunt is over. The values of the one ultimately exclude those of the other. It has been Ballantyne's difficult task to negotiate a route between them.

## The Art of Fiction: *Treasure Island*

> I have begun (and finished) a number of other books, but I cannot remember to have sat down to one of them with more complacency. It is not to be wondered at, for stolen waters are proverbially sweet. I am now upon a painful chapter. No doubt the parrot once belonged to Robinson Crusoe. No doubt the skeleton is conveyed from Poe. I think little of these, they are trifles and details; and no man can hope to have a monopoly of skeletons or make a corner of talking birds. The stockade, I am told, is from *Masterman Ready*. It may be, I care not a jot . . . A few reminiscences of Poe, Defoe, and Washington Irving, a copy of Johnson's *Buccaneers*, the name of the Dead Man's Chest from Kingsley's *At Last*, some recollections of canoeing on the

high seas, and the map itself, with its infinite, eloquent suggestions, made up the whole of my materials. (pp. 195, 199)[11]

Low on income, and still dependent on his father at the age of thirty-one, Robert Louis Stevenson tried his hand at an adventure story. He wrote fifteen chapters in as many days, and when it was complete sent it for publication to a boys' paper, *Young Folks*. Attributed to one Captain George North, the story was announced there in 1881, and emerged in revised form as a novel in its own right two years later. As these passages from his retrospective essay, 'My First Book' (1894), demonstrate, the narrative bears a multiplicity of debts to a whole canon of nineteenth-century adventure fiction. But from the moment of its inception the critical establishment dissociated *Treasure Island* from the popular traditions to which it so obviously claimed allegiance. Praising it for its strength of characterization and its stylish precision, conservative readers found Stevenson's novel a welcome antithesis to the challenge offered by naturalism, represented in Emile Zola's highly controversial fictions. As one reviewer wrote: 'The dramatic verse of the narrative is not less striking than its unflagging spirit. The invention is rich and ready, the dialogue abounds in pith and humour, while the characters – particularly the sailors – are drawn with great force and distinction.'[12] Stevenson's literary associate, W. E. Henley, in the *Saturday Review*, endorsed these views at length:

> Like all Mr Stevenson's good work, it is touched with genius. It is written – in the crisp, choice, nervous English of which he has the secret – with such a union of measure and force as to be in its way a masterpiece of narrative. It is rich in excellent characterization, in an abundant invention, in a certain grim romance, in a vein of what must, for want of a better word, be described as melodrama, which is both thrilling and peculiar. It is the work of one who knows all there is to be known about 'Robinson Crusoe'.[13]

It is as if Stevenson had learned the finest lessons of realism to remodel the romance. Arch rivals, but not altogether enemies, realism and romance competed against one another during the 1880s to define the key debates about fiction of the day. An energetic advocate of romance, Stevenson tells an old story but, as critics would repeatedly point out, with much greater art than ever before.

*Treasure Island* is a remarkably self-conscious fiction. Not only did it draw on a host of earlier, and commercially successful, narratives, it also became the object of the author's critical interrogation. Advertising its contents, the novel is prefaced by a rollicking poem. The first verse runs:

> If sailor tales to sailor tunes,
> > Storm and adventure, heat and cold,
> If schooners, islands, and maroon
> > And Buccaneers and buried Gold,
> And all the old romance, retold
> > Exactly in the ancient way,
> Can please, as me they pleased of old,
> > The wiser youngsters of to-day:

With an eye for the market, this poem is addressed to 'The Hesitating Purchaser', suggesting that Stevenson felt the story inappropriate for a refined adult readership. The poem has a simple function: to remind the buyer of novels that this is an old and long-loved story, taking the adult back to childhood pleasures, those of an unsophisticated kind. The second verse explicitly connects the novel with the work of Kingston, James Fenimore Cooper, and Ballantyne. *Treasure Island*, then, places an extraordinary value on what it means to enjoy a familiar tale – one that reaches back into the past in every sense: to childhood and a line of enduring adventures leading all the way back to *Robinson Crusoe*. Elsewhere, Stevenson emphasizes the link between romances such as Defoe's archetypal narrative and 'child's play' (in an essay of that name):

> It is the grown people who make the nursery stories; all the children do, is jealously to preserve the text. One out of a dozen reasons why *Robinson Crusoe* should be so popular with youth, is that it hits their level in this matter to a nicety; Crusoe was always at makeshifts and had, in so many words, to *play* at a great variety of professions; and then the book is all about tools, and there is nothing that delights a child so much.

And he goes on to add: 'Children think very much the same thoughts and dream the same dreams as bearded men and marriageable women. No one is more romantic'.[14] Apparently, the

playful inventiveness of children – the imaginary making of yet
unrealized worlds – never leaves the adult mind, and it is the duty
of romance to remind readers of that truth. However, Stevenson's
hypothesis discloses one point central to the seemingly natural drives
shaping the conception of 'children's literature': the fact that such
writings are produced by grown-up people who aim to represent
a child's 'world'. Jacqueline Rose explains this issue as follows:
'Children's fiction sets up a world in which the adult comes first
(author, maker, giver) and the child comes after (reader, product,
receiver), but where neither of them enter the space in between',
and so this type of writing 'sets up the child as an outsider to its
own process, and then aims, unashamedly, to take the child *in*'.[15]

Stevenson put pressure on the concept of romance combining the
worlds of adults and children in a manner that gave credence to
the idea that the playful pleasures this genre aroused were eternal,
crossing all cultures and historical periods. Romance, in other
words, served to dissolve a multiplicity of differences. Conservatives
cherished Stevenson's exemplary commitment to a longstanding
tradition of romance in the face of political fictions – British as
well as French; George Moore as well as Zola – that disturbed
their myth-making image of late-nineteenth-century life. So strongly
pledged was Stevenson to the days of yore, he chose to set *Treasure
Island* in the swashbuckling mid-eighteenth century, far away in
time, making it, by curious turns, all the more contemporary to
Victorian Britain.

Telling a good story may be the project of *Treasure Island* but it is
also a feature emphatically thematized throughout the novel. Billy
Bones, the pirate lodged at the 'Admiral Benbow' inn, frightens
the customers with his eerie seafaring tales. Jim Hawkins, the boy
narrator, states:

> Dreadful stories they were; about hanging, and walking the plank,
> and storms at sea, and the Dry Tortugas, and wild deeds and places
> on the Spanish Main. By his own account he must have lived his life
> among some of the wickedest men that God ever allowed upon the
> sea; and the language in which he told these stories shocked our plain
> country people almost as much as the crimes that he described. My
> father was always saying the inn would be ruined, for people would
> soon cease coming there to be tyrannised over and put down, and sent
> shivering to their beds; but I really believe his presence did us good.

People were frightened at the time, but on looking back they rather liked it; it was a fine excitement in a quiet country life. (p. 4)

I brooded . . . over the map [of Treasure Island], all the details of which I well remembered. Sitting by the fire in the house-keeper's room, I approached that island in my fancy, from every possible direction; I explored every acre of its surface; I climbed a thousand times to that tall hill they call the Spy-glass, and from the top enjoyed the most wonderful and changing prospects. Sometimes the isle was thick with savages, with whom we fought; sometimes full of danger-ous animals that hunted us; but in all my fancies nothing occurred to me so strange and tragic as our actual adventures. (p. 36)

As such passages show, the past in which Jim Hawkins lives becomes one of intrepid exploration where fact turns out to be stranger than fiction. Spy-glass in hand, Jim will come up against sights more startling than anything he had dreamed of when pondering maps of far-off islands. To elevate fiction to a higher power than a boy's own imagination: this is the imaginative trick played by romance. The genre sets itself up as something which is beyond the reach of even the most fanciful boyhood mind.

The love of romance affects everybody in *Treasure Island*, so much so that Jim takes his post as cabin-boy on a ship fitted out by the dignitaries of his village, Squire Trelawney and Dr Livesey, whose own desire to hunt down the long-lost treasure laid years ago by the deceased Captain Flint rivals that of the ship's crew, who are ultimately led to mutiny by Long John Silver. In fact, the eagerness with which the squire and the doctor make their plans to set sail conceals the dubious morality guiding their actions. Both men are as wealth-grabbing as the despicable seamen in their plotting for the gold. And it is clear it is the spirit of adventure – story-telling – that obliterates all moral considerations:

'Money!' cried the squire. 'Have you heard the story? What were these villains after but money? What do they care for but money? For what would they risk their rascal carcases but money?'

'That we shall soon know', replied the doctor. 'But you are so confoundedly hot-headed and exclamatory that I cannot get a word in. What I want to know is this: Supposing that I have here in my pocket some clue to where Flint buried his treasure, will that treasure amount to much?'

'Amount, sir!' cried the squire. 'It will amount to this; if we have the clue you talk about, I fit out a ship in Bristol dock, and take you and Hawkins here along, and I'll have that treasure if I search a year.' (p. 32)

In the end, of course, they find their booty. The story could not turn out otherwise.

By rewriting *The Coral Island*, and filling out his altogether more polished script with various textual borrowings, Stevenson opens up a series of events that run almost seamlessly to their conclusion. Any potential obstructions to the plot are removed. 'Women were excluded', he points out in 'My First Book' (p. 195). And natives are nowhere to be seen. Instead, the story is regulated by a repetitive conflict between different classes of men, with two figures who stand at the threshold of both groups, and who communicate the interests of each party to the other. These are Long John Silver and the boy hero, Jim. Both are special in their own right. Caught up in the enemy camp, surrounded by Silver and his unwholesome mates, Jim can win the same kind of admiration that Ralph Rover received from Bloody Bill. Knowing that Trelawney and Livesey sadly suspect that Jim has betrayed them, Silver tells him:

'I'll give you a piece of my mind. I've always liked you, I have, for a lad of spirit, and the picter of my own self when I was young and handsome. I always wanted you to jine and take your share, and die a gentleman, and now, my cock, you've got to. Cap'n Smollett's a fine seaman, as I'll own up to any day, but stiff on discipline. "Dooty is dooty", says he, and right he is. Just you keep clear of the cap'n. The doctor himself is gone dead again you – "ungrateful scamp" was what he said; and the short and long of the whole story is about here: you can't go back to your own lot, for they won't have you. (p. 150)

Jim finally makes his escape. But the point is that Jim, rather like Jack Rushton in *Boys of England*, bears a familiar similarity to the man whose image he must condemn. Silver, likewise, crosses over into the proper realm of middle-class respectability. He knows his mockingly rendered 'dooty'; he is said to be 'genteel' (p. 98); and the squire believes him to be 'a man of substance' (p. 38) because he has a bank account always in credit. He even has pretensions to entering parliament: 'When I'm in Parlyment, and riding in my coach, I don't want none of these sea-lawyers in the cabin a-coming home, inlooked for, like the devil at prayers' (p. 61). Jim, so often positioned, accidentally or not, in the role of spy, has been eavesdropping on Silver's speech. Silver – and, importantly, his name is not gold – inevitably has the lesser value between them. He has the daring but not the moral fibre of the altogether untainted young Jim.

It is obvious how class affiliations divide up Stevenson's cast of characters. David H. Jackson notes how everyone of a lower class than Jim, Trelawney, and Livesey appears childish.[16] Meanwhile, Silver's class pretensions are mocked. What is more, Silver possesses a most uncomplimentary but memorable feature: he has only one leg. (At one point, he becomes in Jim's eyes a 'monster' [p. 76].) One other thing characterizes Silver: his parrot. Ceaselessly, the bird repeats the words 'pieces of eight'. Said to be 200 years old, this venerable creature learned its immortal phrase when watching wrecked plate ships being fished up. Silver says: 'if anybody's seen more wickedness, it must be the devil himself' (p. 54). The parrot, named after Captain Flint who left the treasure behind him on the island, enshrines the whole economy upon which the novel bases itself. *Treasure Island* can only repeat a desire to find treasure – which even Silver knows belongs to the 'devil' – without question. 'Pieces of eight': this phrase comprises the risk of adventure itself. Once learned by heart, it can only be uttered again and again, sustaining a lust for material goods.

In what became a contentious debate about the true purpose of fiction, H. Rider Haggard associated romance with basic human instincts, ineradicable even in a civilized society:

> The love of romance is probably coeval with the existence of humanity. So far as we can follow the history of the world we find traces of and its effects among every people, and those who are acquainted with the habits and ways of thought of savage races will know that it flourishes as strongly in the barbarian as in the cultured brats. In short, it is like the passions, an innate quality of mankind. In modern England this love is not by any means dying out, as must be clear, even to that class of our fellow-countrymen who, we are told, are interested in nothing but politics and religion.[17]

Andrew Lang vigorously supported this view:

The Coming Man may be bald, toothless, highly 'cultured', and addicted to tales of introspective analysis. I don't envy him when he has got rid of that relic of the ape, his hair; those relics of the age of combat, his teeth and nails; that survival of barbarism, his delight in the last battles of Odysseus, Laertes' son. I don't envy him the novels he will admire, nor the pap on which he will feed bearsomely, as Mr John Payne says of the vampire. Not for nothing did Nature leave us all savages under our white skins; she has wrought thus that we might have many delights, among others 'the joy of adventurous living', and of reading about adventurous living.[18]

Both passages base an interest in adventure on barbarism. But this barbaric humanity finds its roots in other qualities as well. Earlier in his essay, Lang associates this 'joy' with a 'childish love of pleasures' that never departs from adult life. Both the child and savage represent both sides of an innate, forever undeveloped, human nature.

Haggard makes a different kind of link. Believing that late Victorian fiction is vitiated by a largely female readership, he scorns women's romance as so 'false', idealistic, and predictable that it is likely to drive susceptible female readers towards the worthless scandalous stories turned out every day by the popular press, itself part of the culture of naturalism and its vicious arousal of sexual passion. Haggard asks: 'Why do *men* hardly ever read a novel?'[19] The answer for him is that novels fail to represent life as it is lived – by which he means, novels too rarely display 'spiritual intensity'. For Haggard, the finest fiction is that which comes from the 'heart', and so, therefore, the romance stands highest in his estimation: 'many of the most lasting triumphs of literary art belong to the producers of purely romantic fiction, witness the "Arabian Nights", "Gulliver's Travels", "The Pilgrim's Progress", "Robinson Crusoe", and other immortal works.'[20] It is, in some respects, paradoxical that one of the contemporary novels he most highly admires is (as he misnames it) 'The Story of a South African Farm' by 'Ralph Iron' (the feminist critic of imperialism, Olive Schreiner). Yet this novel gains a mention in his polemical article because it had attracted attention to the Anglo–Boer conflict in South Africa (and, as chapter 4 explores, Schreiner's novel contains a counter-image of the strong woman whom Haggard would figure so differently in his African romance, *She* [1887]).

Haggard's essay was roundly attacked on all sides in the periodicals. However, his conservative colleagues always championed his and Stevenson's work (often in the same breath), like George Saintsbury: 'I shall not say whether I like *Treasure Island* better than *King Solomon's Mines*, or *King Solomon's Mines* better than *Treasure Island*. I only wish I had drawn the personage of John Silver or written the fight between Twala and Sir Henry'.[21] Haggard, more controversially than Stevenson, stood at the centre of a virulent row about literary standards. Accusations against the indignities of romance flew about in the pages of the periodicals, leading to various charges of immorality and even plagiarism. (All these points are taken up in chapter 4.)

The provenance of this literary debate can be found in Stevenson's earlier essay, 'A Gossip on Romance' (1882):

[P]erhaps nothing can more strongly illustrate the necessity for marking incident than to compare the living fame of 'Robinson Crusoe' with the discredit of [Samuel Richardson's] 'Clarissa Harlowe'. 'Clarissa' is a book of a far more startling import, worked out, on a great canvas, with inimitable courage and unflagging art. It contains wit, character, passion, plot, conversations full of spirit and insight, letters sparkling with unstrained humanity; and if the death of the heroine be somewhat frigid and artificial, the last days of the hero strike the only note of what we now call Byronism, between the Elizabethans and Byron himself. And yet a little story of a shipwrecked sailor, with not a tenth part of the style nor a thousandth part of the wisdom, exploring none of the arcana of humanity and deprived of a perennial interest, goes on from edition to edition, ever young, while 'Clarissa' lies upon the shelves unread.[22]

Rather than consider how shifts of taste, on the one hand, and historical continuities, on the other, may have affected the reduced popularity or longstanding success of either *Robinson Crusoe* or *Clarissa*, Stevenson, like Lang and Haggard, appeals to the fundamental power of incident and action that constitutes a good story. Haggard deplored women's romantic fiction because it distorted life. Yet Haggard spurned naturalism – the deepening and broadening of the psychological and social interests of realism – because it did not pertain to the enduring human spirit. Stevenson, too, prizes above all the heroic feats that persist timelessly (and thus apolitically) in a long line of European narratives. That these stories represent the triumphs of *men*, and have then been absorbed into colonial and imperial history is made almost invisible here.

The *male* investment in these supposedly ungendered – objectively exciting, enduringly popular – adventures runs against the two, rather womanly, terms that entitle his essay: 'gossip' and 'romance'. Useless chatter and fanciful incident, by rather unlikely turns of argument, become the substance of legitimate fictions for male readers. There was, then, in the 1880s a concerted movement among conservatives to mould the idea of the finest novel to a wholly depoliticized and universalized set of masculine terms. The aim was to wrest fiction from women's and, more generally, political interests and implant it back into the heart of every grown-up boy. Haggard, notably, would build on the success of *Treasure Island* by taking its romantic strategies into the depths of Africa – and all in the name of the art of fiction, rather than imperial manhood.

At this time, and with greater intensity than ever before, the novel was being theorized as an object of study, just as 'English' was coming into its own as an academic discipline. Periodicals provided a great deal of space for the discussion of the relative (and often opposed) merits of realism and romance.[23] The beginnings of this important debate can be found in Stevenson's rejoinder to Henry James's well-known essay, 'The Art of Fiction', published in 1884, which takes a sidelong glance at *Treasure Island*. James's article largely forms an even-handed response to Walter Besant's lecture on *The Art of Fiction* that went on sale as a pamphlet in the same year. Besant stakes his argument upon three propositions: first, fiction 'is an Art . . . worthy of admiration'; second, fiction is governed by laws which 'may be laid down and taught with as much precision and exactness as the laws of harmony, perspective, and proportion'; and, lastly, these laws are unteachable to those 'who have not already been endowed with the natural and necessary gifts' to produce such great art.[24]

James's liberal argument against Besant is structured around a single point about the so-called 'laws' regulating a good story. He finds Besant's prescriptions limiting, advocating instead that 'the good health of an art which undertakes so immediately to reproduce life must demand that it be perfectly free'.[25] On this principle of 'freedom', novels should be judged according to whether they fulfil what they set out to do. There is, of course, a self-defeating logic to this view, since the intention has to be inferred from the effect. By adhering to a model of generic conformity or deviation, in order to determine a successfully achieved intention, an alternative set of prescriptions inevitably has to come into play. For James, as long as the novel possesses – in one of his most famous phrases – an 'air of reality (solidity of specification)',[26] the work of fiction shall succeed. It is here that James introduces *Treasure Island* to undermine Besant's presumptions about adventure. 'Mr Besant does not, to my sense, light up the subject by intimating that a story must, under the penalty of not being story, consist of "adventures". Why of adventures more than green spectacles?'[27] Stevenson's novel is held in esteem by James not because it is full of predictable incidents ('murders, mysteries, islands of dreadful renown, hairbreadth escapes, miraculous coincidence and buried doubloons'),[28] points he would return to in his later, expansive essay, entitled simply 'Robert Louis Stevenson' (1887). Rather, for James, *Treasure Island* excels at what it attempts. Yet *how* it succeeds is not – because, in this paradigm, it cannot be – defined. It is too 'free', too full of 'art', to be pinned down.

Stevenson's unsolicited reply to James returns to Besant's prescriptions by similarly defining three categories of fiction: novels of adventure, character, and drama. In his essay, 'A Humble Remonstrance' (1884), he seeks to provide a rationale, and an equal value, to each type. And his views on adventure, once more, stick firmly to a belief in universal childhood experience. Although James disavows that he has ever indulged in fantasies of buried treasure, Stevenson, jocularly enough, finds reason to disagree:

> [James had written:] '*I have been a child, but I have never been on a quest for buried treasure.*' Here is, indeed, a wilful paradox; for if he has never been on a quest for buried treasure, it can be demonstrated that he has never been a child. There was never a child (unless Master James) but has hunted gold, and been a pirate, and a military commander, and a bandit of the mountains; but has fought, and suffered shipwreck and prison, and imbrued its little hands in gore, and gallantly retrieved the lost battle, and triumphantly protected innocence and beauty.[29]

The defence of romance, then, falls within a set of fairly stable parameters. Romance gives pride of place to action, whereas realism focuses on moral choices; romance connects up with childhood experience, whereas realism focuses on the maturation of character; and romance sees itself perpetuating a tradition, whereas Zola and his associates engage with contemporary issues (the fearful *Zeitgeist*). Frequently in Stevenson's correspondence, he makes his loathing for naturalism clear:

> For Zola I have no toleration, though the curious, eminently bour-geois and eminently French creature has power of a kind. I would not give a chapter of old Dumas (meaning himself, not his collaborators) for the whole boiling of the Zolas. Romance with the smallpox – as the great one: diseased anyway and blackhearted and fundamentally at enmity with joy.[30]

Zola's writing stands as a contaminated or perverted form of romance. Although it retains something of the 'power' of that genre, its obsessive concerns with politics and historical change have etiolated it.

Stevenson, however, does not need to be understood entirely within the terms of his own definitions. When turned against its regression into childhood adventure and the romance of the eighteenth century, *Treasure Island* discloses a response to the immediate historical conditions of its production – what Fredric Jameson, not unproblematically, calls the 'political unconscious'.[31] Writing about Stevenson's politics, and the controversies around Gladstone's Home Rule Bill of 1885 – which, at the time of the general election that year, split the Liberals between Unionists and Home Rulers – Christopher Harvie observes that the novel could be read as an unwitting allegory of the threatening scission of Ireland from Britain:

> There is a sense in which *Treasure Island* could be seen as a sort of social parable: an embattled microcosm of civil society – squire, doctor, captain and retainers – being menaced by the lower orders under brutal and materialistic leadership. That the establishment's saved by chance and Jim Hawkins shows the close margin, although the propensity of the pirates (like the Edinburgh working class Stevenson knew) to get smashed out of their minds obviously

helped . . . It may be flippant, but the fact that *Treasure Island*
appealed to adults as well as children suggests a certain affinity
with the squire's embattled party among those groups who were
on 8 February 1886 to have their club windows smashed by mobs
rioting in the West End, or feared for their Irish properties as
cattle-maiming and 'moonlighting' increased. With, added to this,
the feeling that one or two Silvers had already made it in to the
House of Commons?[32]

Elsewhere in his essay, Harvie indicates that the Tory and Liberal
fears of socialism, and the potential subversive force socialism carried
with it, may, to some degree, account for Stevenson's romance of the
1848 revolutions in France, *Prince Otto* (1885). It is possible to see
how several connected histories seize on the fabric of Stevenson's
text. Perhaps in *Treasure Island*, the island may figure as Ireland
(a colony), as much as it represents a realm of far-off plunder:
a narrative space where many dreams of empire come together.
There is not any final resolution to these always potential historical
pressures. However, towards the end of Stevenson's canon, the
contemporary historical elements exiled from his romances return
– as repressions tend to – and expose the rather vain pretensions
of adventure when placed in the critical hands of James, Lang, and
Haggard.

In Stevenson's later fiction, the dream of adventure would fall
by the hollowness of its own convictions. In two later works, *The
Beach of Falesá* (1892) and *The Ebb-Tide* (1893), both set in the
South Pacific, the island story witnesses grown men abandoned
to the 'realism', one might call it, of imperial politics. He claimed
that *The Beach of Falesá*, a collaboration with his stepson which he
eventually found difficulty in publishing, would mark a break with
his earlier writings. The following extract from his correspondence
to Sidney Colvin gives a good idea of the deliberations Stevenson
went through when composing his work:

One of the puzzles [with the draft he is writing] is this: it is a first
person story – a trader telling his own adventure in an island. When
I began I allowed myself a few liberties, because I was afraid of the
end; now the end proved quite easy, and could be done in the pace;
so the beginning remains a quarter tone out (in places); but I have
rather decided to let it stay so. The problem is always delicate; it

is the only thing that worries me in first person tales . . . There is a vast deal of fact in the story, and some pretty good comedy. It is the first realistic South Sea story; I mean with real South Sea character and details of life. Everybody else who has tried, that I have seen, got carried away by the romance, and ended in a kind of sugar candy sham epic, and the whole effect was lost – there was no etching, no human grin, consequently no conviction. Now I have got the smell and look of the thing a good deal. You will know more about the South Seas after you have read my little tale than if you had read a library.[33]

Romance, as a genre, always staked some claim on historical veracity but here Stevenson recognizes only too clearly how the compulsions of the adventure story can turn the bitterest of truths into the lightest of confections. His stress is very clearly placed on the factuality of realism. Although his interest remains in 'adventure', his choice of a first person narrator indicates his interest in presenting a more immediate, and thus realistic, kind of viewpoint. *The Ebb-Tide* (1893) indicates a further shift away from romance. The very first sentence underlines the fragmented existence of white migrants trying to make a living there: 'Throughout the island world of the Pacific, scattered men of many European races and from almost every grade of society carry activity and disseminate disease'.[34] The mixing of classes and races marks the degeneracy so deeply felt at home and abroad in the 1890s, and that was a topic often placed at the centre of discussions of naturalism. In *The Ebb-Tide* the vision is, in some ways, akin to the disturbing scenario opened up in *Dr Jekyll and Mr Hyde* (1886) where the pleasure of creating an 'impenetrable mantle' (p. 86) – a dream of becoming invisible by creating another identity – is described, tellingly, as an 'adventure' (p. 89). But once Jekyll has 'like a schoolboy' sprung 'headlong into the sea of liberty' (p. 86), all he can do is commit murders. Hyde is the one cryptically hiding in the demonic adventurer whose name authorizes death (*Je Kyll* – 'I kill'). Whether on an island or in the gothic streets of Jekyll's London, the savage insticts of adventure finally spin out of control.

During the course of the 1880s and early 1890s, Stevenson's work demonstrates how his zeal for adventure was attenuating in its interest in 'child's play' and the excitements of romance, and began to transmogrify into a narrative that was proving more and more difficult to tell. 'Getting to the story, having it told, is complicated, far from easy', writes Stephen Heath of *Dr Jekyll and Mr Hyde*.[35] Focusing on the grotesquely distorted male sexuality that fills out this highly misogynistic narrative, Heath remarks that the story lacks a reason for beginning as it does. It is certainly not self-evident why a little girl should be running through the streets of London at night, only to collide with Mr Hyde who cruelly tramples upon her body. Why should child's play have turned into child murder?

With that question in mind, it could be argued that *Dr Jekyll and Mr Hyde* magnifies the unreasoned sources of an interest in violence that haunted the colonial escapades of *Treasure Island*, where the monstrous Silver roved. Perhaps by the end of his career – long out of Britain, immersed in the complexities of imperialist politics as European nations vied for control of Samoa – Stevenson had come to acknowledge the cultural imperatives driving British boys towards the risks involved in adventure. The romance of *Treasure Island* had collapsed under the brutal realism of the equally far-off Samoa. The trajectory of Stevenson's oeuvre traces a larger pattern of disillusionment in adventure fiction as it travels, more and more sluggishly, away from the Crusoe myth towards the restless forms of alienation to be located in literary modernism. As chapter 4 suggests, the emergence of modernism is intimately involved with the decline of empire.

## Notes

1 Captain Marryat, *Masterman Ready*, Everyman's Library (London: Dent, 1970). All references to this edition are included in the text. For an account of the genealogy of the Robinsonade, see Martin Green, 'The Robinson Crusoe Story' in Jeffrey Richards, (ed.), *Imperialism and Juvenile Literature* (Manchester University Press, 1989), pp. 34–52.
2 Joseph Conrad, 'Tales of the Sea', *Outlook*, 4 June 1898, reprinted in *Notes on Life and Letters* (London: Dent, 1924), pp. 53–7.
3 William Hurton, 'Marryat's Sea Stories', *Dublin University Magazine*, 47 (1850), p. 295.
4 Patrick Brantlinger, *Rule of Darkness: British Literature and Imperialism, 1830–1900* (Ithaca: Cornell University Press, 1988), p. 50.
5 'Marryat's Sea Stories', p. 304.

6    Peter Hulme, *Colonial Encounters: Europe and the Native Caribbean, 1492–1797* (London: Methuen, 1986), pp. 182–3.
7    On the representation of the Fijians within the context of Victorian ethnology, see George W. Stocking, Jr., *Victorian Anthropology* (New York: The Free Press, 1987), pp. 87–92. This book is the definitive work on Victorian concepts of race and savagery.
8    Anonymous, 'Coral Rings', *Blackwood's* 74 (1853), p. 360.
9    R. M. Ballantyne, *The Coral Island: A Tale of the Pacific Ocean* (London and Glasgow: Blackie, n.d.). All references to this edition are included in the text.
10    Ballantyne, *The Gorilla Hunters* (London and Glasgow: Blackie, n.d.). All references to this edition are included in the text. (My copy was awarded as a Methodist Sunday school prize in 1946; this unremittingly racist narrative was clearly thought of as sound reading until the Second World War.)
11    Robert Louis Stevenson, 'My First Book' (1894), reprinted in *Treasure Island*, (ed.) Emma Letley, *The World's Classics* (Oxford: Oxford University Press, 1985). All references to this edition are included in the text. The discussion that follows is indebted to Letley's introduction to *Treasure Island* (pp. vii–xxiii). By 'Johnson's *Buccaneers*', Stevenson means Captain Charles Johnson, *A General History of the Robberies and Murders of the Most Notorious Pirates* (1724).
12    Anonymous, Review of *Treasure Island*, *Academy*, 24 (1 December 1883), p. 362, reprinted in Paul Maixner (ed.), *Robert Louis Stevenson: The Critical Heritage* (London: Routledge and Kegan Paul. 1981), p. 129.
13    W. E. Henley, Review of *Treasure Island*, *Saturday Review*, 56 (8 December 1883), pp. 737–8, reprinted in *The Critical Heritage*, ibid., p. 132.
14    Stevenson, 'Child's Play' in *Virginibus Puerisque and Other essays in Belles Lettres*, Tusitala Edition ([1881]; London: William Heinemann, 1914), pp. 110–11.
15    Jacqueline Rose, *The Case of Peter Pan or The Impossibility of Children's Fiction* (London: Macmillan, 1984), pp. 1–2.
16    David H. Jackson, '*Treasure Island* as a Late Victorian Adults' Novel', *Victorian Newsletter*, 72 (1987), p. 29.
17    H. Rider Haggard, 'About Fiction', *Contemporary Review*, 51 (1887), p. 172.
18    Andrew Lang, 'Realism and Romance', *Contemporary Review*, 52 (1887), p. 689.
19    Haggard, 'About Fiction', p. 177.
20    ibid., p. 180.

21  George Saintsbury, 'The Present State of the Novel', *Fortnightly Reviews* NS 42 (1887), p. 411.
22  Stevenson, 'A Gossip on Romance' (1882), *The Works of Robert Louis Stevenson* (London: Chatto and Windus, 1911), Vol. 9, p. 140.
23  Important essays concerning the late Victorian dissension between realism and romance include [Alfred C. Lyall], 'Novels of Adventure and Manners', *Quarterly Review*, 179 (1894), pp. 530–52 and 'History and Fable', *Quarterly Review*, 178 (1894), pp. 31–51; and [William Barry], 'Realism and Decadence in French Fiction', *Quarterly Review*, 170 (1890), pp. 57–89. For a concise and informative introduction to critical questions raised for Victorians by these contending genres, see Kenneth Graham, *English Criticism of the Novel 1865–1900* (Oxford: Clarendon Press, 1965), pp. 19–70. A wide-ranging survey of the changing shape of late Victorian fiction is Peter Keating, *The Haunted Study: A Social History of the English Novel 1875–1914* (London: Secker & Warburg, 1989).
24  Walter Besant, *The Art of Fiction* ([1884]; London: Chatto and Windus, 1902), pp. 5–6.
25  Henry James, 'The Art of Fiction', reprinted in Edwin M. Eigner and George J. Worth, (eds), *Victorian Criticism of the Novel* (Cambridge: Cambridge University Press, 1985), p. 199.
26  ibid., p. 202.
27  ibid., p. 208.
28  ibid., p. 209.
29  Stevenson, 'A Humble Remonstrance', reprinted in *Victorian Criticism of the Novel*, p. 218.
30  Letter to Alexander Ireland, March 1882, *The Letters of Robert Louis Stevenson*, Vol. 2, Tusitala Edition, (ed.) Sidney Colvin (London: Heinemann, 1924), p. 190.
31  Fredric Jameson, *The Political Unconscious: Narrative as a Socially Symbolic Act* (London: Methuen, 1981). This important study has been widely criticized for staying within the Marxist reflection-model of historical subtext/textual surface – to be found in Georgy Lukács's work – that Jameson seeks to undo. Ian Hunter points out that even if Jameson recognizes that 'history' is continuously retextualized, and must be posited only as an 'absent cause', it remains, in Hunter's words, as a 'pre-theoretical projection of the purely formal narrative processes of textualisation . . . But it is simultaneously the underlying form which determines the process of textualisation itself': *Culture and Government: The Emergence of Literary Education, Language, Discourse and Society* (London: Macmillan, 1988), p. 240. That said, the notion of a 'political unconscious' focuses the need to

concentrate on the historical displacements and projections within fictional narratives.

32  Christopher Harvie, 'The Politics of Stevenson' in Jenni Calder, (ed.), *Stevenson and Victorian Scotland* (Edinburgh: Edinburgh University Press, 1981), pp. 120–1.
33  Letter to Sidney Colvin, 28 September 1891, *The Letters of Robert Louis Stevenson*, Vol. 4, pp. 100–1.
34  Stevenson, *Dr Jekyll and Mr Hyde and Other Stories*, (ed.) Jenni Calder (Harmondsworth: Penguin Books, 1979). All references to this edition are included in the text.
35  Stephen Heath, 'Psychopathia Sexualis: Stevenson's Strange Case' in Colin MacCabe, (ed.) *Futures for English* (Manchester: Manchester University Press, 1988), p. 95. On the question of male sexuality, see also Elaine Showalter, 'Syphilis, Sexuality, and the Fiction of the Fin de Siècle' in Ruth Bernard Yeazell, (ed.), *Sex, Politics, and Science in the Nineteenth-Century Novel*, Selected Papers from the English Institutes, 1983–84, New Series No. 10 (Baltimore: The John Hopkins University Press, 1986), pp. 100–3, and 'Dr Jekyll's Closet' in *Sexual Anarchy: Gender and Culture at the Fin de Siècle*, (New York: Viking, 1990), pp. 105–26.

# 4

# A Man's World

## Scrambling for Africa: Haggard and Henty

There, not more than forty or fifty miles from us, glittering like silver in the early rays of the morning sun, soared Sheba's Breasts; and stretching away for hundreds of miles on either side of them ran the great Suliman Berg. Now that, sitting here, I attempt to describe the extraordinary grandeur and beauty of that sight, language seems to fail me. I am impotent even at its memory. Before us rose two enormous mountains, the like of which are not, I believe, to be seen in Africa, if indeed there are any to match them in the world, measuring, each of them, at least fifteen thousand feet in height, standing not more than a dozen miles apart, linked together by a precipitous cliff of rock and towering in awful white solemnity straight into the sky. These mountains, placed thus, like the pillars of a gigantic gateway, are shaped after the fashion of a woman's breasts, and at times the mist and shadows beneath them take the form of a recumbent woman, veiled mysteriously in sleep. Their bases swell gently from the plain, looking at that distance perfectly round and smooth; and upon the top of each is a vast hillock covered with snow, exactly corresponding to the nipple on the female breast. The stretch of cliff that connects them appears to be some thousands of feet in height and perfectly precipitous, and on each flank of them, so far as the eye can reach, extend similar lines of cliff, broken only here and there by flat, table-topped mountains, something like the world-famed one at Cape Town – a formation, by the way, that is very common in Africa. (pp. 56–7)[1]

In this detailed descriptive passage from Haggard's best-selling *King Solomon's Mines*, the intrepid Allan Quatermain casts his astonished eyes across the sexual geography of a dark and unexplored continent. Equipped with a map that once belonged to a fictional sixteenth-century Portuguese adventurer, Quatermain has reached this imposing hinterland while undertaking a type of journey that remained a mesmerizing source of interest to the European mind right up until the 1890s. Like Haggard's novel, Henry Morton Stanley's *Through the Dark Continent* (1878) and *In Darkest Africa* (1890) – the latter comprising two hefty volumes charting an eventful route across the Congo – was appreciated by a very wide audience. (*In Darkest Africa* sold no less than 150,000 copies.) From the celebrated travelogues of Mungo Park, who in 1796 was probably the first European to follow the slave caravan up the Niger, the nineteenth-century reading public eagerly consumed an unending number of records concerning the white man's (and, on occasions, woman's) heroic exploits in Africa. Every corner of the continent was invaded, often with missionary intentions. David Livingstone (whom Stanley notoriously discovered to be alive, after fifteen years' absence, in 1871), embodied both the courageous explorer and the zealous missionary worker. If conversion and exploration frequently went hand in hand, they were just as often followed by imperial annexation. From roughly 1875 to 1895, Europe relentlessly acquired sections of Africa. To take a handful of representative examples: Britain took over Zanzibar in 1888, the East Africa Protectorate (now Kenya) in 1895, Egypt in 1882, and the Soudan in the same year. This chapter examines how and why different kinds of adventure fiction fixed their gaze on a continent that had come to symbolize the highest achievements of empire. Africa, perceived as the most degraded and dangerous corner of the world, was correspondingly considered to present the greatest challenge to its conquerers. No other continent at this time could rival it in terms of ideological value.

But one important question arises from the European struggle to dominate as much of the 'dark continent' as possible. Was the intense European interest in Africa driven by economic considerations as well as by the state-led interests of foreign policy? The reasons behind the accelerated 'scramble' for territory – among Britain, Germany, France, and Italy – have been widely debated ever since J. A. Hobson put forward his contentious attack on the economic motives of imperialism in 1902, pointing out that capitalist overproduction and corresponding underconsumption at home inevitably led to a ruthless search for new markets. Hobson emphasized that, although there were for imperial powers no significant gains from trade with the colonies, it was certainly true that industries producing armaments clearly benefited from the coercive arrogation of territory. Africa was inevitably a site of military conflict between rival European nations. The Ashanti War (concerning the Gold Coast) that took place in 1874–75 was followed by the first of the Anglo–Boer wars in 1881. Thereafter, the 1880s and 1890s witnessed the ravaging of Egypt as British armies followed the Nile towards Khartoum. Surveying the scope of British trade with its ever-spreading empire, Hobson believed that the aggressive exploitation of imperial markets could be halted by the reform of capital: namely, the removal of preferential tariffs and thus the renewal of an earlier phase of Cobdenite free trade.

Hobson's was an influential thesis stemming from radical liberal concerns with the withdrawal of state intervention from economic policy at the turn of the century. In 1917, even though he rejected Hobson's advocacy of *laissez-faire*, Lenin drew on Hobson's account of domestic underconsumption to claim that imperialism marked a shift from the colonial export of goods to the monopolistic export of capital. For Lenin, therefore, empire achieved the highest stage of capitalism.[2] Although there is much evidence to support Hobson's and Lenin's interrelated arguments, both writers have been criticized for their economic determinism, whereby the exchange of capital and labour is said to override all other concerns. It may also be contended that Lenin, writing in the wake of the multiplicity of European incursions into Africa, was largely inattentive to the cultural mechanisms – that is, the prevailing systems of representation – driving armies deeper and deeper into the heart of darkness. Although empire was undoubtedly an economic resource for Britain, the monopolization of markets by the use of trusts, cartels, and syndicates was not solely the guiding spirit leading fictional heroes such as Quatermain into a lavishly mythologized world of tyranny and cannibalism. Surely the popular narratives of empire discussed in this book were not only produced by, but also productive of, the doctrine of imperialism?

The myth of the dark continent had been accumulating a host of negative associations during the fifty or so years since the abolition of slavery in Britain. And the darker the continent became the more the desire grew to acquire huge tracts of land. In *Rule of Darkness*, Brantlinger rightly claims that 'abolitionism contained the seeds of empire'. The Emancipation Act of 1833, which was the belated culmination of a long battle by radicals to secure fundamental human rights, marked a decisive break with the colonial system. Certainly, British trade with its former slave colonies would not noticeably increase thereafter for the rest of the century. But, as Brantlinger adds, although 'the Negro was legally freed . . . in the British mind he was still mentally, morally and physically a slave'.[3] Indeed, it was as though the emancipation of slaves had, in some quarters, freed the racist mind of its guilty conscience, enabling prejudices to be openly expressed. Many eminent Victorians championed the ideal of white supremacism. Brantlinger draws attention to Charles Dickens who, in the pages of the family magazine *Household Words* of 1853, was moved to write of the native American: 'I beg to say that I have not the least belief in the Noble Savage, I consider him a prodigious nuisance, and an enormous superstition. His calling rum fire-water, and me a pale face, wholly fail to reconcile me to him. I don't care what he calls me. I call him a savage, and I call a savage a something highly desirable to be civilized off the face of the earth.'[4] Dickens's prejudices would be underwritten by apparently scientific accounts of racial differences and thereby extend to all people of colour around the world.

The image of the African, in particular, had been increasingly distorted since the earliest phases of colonial slavery. As the nineteenth century wore on, evangelists, explorers, and anthropologists produced writings that put together a picture of Africa as the most savage place in the world, averting their gaze from the highly organized composition of many African societies. It has to be remembered that as wars were successively waged in practically every part of the continent, ethnologists were measuring African heads to establish a hierarchy of racial types. In France, anthropometry and, more particularly, craniometry began with Paul Broca's investigations of 1861. Francis Galton's hereditarian interests in measuring skulls and bodies were put on public display in the laboratory he established at the International Exposition of 1884. Even Gladstone queued up to have a measuring-tape placed around his head. (Similar craniometrical exercises would be used to discriminate between persons on the grounds of gender. They were also deployed to make distinctions between law-abiding and criminal types.)[5] It is not so surprising, then, that Haggard should image Africa in such bodily terms. By mid century, Africans were almost uniformly referred to as 'niggers'. A matter of decades later, with pictures of narrow foreheads and ape-like features impressed upon the European mind, earlier prejudices were scientifically legitimated.

Dorothy Hammond and Alta Jablow note that the world 'nigger' was borrowed from the Indian empire, equating a common subordinacy between all Black peoples.[6] (In fact, it was the panicked British response to the Indian Mutiny of 1857 that is often claimed to have brought this term of racial abuse into common currency. Never before had Black peoples been so distrusted.) Enshrining darkness, both of their skin colour and of their homeland, African men and women would come to represent the complete antithesis of white cultural values. As popular fiction of the time indicates, however, the qualities attributed to Africans indubitably projected disturbances within the white mind. Darkness was, in many respects, a deepening shadow cast by whiteness. For Victorians, the picture of a miserably unenlightened Africa brought together a number of interrelated European anxieties about religion, sexuality, and history on to this highly physicalized terrain. Their untiring journeys across the desert, along the river, and into the jungle were just as significantly travels into two troublesome zones: first, the urban squalor of major cities, and second, what were increasingly recognized as the unknown underworld passages occupying the labyrinthine depths of the supremacist psyche. Both of these shadowy territories, and the threats they posed, need to be looked at briefly in turn.

General Booth, the founder of the Salvation Army, deliberately referred to the East End of London and other deprived areas as 'darkest England'. He named it thus in direct response to the title Stanley gave to his popular record of his travels published in the same year. Booth's analogy is, by his own admission, rather strained but it plainly indicates how the dark continent served as a vivid metaphor for the insanitary world that plagued the late Victorian social conscience:

As there is a darkest Africa is there not also a darkest England? Civilization, which can breed its own barbarians, does it not also breed its own pygmies? May we not find a parallel at our own doors, and discover within a stone's throw of our cathedrals and palaces similar horrors to those which Stanley had found existing in the great Equatorial forest?

The more the mind dwells upon the subject, the closer the analogy appears. The ivory raiders who brutally traffic in the unfortunate denizens of the forest glades, what are they but the publicans who flourish on the weakness of our poor? The two tribes of savages, the human baboon and the handsome dwarf, who will not speak lest it impeded him in his task, may be accepted as the two varieties who are continually present with us – the vicious and lazy lout, and the toiling slave. They, too, have lost all faith of life being other than it is and has been. As in Africa, it is all trees, trees, trees, with no other world conceivable; so is it here – it is all vice and poverty and crime.[7]

To explain the design of his New Jerusalem, Booth had inserted at the start of his book a fold-out illustration depicting a raging sea of unemployment, homelessness, prostitution, and every other imaginable vice and form of deprivation set against a rich and plentiful land free from crime, drink, and shame. In this glorious vision, 'the city colony' and 'the farm colony' – honest trading and justly rewarded labour – are shown to thrive among those upright bastions of philanthropy: cheap food depots and homes for inebriates. Beyond the pastoral fields of England lie the New World, the British colonies, and foreign lands with steamboats speeding towards them. Towards the top of the page, above the crowded housing of the city, the bright horizons of the outlying colonies appear. Salvation, in the figure of a lighthouse, sends out its beacons of spiritual light across a storm-tossed ocean that grows darker and darker towards the bottom margin. Everywhere lifeboat crews are reaching out to the benighted '3,000,000 in the sea'. This picture demonstrated all too graphically how in the cavernous shadows of this uncharted landscape lay the sources of sexual desire: the primitive, untameable, even barbaric forces that rebelled against the constraints of civility, and thus against God. Illustrations like this one sketched in the outlines of the repressions that would in later decades comprise psychoanalysis, awakening a 'mental fright' in Freud's *The Interpretation of Dreams* (1900). (In one of his many accounts of the memory-traces inscribed across his night-time adventures into sleep, Freud recalls the overwhelming power of Haggard's myth of the eternal feminine, *She* [1887].)[8] Africa, the East End, the unconscious – each aspect of darkness was metonymically linked to the other in the imperialist imagination.

Quatermain's fetishistic description of Sheba's breasts bears out a number of these points about the darkness associated with Africa and its restless sexuality. But rather than banish sexual desire to the vicious depths of Booth's turbid ocean, Haggard's narrator fixes his gaze on this shapely landscape. Every feature is sexualized. To begin with, he rather crudely uses the word 'impotent' to express his diminished state of mind in the face of this amazing spectacle. Yet this word, even if it denotes a loss of mental power, endorses the erotic investment in this seemingly alien world. Given that the mountainous breasts 'swell gently from the plain', it would seem that this incredible geographical setting literally embodies passion. Although this landscape may seem outlandish in conception, it in fact presents a far from unfamiliar scene. The narrative permits the eye to travel the length and breadth of cliffs and mountains while picturing parts of the female anatomy that, banished from public view in Britain, could be found in obscene publications. Yet, as this story is a romance, it assumes that it will not be confused with the male genre it closely resembles: pornography.

Haggard's adventure, however, has ample licence to make the most of its phallic pleasures (even if the hero is, in one sense, 'impotent') because the story is set in Africa, a world commonly held to be one of contemptibly naked and therefore oversexed peoples. It would be unimaginable to depict rural Britain in this manner. Yet here is a late nineteenth-century example of a longstanding tradition associating femininity with unconquered territory. The point is, as in modern pornography, the exceptionally detailed description of this landscape exploits synecdoche. Sheba's body is ritually taken to pieces. The feminine inferiority of Africa is laid out, part by part, for the inspection of this type of male gaze. Appropriately enough, she is lying on her back. To sum up: this representation of Sheba's breasts bears out a consistent piece of logic: as Europe is to Africa so is man to woman. In both novels discussed in this chapter, Haggard equates whiteness with male power, and blackness with female weakness. Yet, as each narrative reveals, it proves very difficult to keep these hierarchies in place.

The association of African darkness with European female sexuality was a nineteenth-century commonplace. Two related images are of central importance here: one is the attributed sexual immodesty of African men and women (which continually shocked the missionary mind); the other is the internalized fear of prostitution on city streets (the prostitute functioned as a powerful symbol of social chaos). Sander L. Gilman has examined this link in relation to a wide range of European visual and textual representations of African female sexuality. Lending a significant inflection to Kipling's well-known phrase, he states: 'The "white *man's* burden" thus becomes his sexuality and its control, and it is this which is transferred on to the need to control the sexuality of the Other, the Other as sexualized female. The colonial mentality which sees "natives" as needing control is easily transferred to "woman" – but woman as exemplified by the caste of the prostitute'.[9] Haggard's later, and equally popular, work of fiction, *She*, centres on the unfulfilled sexual desires of a woman who murders members of her people at whim. Hers is a vengeful, demonic sexuality. And, like the supposed degeneracy of the infectious prostitute, her uncontrollable sensuality consumes her from within. Haggard clearly viewed sexual feelings as an unconquerable force. For him they amounted to 'the most powerful lever with which to stir the mind of man'.[10] It is noticeable, however, that his male heroes are far from sexual beings. The sources of passion are to be found in those mutually reinforcing worlds of otherness: woman and Africa. Manly in the extreme, Haggard's heroes find themselves opposed to the warring forces of unleashed desire. Yet their potent resistance underwrites their strong attraction to the temptations they ostensibly manage to repel.

Throughout *She* and *King Solomon's Mines*, women perform two, rather predictable, functions: they are either dutifully passive ('veiled mysteriously asleep') or punishingly domineering (taunting their male subjects). Pushed to the erotic extremes of virginity or promiscuity, Haggard's women are stranger still to the white male gaze because they are Black. For example, when commenting on the caring attitude of Foulata, a young African woman who nurses one of the adventurers back to health, Quatermain declares: 'Women are women all the world over, whatever their colour. Yet somehow it seemed curious to watch this dusky beauty bending night and day over the fevered man's couch, and performing all the merciful errands of a sick-room, swiftly, gently, and with as fine instinct as that of a trained hospital nurse' (p. 142). He is trying to resolve a glaring cultural contradiction. How can this kind and thoughtful Black woman exist? What exactly was she? A savage with a sexual appetite or an emblem of universal virginity? Or, simply, a woman with natural instincts for nurturing and motherhood, qualities that may seem opposed to a voracious sexuality? In these respects, *King Solomon's Mines* raises a set of questions about race and gender at a remove from the work of adventurous romance upon which it was apparently modelled, *Treasure Island*. These fictions, if embedded in many of the most damaging assumptions of dominant Victorian sexual ideology, voiced beliefs that bourgeois propriety demanded were best kept silent. For all the fame these novels brought to Haggard, making him into probably the most highly paid author of his day, he was, like Quatermain, treading on perilous ground. Many of his contemporary readers found the violent passage between Sheba's breasts an infringement of good taste. From their beginnings, Haggard's African stories, although politically conservative in conception, courted controversy.

Dedicated to 'all the big and little boys who read it', *King Solomon's Mines* was primarily aimed at the juvenile market. Having read through the manuscript, Lang informed Haggard that it might be possible to place the novel with Harper's *Boys' Magazine*. Instead, it went to Cassell's who performed a successful advertising campaign that guaranteed the book a wide number of reviews. (Fly-posters informed the public that this was 'the most amazing story ever written'. They seem to have believed it.) At a time when the size and pricing of novels was changing, Haggard's single-volume work reached a larger public than the three-decker novels that were becoming expensive by comparison. 31,000 copies were sold within a year, andd so its distribution extended well beyond the intended juvenile readership. As his article 'About Fiction' indicates, Haggard was concerned to promote a type of romance that drew on a specifically masculine (not just male) group of readers.

Haggard achieves his aims in producing a thrustingly masculinist narrative by depicting his hero as the least literary of men. The opening paragraphs make much of this issue. Quatermain begins his tale with this series of disavowals: 'I am a timid man, and dislike violence; moreover I am almost sick of adventure. I wonder why I am going to write this book; it is not in my line. I am not a literary man, though very devoted to the Old Testament and also to [those mid-Victorian favourites, R. H. Barham's] *The Ingoldsby Legends*' (1840) (p. 13). Quatermain, therefore, has no artistic or intellectual pretensions. He knows his Bible (probably those parts meting out violent judgements) and muses over popular writings.

Quatermain's narrative is, however, framed by an editor who provides marginal annotations wherever necessary, either to correct the hero's mistakes, or to draw the reader's attention to an illuminating quotation from great works of literature. (A similar editorial structure also informs *She*.) For instance, when searching for the treasure-trove of diamonds inside the mines, Quatermain and Sir Henry Curtis speculate on the mythological significance of the colossi that surround them. The hero relies on Sir Henry's classical education to understand the myth of Ashtoreth (or Astarte, depending on which culture she appears in). At this point, the editor footnotes an apposite passage from the first book of *Paradise Lost*. Editorial interventions of this kind may seem inconsequential. But their persistence throughout this narrative begs questions about literary authority. Why usher Milton into this adventure?

*King Solomon's Mines* adds on secondary erudition for two reasons: first, to make weight for the protagonist's apparent lack of learning; and, second, and more importantly, to demonstrate that the extraordinary scenes such as the ones on view here have their origins in Britain's literary heritage. In this manner, the editor (who presents the book to the public) enhances the status of the work at his command. Editor and adventurer, therefore, cannot be confused. But, taken together, these two male voices work together to tell an 'amazing' story. Appropriate quotations ennoble adventurous deeds, while the deeds themselves take their meaning from the great cultural documents of the past. Learned gentlemen and manly explorers are mutually supportive. Two different kinds of masculinity, then, are endorsed at both the centre and the margins of the book. As each novel demonstrates, these men need one another.

The fact that Quatermain has few pretensions to learning has to be balanced against the shocking incidents he witnesses. As the following outline indicates, the story is thin on plot. It relies chiefly on sensational incident. Accompanied by Captain Good (a naval officer) and Sir Henry (a gentleman) in search of George Neville (Sir Henry's long lost brother), Quatermain finds the body of José Silvestra preserved in the ice of a cave. (Silvestra has been dead for 300 years.) They take the map they find upon his body and, apart from being waylaid by a fearful confrontation with a bull elephant, all three successfully reach Kukuanaland. They are also accompanied by the noble Zulu, Umbopa. When they meet King Twala, who ritually sacrifices his people with the aid of the witch Gagool, they discover that Umbopa is in fact the rightful heir to Twala's kingdom, and has returned to stake his claim to the throne. Battles ensue, Umbopa (now known as Ignosi) triumphs, and the white explorers head for the mines. In this gothic underworld, they find themselves entrapped by Gagool. Tension mounts as they struggle to find an exit. When free, they return to base, discovering Sir Henry's brother on the way. Their mission, therefore, resists the forces of nature (the bull elephant), overcomes tyranny (the reign of Twala), and outwits female evil (the death of Gagool).

Quatermain, claiming at the start to be nothing more than a 'poor travelling trader', prefaces these episodes of considerable violence with these words: 'I have never slain wantonly or stained my hand in innocent blood, but only in self-defence' (p. 14). Instead, each man has his mission: Quatermain to lead; Sir Henry to perform his duty (by rescuing his brother); and Captain Good to support the other two. Between them, they combine the best of qualities to ensure their eventual success. Quatermain is fearless; Sir Henry erudite; and Good lives up to his name, bringing moments of light comedy to bear on the story. (Much is made of Good's loss of his trousers when he reaches the realm of Twala, king of the Kukuanas. He has to remain without this article of clothing lest the suspicions of these imaginary Africans are aroused. Quatermain tells Good: 'If you change any of these things the people will think that we are impostors . . . If they begin to suspect us our lives will not be worth a brass farthing' [p. 73]). Morally speaking, the narrative buoys itself up by ensuring that the adventurers get the chance of finding the diamonds yet only have enough time to fill their pockets with sparing handfuls of them. Quatermain, it should appear, is not a greedy man. But that is the reassuring end of the story and not its incredibly violent passage in between. At a pivotal point in the novel 200 Kukuanas are massacred.

Armed with rifles, the white men always save themselves from injury. Confronted by the 'horrid apparition' of an African armed with a spear, Quatermain recounts a quick turn of events: 'he took a header right over my prostrate form. Before he could rise again, *I* had risen and settled the matter from behind with my revolver' (p. 122). By contrast, when not speared (or eaten) by each other, Black people either die at the hands of white men or are tragic victims of fate. One servant, Khiva, is trampled to death by the rampaging elephant. His white masters, needless to say, escape unharmed. Not even Foulata, who has fallen in love with Good, survives (she is stabbed, in a climactic struggle, by Gagool), and so any threat of miscegenation is avoided. When in the presence of his Black enemies, Quatermain is not unused to protecting his life by relying on the enduring power of his 'imperial smile' (p. 71). Time and again, the narrative introduces this adjective whenever issues of racial superiority are at stake. His ability to trick the cannibals turns out to be an essential characteristic of empire. The only Africans who win respect are the Zulu princes, such as Umslopogaas in *Allan Quatermain* (1887), or Ignosi, who restores order to Twala's vicious kingdom. Brian V. Street points out that this figure, admired for his athletic physique, 'has many of the qualities of the English gentleman – honour, dignity and courage'.[11] The Zulus of course, were the most successfully militarized of African peoples in Southern Africa, and had beaten the British at the humiliating battle of Rorke's Drift in 1879. Haggard was filled with admiration for the tenacious fighting spirit of the Zulus. But this noble quality does not always cleanse Ignosi and Umslopogaas of the taint of savagery. If heroic and faithful, Umslopogaas cannot outlive the likes of Quatermain. This prized African warrior dies an honourable death fending off an approaching army.

Surveying Haggard's substantial body of adventure fiction, Wendy R. Katz emphasizes how the racial disposition of the Africans is repeatedly compounded by their despicable involvement with supernatural forces. However, when attempting to purge these communities of their abhorrent customs, the explorers resort to the very forms of superstition they seek to denounce. Missionary fervour, whether explicitly Christian (in *Allan Quatermain*), or exclusively imperialist (in *King Solomon's Mines* and *She*), actually relies on using one kind of evil to defeat another. The example Katz cites is where Quatermain informs Twala that his men have been sent from the stars, and that their rifles perform the work of magic.[12] By making deceptive use of their knowledge of astronomy, the white explorers are able to predict an eclipse, and they persuade Twala and even Ignosi that this phenomenon proves their supremacy. When the eclipse comes, the adventurers see that their prophecy has been fulfilled: "'The moon is dying – the white wizards have killed the moon", yelled the prince Scragga. "We shall perish in the dark"' (pp. 110–11). At this instant, Scragga tries to spear Sir Henry. But Sir Henry, with the wisdom of foresight, is saved by the chain-mail he has been wearing beneath his shirt. In self-defence, he grasps Scragga's spear and slaughters the African. Under the cover of nightfall, the white men leave this scene unnoticed. This is a typical episode demonstrating how one structure remains firmly in place throughout these novels: a desire to rid the world of this heart of darkness rests on a desire for it.

*She* follows an almost identical pattern to *King Solomon's Mines*. This novel, however, finds something far more terrifying than Twala and Gagool in its midst. This is a story of relentless sexual warfare where opportunities for gratuitous racism take on newer and larger proportions. Masculinity is glorified; femininity is vilified. 'Like Cain . . . branded by Nature with the stamp of abnormal ugliness' (p. 197), Ludwig Horace Holly, narrator and master of the journey that comprises *She*, openly admits he is 'a bit of a misogynist' (p. 257). His distaste for Africans is similarly in evidence. Remarking on the physiognomy of the Amahagger tribe, he states:

> Generally their appearance had a good deal in common with that of the East African Somali, only their hair was not frizzed up, and hung in thick black locks upon their shoulders. Their features were aquiline, and in many cases exceedingly handsome, the teeth being especially regular and beautiful. But notwithstanding their beauty, it struck me that, on the whole, I had never seen a more evil-looking set of faces (p. 248).

This description displays that combination of attraction and repulsion structuring the vision of everything to be found in Haggard's Africa. It is noticeable how the Amahagger are neither basely

African (with 'the thick lips' and 'fat cheeks' that lend a 'terrifying expression' (p. 236) to the Black image mentioned earlier in the novel) nor nobly European. They are sufficiently 'aquiline' to be loved; but adequately Black to be loathed. The ambivalent racism to be found in these words is further complicated in the sexual representation of She Herself. Ayesha, alias She-who-must-be-obeyed, and who is historically linked with Europe, famously loses her beauty at the end to shrivel up into nothing other than a 'monkey' (p. 402). For all his 'misogyny', Holly discovers that he has fallen 'absolutely and hopelessly in love with this white sorceress' p. 308). His aversion to women is linked to his fascination for them. Given this double movement of abhorrence and adoration, there is much in this novel that could even in its own day be categorized as perverse.

In their extensive analysis of Her astonishing hold over the late Victorian imagination, Sandra M. Gilbert and Susan Gubar identify in *She* not only the widely circulated image of the *femme fatale* – gracing the walls of many an art gallery and filling out the lines of a host of woman-hating poems – but also the icon of an 'anti-Victoria', one who would, according to Holly, 'assume absolute rule over British dominions' (p. 376). Certainly, Victoria was exerting more representational power over her empire than earlier in the century, as the Jubilee celebrations of 1887 and 1897 indicate. Moreover, emerging suffragist and native demands for independence created, as Gilbert and Gubar note, a link between the forms of resistance voiced by both groups.[13] Female authority and female vulnerability, then, shape the contours of this particular version of empire. Victoria was clearly the most important symbol of imperial rule but the potency invested in imperialism was not entirely compatible with her gender. Juxtaposed in this manner, the connection between Victoria and Ayesha makes it possible to see how the impostures of empire are, in some significant respects, translated on to this sexualized representation of Africa.

Everything brutal about British imperialism – the wars, the massacres, the destruction of cultures – is displaced into the very heart of the continent the Victorians sought to conquer. Notably, Ayesha's land is called Kôr, which suggests various connotations (core, *coeur*, Cora; the centre, the seat of passion, and the queen of the underworld). And the name, Ayesha, which refers to Muhammad's second wife, suggests that this story also has something of a holy war between Islam and Christianity in mind. By all accounts, Her Africa resonates with a mighty corpus of European and Asian religions and legends. Instead of becoming the object of imperial domination, Her country, with no apparent history of its own, turns into the subject of it. 'My empire is of the imagination', says She (p. 319). But the imagination that fashions her lethal words, and substitutes sexual for military power, is clearly that of British imperialism. Throughout *She*, it seems that the murderous female heart of Africa is to take the blame and burden for the wrongs of the European past and the imperial present.

There is a further response to the internal crises of domestic Britain, particularly sexual ones, to be located in this book. At the same time as the *fin de siècle* cult of misogyny, there was a mounting concern about sexual relations between men. The Labouchère amendment to the Criminal Law Amendment Act of 1885 outlawed sexual relations between men (acts of 'gross indecency'), even in private. (Oscar Wilde was tried under this law ten years later. He was sent to gaol for two years with hard labour.) This notorious amendment – later known as the 'blackmailer's charter' – formed part of legislation raising the age of consent for girls from thirteen to sixteen years. Viewed within the context of the punitive Criminal Law Amendment Act, Labouchère's clause was a defining feature of new perceptions about sexual desire and sexual morality. There is, of course, no explicitly homosexual content in any of Haggard's novels. But their homoerotic elements are legion, and they are designed to rise up as a superior amatory force against the love of woman. Wayne Koestenbaum provocatively argues that, along with Stevenson's work, 'Haggard's romances made room for pederasty by excluding marriage'.[14] Haggard takes great pains to banish women from the early part of *She*. Yet try as he might to keep women away from the boy in his charge, Holly leads his young ward on an expedition towards a final confrontation with Her: the ultimate in feminine evil. In this manner, the novel reads like an initiation into manhood where sexual temptation stands as the greatest sign of weakness in men. Yet it is a test that, implicitly, all boys must endure.

Holly, a university don (and therefore debarred from marrying) is most implausibly entrusted with the keeping of a male child. The young Leo Vincey, age five, is put into Holly's care by the boy's father. Vincey senior has spent much of his life researching his family history. Before he dies of tuberculosis, Vincey senior tells Holly of his great ancestor, Kallikrates (a Spartan, mentioned in the annals of Herodotus). Vincey's will contains precise instructions about what to make of the contents of a chest containing documents in Greek and Latin, and details of an expedition to be undertaken into the depths of Africa. Young Leo – 'the handsomest fellow I have ever seen' (p. 193) – resembles a 'Greek god' (p. 206). Believing that the 'boy was old enough to do without female assistance', Holly arranges for 'a suitable male attendant' to look after Leo (p. 205). The first sentence Leo utters to his father seals the homoerotic bond set against Her sexually consuming energies: 'I like you . . . you is ugly, but you is good' (p. 205). As Holly goes on to say, 'Few sons have been loved as I love Leo' (p. 206). Love between these men by far surpasses that which Ayesha shows for Kallikrates (Leo's ancestor sixty-five generations ago). In Leo, Ayesha sees the reincarnation of her lover of 2,000 years before, and there is sufficient documentary evidence provided at the start to prove that She is right.

An elaborate historical apparatus, then, is set in place to link past and present together. The novel drew on those powerful metaphors of ancient empires against which Britain was regularly compared, especially to arouse fear of future decline. In one of the closing chapters, She asks Holly about Britain, and a politically contentious dialogue opens up with the following question:

> 'And now tell me of thy country – 'tis a great people, is it not? with an empire, like that of Rome! Surely thou wouldst return thither, and it is well, for I mean not that thou shouldst dwell in these caves of Kor. Nay, when once thou art even as I am, we will go hence – fear not but that I shall find a path . . . For thou [Kallikrates] shall rule this England – '
> 'But we have a queen already', broke in Leo, hastily.
> 'It is naught, it is naught', said Ayesha; 'she can be overthrown'.
> At this we both broke out in a exclamation of dismay, and explained that we should as soon think of overthrowing ourselves.
> 'But here is a strange thing', said Ayesha, in astonishment; 'a queen whom her people love! Surely the world must have changed since I dwelt in Kôr'.

> Again we explained that it was the character of monarchs that had
> changed, and that the one under whom we lived was venerated and
> beloved by all right-thinking people in her vast realms. Also, we told
> her that real power in our country rested in the hands of the people,
> and that we were in fact ruled by the votes of the lower and least
> educated classes of the community.
>   'Ah', she said, 'a democracy — then surely there is a tyrant, for I
> have long since seen that democracies, having no clear will of their
> own, in the end set up a tyrant, and worship him'.
>   'Yes', I said, 'we have our tyrants'. (p. 375)

Together, the older and younger man rally to the defences of their
country lest She should finally reign over a great imperial power.
But defined against this concern about tyranny is an intolerance
towards democracy. Haggard is certainly displaying his extremely
conservative colours here. According to Holly, since democracy lies
in the hands of the ignorant majority it is a weapon that can be
turned against the interests of the people who seek to benefit from
it. (Universal male suffrage for adult men was accomplished two
years before this novel went on sale.) Like many thinkers of the
far right, Haggard wished to place political leadership above party
strife. However, the form this polemic takes leads Holly not away
from She but places him in agreement with her. There is, it seems,
something politically desirable in the terrible image She concocts.
Although She represents one form of tyranny (from above), She too
acknowledges that tyranny can rise up (from below). Undoubtedly,
for Haggard's men, adversaries are to be found everywhere: in
Africa, in sexuality, and even in the working class.

Controversy raged around these fictions. Yet nearly all of Haggard's fiercest critics found much to praise in his writing. Even
the reviewer who considered 'the story of *She* . . . one of the
most repulsive ever conceived' none the less enjoyed the 'author's
genuine admiration of manly pluck and fighting skills when athletic
skills are apt to be overrated'. The 'rapidity' of the story marked
its special appeal.[15] The most concerted attack on his work was led
in the pages of the *Fortnightly Review*, and there was a cross-fire
of opinions between this journal and the *Contemporary Review*. In
'The Fall of Fiction', William Watson pointed to the far-fetched
quality of some of the most horrific incidents. (Attention is paid to
the death of Gagool. How did she come to be crushed by a secret

moving rock which only she knew how to operate?) However, it was, by and large, on moral grounds that these novels were condemned. Taking note of Haggard's 'eminent offences against good taste and good sense', Watson was concerned about their appeal to 'public taste'. He thought these books were addictive. To make his point, and no doubt sharing some of General Booth's concerns about the working classes, Watson drew a comparison with alcohol:

> There is among the very poor in our large cities a class of persons who nightly resort to the gin-shop to purchase a mixture of every known liquor, the heterogenous rinsings of a hundred glasses. The flavour of this unnameable beverage defies imagination, but the liquor has for its lovers one transcendent virtue – it distances all rivalry in the work of procuring swift and thorough inebriation. Its devotees would not thank you for a bottle of the finest Chateau Yquem, when the great end and aim of drinking – the being made drunk – can be reached by such an infinitely readier agency. The taste for novels like Mr Rider Haggard's is quite as truly the craving for coarse and violent intoxicants because they coarsely and violently intoxicate. But the victims of this thirst are without the excuse which the indigent topers to whom we liken may plead. The poor tippler might say that he bought his unutterable beverage because he could not afford a better. But the noblest vintages of literature may be purchased as cheaply as their vilest substitutes. (p. 336)

Watson bases his analogy on assumptions similar to those guiding the debate about literacy and literary education analysed in chapter 1. The issue at stake here, however, concerns not so much those numerous and impoverished gin drinkers who doubtless wasted their money on penny dreadfuls. Rather, Watson is perturbed by the lowering of standards among respectable readers who should have enough good sense to buy 'meritorious' instead of 'meretricious' fiction.[16] Adventures like Haggard's apparently threaten to turn the bourgeoisie over to the inebriate working classes.

On the basis of this assault on Haggard, Lang championed him, and Watson made this final reply:

> Mr Lang warmly defends Mr Haggard's taste for blood. 'Without shedding blood', he says, 'you cannot fight your way through undiscovered Africa'. Well, Mr Haggard's is indeed an 'undiscovered Africa', for it is an Africa that has no existence. Does not every reader

see that Kôr, and Kekuanaland, and the city in *Allan Quatermain*, are localities so essentially *in nubibus* that there was no artistic necessity to parade realistic means of conveying thither?[17]

Lang contested such views by claiming that adventure drew out 'our mixed condition, civilized at the top with the old barbarian under our clothes'. He added: 'Culture is saddened at discovering that not only boys and illiterate people, but even critics not wholly illiterate, can be moved by a tale of adventure'.[18] For Lang, literary merit was not the problem. Rather, it was the content that mattered. He could, therefore, claim to admire Haggard's and Stevenson's books for boys better than those they wrote for an exclusively adult market (such as *Mr Meeson's Will* [1888] or *The Strange Case of Dr Jekyll and Mr Hyde*). Lang's adaptation of atavistic racial theories was clearly put in the name of empire. For him, literary merit was irrelevant to communicating the innate violence in every man. This natural will-to-power was celebrated in one of his poems: 'King Romance is come indeed!'[19] And the celebrity of *She* in particular was not simply because of its remarkable sales and the furore it created in literary circles. Its violence also met with mockery.

Shortly after its publication, *She* was the subject of several parodies. (One American company brought out no less than four in one year.) Not only did *Punch* perform its usual duty in sending up this *cause célèbre*, Longman also published an extended and good-humoured response to the novel by Lang and a collaborator, W. H. Pollock. Entitled '*He*', by the author of '*It, King Solomon's Wives, Bess, Much Darker Days, Mr Morton's Subtler, and Other Romances*' (each part of the subtitle pretending to deride Haggard's novels), this counter-version of the original romance takes place in Grub Street not Africa. Koestenbaum notes how the parody inverts key terms and locations:

> The purpose of *He* was to unsex *She*; Lang and Pollock, however, do more than repudiate strong women. They question gender itself by uniformly reversing the sexes of all the characters in *She*, turning She into He, Holly into Polly, and Leo into Leonora. The collaborators even make a man of Queen Victoria; dedicating the work to Haggard's fictional hero, Allan Quatermain, they unsex Victoria by saying that 'His Majesty is a Merry Monarch'.

They replace *She*'s matriarchal kingdom of Kôr with the world of masculine literary clubs.[20]

Making men into women, women into men, and Africa into England, these parodists were laying bare the cultural text that brought *She* into the public eye. *She* was a product of the close bonds between men that held the conservative literary world tightly together, and Lang was a constant mentor to Haggard during the preparation of five of the novels Haggard published in the 1880s. They jointly produced a romance, *The World's Desire*, in 1890. Lang and Pollock's *He*, therefore, was doing two related things at once. First, it added a further layer of male conspiracy against the female power eagerly ignited and promptly vanquished in Haggard's romance. Second, it revealed how homosocial relations between men were generating their imperial strength by opposing themselves to what were projected as formidable forms of female authority such as the figure of 'new woman' first embodied in Schreiner's heroine, Lyndall, in *The Story of An African Farm* (1883), a work Haggard admired.

Flattery from inside Haggard's coterie was matched outside his circle by repeated accusations of plagiarism. One article in *Time* enumerated Haggard's many borrowings, and concluded: 'the English press which has trumpeted its success must be utterly corrupt, and the people who have listened and believed must be very ignorant and wholly devoid of judgement'.[21] Another review pointed out at length how *Allan Quatermain* had lifted and modified passages from E. F. Smith's record of his travels around the world, *The Cruise of the Falcon* (1882). In an ironic turn of events, a story Smith subsequently published in *Cassell's Saturday Magazine* was criticized by one commentator for abstracting large parts of *Allan Quatermain*.[22] The imperial imagination, it seemed, had no scruples about appropriating other people's property. Romance knew no bounds since its duty was to follow the dictates of something that stood over and above the interests of individuals: the empire.

The writer who could make the least claim to originality in this era of books for 'big and little boys' was G. A. Henty. Producing 103 volumes between 1868 and 1902, no other author could with equal success sustain the attention of boy readers. His adventure fictions, produced three times a year for the publishing house Blackie, outnumber even Haggard's, as do their sales figures, which may run to a total of 25 million copies. Yet if they cover much of the same territory as Haggard's romances, they are altogether different in their preoccupations. Here the *femme fatale* is not in evidence but the heroic deeds of great men certainly are. Henty's chief resource was the detailed annals of imperial history, particularly contemporary military campaigns, where his valiant boy heroes were placed in the lauded company of the bold and the brave, as his titles show: *With Clive in India: or the Beginnings of an Empire* (1884), *With Roberts to Pretoria: A Tale of the South African War* (1902), and *With Kitchener in the Soudan: A Story of Atbara and Omdurman* (1903).

It goes without saying that each story makes empire into an adventure. Fiction serves as an alibi for relating the precise movements of the army. Henty's writings fed a widespread interest in the African 'scramble' for new lands. G. W. Steevens' *With Kitchener to Khartoum* (1899), an account of Kitchener's campaign by a journalist from the *Daily Mail*, met the demands of a growing market for imperialist propaganda. Henty's writing had similar aims. In *Boy's Own Paper* for 1902, Henty claimed it was his task to 'inculcate patriotism in my books', and added: 'I know that very many boys have joined the cadets and afterwards gone into the army through reading my stories'.[23] Passages of his prose read like instructions for the cadets corps. Correct handling of weapons; proper execution of commands; attention to codes of conduct: all these points insist on conformity, obedience, and respect. But these works, if inculcatory in intention, do not read like moral tracts. Instead, imperial history of this kind, reported daily in the popular Tory newspapers, lent itself to an exciting episodic structure. Since the moral mission of empire formed the most basic of all assumptions in this kind of adventure, it remained very much in the background of the narrative. Emphasis fell on the complexities of action: reconnoitring enemy territory; planning the logistics of battle; carrying out a successful raid; and so on. Moreover, in *With Kitchener in the Soudan*, Henty has to go to ingenious lengths to situate his boy hero in a suitable position to maximize the excitement of the military advance down the Nile. For his protagonist, Gregory Hilliard, there is a special reward for serving his country so well.

The novel opens some twenty years before Kitchener's bombardment of Omdurman in 1898. Henty's narrator tells how the aristocratic Gregory Hartley marries a clergyman's daughter against the wishes of his parents. Hartley, therefore, cannot draw any income from his father. He turns to writing, and fails to make a living. Concerned for his wife's health, and for employment of some kind, he is prepared to move to a warmer climate by taking a post as a messenger to a commercial enterprise in Egypt. Having stepped down in the world, he changes his name to Hilliard (which is, in fact, his middle name; strictly speaking, he has not dishonourably given a false identity).

The action moves briskly to events in 1882. At that time, the British and French joint administration of Egypt had entered a new crisis. Egypt was unable to pay off the debts which had accumulated around the Suez Canal. In 1881, Arabi Pasha mounted a people's revolt against the government, demanding an Egyptian role in the administration of the country's budget. In June the following year, riots led to the deaths of fifty Europeans in Alexandria. All of these events are closely observed in Henty's narrative. Rather hurriedly, the narrator shows how changes in the Egyptian economy force Hilliard out of commerce and into the Egyptian army. Consequently, he follows Wolseley to relieve Gordon's siege at Khartoum. Gordon's campaign had been to suppress the Sudanese slave trade, and he had met with the fierce resistance of the Mahdites, followers of the prophet Mahdi who led the Dervishes into a jihad (holy war) against the British forces. Wolseley arrived two days too late, and many British and Egyptian lives were lost. The narrative gives this explanation:

> [Gordon's] requests for aid were slighted. He had asked that two regiments should be sent from Suakim to keep open the route to Berber, but Mr Gladstone's government refused even this slight assistance to the man they had sent out, and it was not until May that public indignation at this base desertion of one of the noblest spirits that Britain ever produced caused preparations for his rescue to be made. (p. 51)[24]

Gordon was speared through the middle, and then beheaded. His head was left on display. Kitchener's campaign twelve years later aimed not only to secure Soudan to the British crown but also avenge Gordon's death. It was to mark the triumph of imperialism over Gladstone's Liberalism. In an article considering 'The Ethics of Empire' in 1897, one writer pointed to the murder of Gordon as the ultimate proof that liberal-minded 'sentiment' should not 'sway the counsels of empire'. The Dervishes's barbarism was said to be far greater than any atrocity the British might commit against them.[25]

Henty structures his narrative around these two politically charged events. Hilliard senior dies aboard a wrecked steamer on the Nile during the time of Gordon's siege. As the intervening years pass by, Hilliard junior grows up to serve the Egyptian army as it steadily advances towards Fashoda. Young Gregory Hilliard wins favour with his superiors because of his linguistic skills. With foresight, his mother (who finally dies from ill-health) saw 'that if the Soudan was ever reconquered the knowledge of the tribal languages [would] be of immense benefit to her son . . . Thus Gregory, almost unconsciously, acquired several of the dialects used in the Soudan. Arabic formed the basis of them all, except the negro tongue' (p. 54). These languages work to his advantage. Indeed, his ability to speak Arabic amounts to a classical education. A large part of the European interest in annexing Egypt was bound up with a longstanding recognition of the cultural significance of this nation, as Edward W. Said observes:

> Because Egypt was saturated with meaning for the arts, sciences, and government, its role was to be the stage on which actions of world-historical importance would take place. By taking Egypt, then, a modern power would naturally demonstrate its strength and justify history; Egypt's own destiny was to be annexed, to Europe preferably. In addition, this power would also enter a history whose common element was defined by figures no less great than Homer, Alexander, Caesar, Plato, Solon, and Pythagoras, who graced the Orient, in short, existed as a set of values attached, not to its modern realities, but to a set of valorized contacts it had had with a distant European past.[26]

Acquaintance with native Egyptian customs and languages turns out to be one of the great fortunes of empire for Gregory Hilliard. His orientalist knowledge dignifies his status, and it plays a strategic role in assisting the army on its hazardous route to Khartoum.

Like Kipling's Kim, Hilliard can both speak and act like the native. Confident and plucky, he approaches General Hunter with a plan for interloping in the enemy camp. Not only does he intend to discover the movements of Mahmud's forces, but he also wishes to glean information about the circumstances that sealed his father's fate many years ago:

> 'I talk Baggara better than the negro dialect that passes here. It is among the Baggara that I am likely to learn something of my father's fate; and as the old nurse from whom I learnt these languages had been for a long time among that tribe, she devoted, at my mother's request, more time to teaching me their Arab dialect than any other, and I am convinced that I could pass unsuspected among them as far as language is concerned. There is no great difference between Arab features and European, and I think that when I am stained brown and have my head partly shaved, according to their fashion, there will be little fear of my being detected. As to costume, that is easy enough. I have not seen any of the Dervishes yet, but the natives who have come from El Obeid or any other neighbourhood where they are masters, could give me an account of their dress, and the way in which they wear the patches on their clothes, which are the distinguishing mark of the Mahdists'. (pp. 104–5)

Alert in every respect, Hilliard misses nothing. Linked together in this manner, these sentences pay unfaltering attention to detailed procedures, ensuring that all possible outcomes are covered. This model of boyhood, as chapter 5 demonstrates, lay at the heart of Baden-Powell's Scout movement. Predictably, Hilliard's spy mission is successful. He discovers the Mahdites's plans, and safely returns to the army encampment. After the battle of Atbara, the regiments make their final advance to Omdurman.

Omdurman counts among the most celebrated of imperial victories, and it restored public faith in empire after the calamity of Jameson's Raid in 1895, as well as firmly re-establishing the British hold on the Soudan after Gordon's shocking death in 1885. After the massacre (when 11,000 Dervishes were killed in four hours), Gregory draws this conclusion:

> [H]e could not but feel sorry for the valiant savages who under so awful a fire still pressed forward to certain death, their numbers

withering away at every step until they dwindled to nothing, only
to be replaced by a fresh band, which darted forward to meet a
similar fate; and yet, when he remembered the wholesale slaughter
at Metemmeh, the annihilation of countless villages and of their
inhabitants, and, above all, the absolute destruction of the army
of Hicks Pasha, the capture of Khartoum, the murder of Gordon,
and the reduction to a state of slavery of all the peaceful tribes of
the Soudan, he could not but feel that the annihilation of these
human tigers and the wiping out of their false creed was a necessity.
(p. 238)

These sentiments are endorsed by the response of Hilliard's faithful
Arab servant, Zaki, who also feels avenged since his people, once
enslaved by the Mahdites, are now freed. This discourse obviously
draws on a language of emancipation reaching back to an earlier
colonial era waging Christian war against Islam. Christianity reigned
victorious at Khartoum. After playing the national anthem, the Khe-
dive's hymn, the dead march, and 'Toll for the Brave', 'minute-guns
were fired, and four chaplains – Anglican, Presbyterian, Methodist, and Catholic – by turns read a psalm of a prayer'. Finally,
'the Soudanese bands played Gordon's favourite hymn, "Abide
with me"' (p. 245). Guided by the justice meted out in the Old
Testament, this glorious spectacle marked the highest point of a
just war. And that was precisely how the British public viewed
this achievement. Kitchener left Khartoum for Fashoda where he
confronted the French general, Marchand. Conflict was avoided.
Britain, then, had prevailed not only over the Dervishes but also
over its main European rival. Later, Kitchener campaigned for
monies to establish a college in Gordon's name at Khartoum.

Radical opposition to these events in the Soudan, however, was
loudly voiced in parliament. In 1898, a contentious argument
attended the presentation of a bill for the dispensation of a
grant to Kitchener for his military deeds. Members of all political
persuasions in the house were horrified by the enormous number
of deaths on the enemy side. Yet one point, suppressed in Henty's
narrative, occupied the main part of the debate. The leader of
the Radicals, John Morley, objected to the exhumation of the
Mahdi from his tomb in Omdurman. The prophet had died
from smallpox shortly after the murder of Gordon. It was left
to Gordon's nephew to ransack the tomb, disperse the remains of

the Mahdi's body, and create souvenirs out of the prophet's nails. Having heard various reports about this incident, Morley stated: 'You send your soldiers to civilize savages. Take care the savages do not barbarize your soldiers'.[27] Defending Kitchener's grant, one member was moved to quote Kipling's view of 'fuzzy-wuzzy' – 'all 'ot sand and ginger when alive, / And generally shammin' when 'e's dead' – claiming that such were 'the men with whom our regiments have to deal'. These views were asserted in the same sentence which declared that 'there never was any cruelty at all with regard to the wounded on the battlefield'.[28] In these terms, death could never approach cruelty. It was, instead, an appropriate punishment for a lesser race.

Although these details are absent from *With Kitchener in the Soudan*, wounded men do make their appearance by a complicated route. Two chapters are devoted to the skill and bravery of Hilliard senior in nursing the Mahdites. He even manages to amputate an arm. These details are revealed in the papers belonging to him which his son locates many years later under a rock in the desert. Having entered the enemy camp as a Dervish, as his son would in later years, Hilliard senior does a noble deed to an Arab at the time of Gordon's campaign. He says he had once thought of training as a surgeon, and had attended classes at university. This experience gives him the opportunity to practise what he had only been able to imagine:

'The tourniquet was first put on the arm and screwed tightly. Then I administered the chloroform, which took its effect speedily. My nerves were braced up now, and I do think I made a fair job of it – finding and tying up the arteries, cutting and sawing the bone off, and making a flap; a few stitches to keep this together and it was done and to my relief the Arab, who had lain as rigid as a statue, winced a little when the last stich was put in.' (p. 296)

Even if this proves to be an act of charity, it enables the boy reader to witness the dismemberment of an Arab body. Adept at removing bullets, Hilliard senior provides all the physical detail missing from the battle scenes. (In fact, descriptions of the battles almost solely attend to the exact numbers of soldiers and armed weapons involved.) Metaphorically speaking, this journal has a special healing power of its own since its discovery brings together father and son, and provides a philanthropic vision of imperial warfare. In this respect, the narrative creates a neat symmetry between these two epochal events, as if they existed in a mutually supportive order. Hilliard's good and self-sacrificing deeds during the campaign of 1885 are vindicated by the victory celebrated thirteen years later.

There are further comforting (and carefully plotted) aspects to the story. Just as the Mahdi's body was Kitchener's reward, so too does young Hilliard receive his own prize. The final pages are turned over to unexpected news. One of the colonels had received information confirming that the boy is not the son of an army Pasha but is in fact the Marquis of Langdale, and that his real name is Hartley. And so he returns with Zaki to London, and this orphan of empire takes his rightful place at the top of the social ladder. In the end, 'Gregory is learning the duties of a large land-owner' (p. 384). He may have had only a minor role in the Soudan but it was clearly an ideal training-ground for him to learn how to run his personal estate. The connection between the power of the landed classes and imperialism was still very strong in the late nineteenth and early twentieth centuries. Haggard wrote extensively on the condition of a degenerating Britain in *Rural England* (1902). He looked to the 're-creation of a yeoman class, rooted and supported by the soil'.[29] Henty's boys were undertaking the task of securing that vision, if without Haggard's fatalistic overtones. But already, at the apogee of empire, a contradictory perspective was emerging, angling its gaze at the ideological functions of these conservative fictions. It is at this point that it is appropriate to turn to the best known interrogation of the popular adventure into Africa: Conrad's novella, *Heart of Darkness* (1898).

## Conrad's Man

Even on a cursory reading of what is still a fiercely debated narrative, *Heart of Darkness* bears a number of superficial resemblances to the kind of seafaring story celebrated – to recall an example that Conrad admired – in Captain Marryat's fiction. This brief tale (approximately 30,000 words) similarly follows a path cut by Haggard and Henty into the remote interior of Africa. One of the central points of critical discussion about this novella concerns the extent to which Conrad's unconventional narrative technique undermines the racist assumptions to be found, for example, in popular imperialist fiction. That said, in many critical commentaries *Heart of Darkness* is so highly regarded as a pre-eminent example of great literary writing that analyses of its racial outlook often dissociate it entirely from the tales of adventure it seems to interrogate. Direct comparisons between the two are rarely made. Since *Heart of Darkness* is a canonical work, and has thus become a permanent fixture on many educational syllabuses, the amount of critical attention given to this relatively slender volume is greater by far than that accorded to writers exploiting the juvenile fiction market.

Criticism has gone to remarkable lengths to reveal new sources for this technically complex representation of an unnerving journey up the Congo. Careful research has demonstrated Conrad's aesthetic choices (his 'Impressionism'), his interweaving of Western and Eastern myths (the interest in Buddhism), the use of classical mythology (the appearance of the three fates: Clotho, Lachesis, Atropos), and, concomitantly, his extension of more modern patterns of myth (Romantic Prometheanism, for example). Indeed, *Heart of Darkness* is so infused with studied allusions to the burden of European culture reaching far back before the era of modern imperialism that Marlow's story of his encounter with the mysterious Mr Kurtz has regularly been regarded as one of remarkable philosophical magnitude. Throughout, there are many gestures made towards metaphysical concepts that would seem to operate with an altogether higher purpose in mind than the brutal actions taking place in a country gone to waste in the hands of a tinpot tyrant.

In the large corpus of criticism, a number of individual words have been systematically raised to the level of resonant symbols. The reference to the 'Intended', made by Kurtz, the ivory-trader whom Marlow, the protagonist, finds in the middle of the jungle, is a case in point. The 'Intended' might mean Kurtz's mission in life, his fiancée, a god-like power guiding his fate or all three things at once. It is the multiplicity of meanings generated by such philosophical inflections that amplify the grandeur of the novella.

None of these meanings has been hallucinated by Conrad's critics. All can be easily discovered. But it is the political priority which these features are given by commentators on the story that causes greatest disquiet in Conrad criticism. Key motifs and telltale phrases are time and again reordered to create (or recreate) arguments about whether the story is racist or anti-racist, imperialist or anti-imperialist. But since the conception of *Heart of Darkness* is so evidently in the philosophical grip of the very problems its critics are often seeking to resolve, it proves enduringly difficult to decide whether Conrad – however we designate him: as author or as text – is an apologist for imperialism or not. Ingenious arguments often state that, by virtue of the cultural conditions in which he wrote, Conrad was inescapably subjected to, and thereby a perpetuator of, imperialist ideology, in spite of what views he might have claimed to the contrary.

The latter critical position receives scrupulous attention in Benita Parry's introduction to *Conrad and Imperialism*. Parry focuses on the imperialist residue that remains in many of Conrad's works, showing how these stories deliberately subvert many of the hierarchically organized sets of images inscribed on the European mind. She analyses the binary Manicheanism (theorized by Frantz Fanon) that tries to split apart the white supremacist self from its blackened others:

> By transforming the characteristic genres of colonial fiction into vehicles for reflecting on the precepts, values and habits of thought native to these categories and the narrative mediations defamiliarizing conventional perceptions, disjunctions between the established morality and moral principle are displayed, while ethical absolutes are revealed to be pragmatic utilities for ensuring social stability and inhibiting dissent. These innovations from within the forms of the given mode produce a contrapuntal discourse where the authentic rendering of imperialism's dominant ideological categories is undercut by illuminations of the misrecognitions and limitations in a form of cognition that saw the world in black and white and admitted only a restricted area of reality to its purview. Yet, competing with exposures of imperialism's Manicheanism and tunnel-vision, there

are fantasy representations of the colonial universe seen across a metaphysical divide which acts to endorse racial solidarity, invite the closing of ethnic ranks, and confirm western codes as human norms and the ultimate measure of moral standards.[30]

As Parry states, in Conrad's writing a host of conventional imperialist assumptions about the dark continent are turned in upon themselves. And, what is more, in *Heart of Darkness* empire is viewed through a decentred narrative structure. Instead of employing an omniscient narrator, Conrad situates his main narrator, Marlow, within a larger first-person framework. That is, the novella opens with an unnamed speaker who proceeds to report (no matter how implausibly) Marlow's own extended autobiographical recollections of his time in the Belgian Congo. This redoubling of first-person narrative perspectives was, to say the least, uncommon in fiction in the late 1890s, and may have struck readers encountering it for the first time in the conservative journal *Blackwood's* as avant-garde. Not insignificantly, the narrative structure is as peculiar as the experiences it recounts.

This off-centred narrative technique has, typically for Conrad, paradoxical results. On the one hand, the use of the first person provides an intimate, immediate, almost confessional outlook on empire. Yet, on the other, given that the story is set within a complex narrative frame (with one first-person narration enclosing another), the putative authenticity of the inset narrator, Marlow, is constantly drawn into question. Every now and again, the unnamed narrator of the outer frame remarks on how Marlow's story has been received by his audience aboard *The Nellie* – the ship upon which the story is told, not the ship upon which the events in the story took place. Marlow, then, both narrates and has his story narrated for him. This narrative structure enables Marlow to be put on show as a storyteller. As the first narrator states:

'The yarns of seamen have a direct simplicity, the whole meaning of which lies within the shell of a cracked nut. But Marlow was not typical (if his propensity to spin yarns be excepted) as to him the meaning of an episode was not inside like a kernel but outside, enveloping the tale which brought it out only as a glow brings out a haze, in the likeness of one of those misty halos that, sometimes, are made visible by the spectral illumination of moonshine.' (p. 9)[31]

This passage is one of several examples which foregrounds both the mode and the manner of Conrad's intricate narrative technique. There are important aesthetic considerations at stake here. The narrator metaphorically turns inside out traditional nineteenth-century beliefs in meaning as something that has to be prised from its container. For Victorians, given the amount of philological research they undertook, the meaning of meaning itself was associated with concepts of depth or deep-rootedness (like the roots of words). The narrator insists, however, that the meaning of Marlow's tale lies not in its underlying symbolism but, instead, on its misty, rather ghostly surface. Given that Marlow's narration glows with an almost magical aura in unusual conditions of light, it may be inferred that readers and listeners to this story need to be especially sensitive to phrases and expressions that may at first appear, superficially, opaque. Ian Watt has taken the greatest pains to demonstrate how and why these multiple references to 'halos' and 'haze' link *Heart of Darkness* with the discoveries of Impressionism in painting. (Virginia Woolf would confirm the link between Impressionism and literary Modernism in her article on 'Modern Fiction', published in 1919, where she stated that life was not a 'series of gig lamps symmetrically arranged' but, instead, 'a luminous halo, a semi-transparent envelope surrounding us from the beginning of consciousness to the end.')[32]

Impressionism constructed a view of 'primitive' art to challenge the aesthetic orthodoxies of the time (such as the narrative and historical types of painting that still dominated national exhibitions). It is perhaps not surprising that in the elite world of painting this new interest in examining basic representational structures – of colour and line, in particular – emerged at a time of imperial expansion. Yet it was not the project of Impressionism to draw on either African or Asian aesthetics. The point of this movement was to place more responsibility on the viewer to produce the 'impression', the overall play of light, shadow, and shape, to be found on the canvas. In the 1890s, then, Conrad was certainly not alone in reacting against the prevailing depth-model of his time which governed late Victorian realism and its more shocking outgrowth, naturalism (the novels of George Gissing and George Moore, for example). The aesthetics of the surface engaged many radical thinkers. Oscar Wilde, the most scandalous aesthetician of his day, would write in the preface to his only novel, *The Picture of Dorian Gray*, in 1891: 'All art is at once surface and symbol.'[33] In *Heart of Darkness*, the onus is upon the reader to form impressions of the shimmering symbols that lie upon its textual surface. Likewise, 'impressions' are gradually built up as Marlow becomes aware of the shape of things around him: 'No sooner had we entered it [the western passage of the river] than I became aware it was much narrower than I had supposed. To the left of us there was the long uninterrupted shoal and to the right a high steep bank heavily overgrown with bushes' (p. 45). Unlike Marlow's heroic forebears in popular fictions of empire, he is not the master of his environment. Instead, its 'shadows' steal upon him. The 'direct simplicity' of the familiar 'yarn' had disappeared to enable a self-consciously skewed perspective of empire to emerge.

Marlow's framed narrative in itself repeatedly inverts commonplace views of imperialism. From the outset, the degeneracy of empire is made clear in a striking comparison with the Roman invasion of Britain. Here Marlow is speaking:

> 'It was just robbery with violence, aggravated murder on a great scale, and men going at it blind – as is very proper for those who tackle a darkness. The conquest of the earth, which mostly means the taking it away from those who have a different complexion or slightly flatter noses than ourselves, is not a pretty thing when you look at it too much. What redeems it is the idea only. An idea at the back of it, not a sentimental pretence but an idea; and an unselfish belief in the idea – something you can set up, bow down before, and offer a sacrifice to . . . ' (p. 10)

The fate of the Roman empire was regularly held up by late Victorians and Edwardians as a warning to the tragedy that might befall Britain's territories around the globe. As a contributor to the *Fortnightly Review* put it: 'England has reached the limit of empire, and her greatest need is a Hadrian who would recognize that fact and strongly attempt the policy to which it points. Her question, whether in respect of dominion or trade, is no longer one of extension, but one of existence.'[34] But Marlow indicates that both modern imperialism and that of its classical ancestors was unethical and misguided. However, the logic of this passage takes an unexpected turn. Marlow claims that the only way to understand the inhumanity of empire is the sacrosanct 'idea' enshrining it. He says this 'idea' (religiously) 'redeems' imperialism. But for whom? It is up to the rest of the narrative to provide the information to judge the answer to this question. Yet it remains a question that is unresolved.

The 'idea' draws everyone within its magnetic field of forces. Each actor in this drama serves its overriding purpose. King Leopold runs the country; Kurtz collects the ivory; the manager labours to keep the ivory trade in business; and Marlow supports the manager's work. But the system is clogged up with bureaucracy (the manager), and business fails to run smoothly (Kurtz has been withholding rather than supplying the goods). One figure, the Russian 'harlequin' (named as such because, in rags, he wears patched-up and particoloured clothing) is symbolically one of the clowns playing an absurdly lively role in a nation struck by famine and disease – all in the name of producing valuable trade for the inflated ambitions of Belgium:

> 'Glamour urged him on, glamour kept him unscathed. He surely wanted nothing from the wilderness but space to breathe in and to push on through. His need was to exist and to move onwards at the greatest possible risk and with a maximum of privation. If the absolutely pure, uncalculating, unpractical spirit of adventure had ever ruled a human being, it ruled this be-patched youth. I almost envied him the possession of this modest and clear flame.' (p. 55)

Marlow all too clearly recognizes that the fantasy of adventure (its 'glamour') is at odds with the extreme 'privation' brought about by the white man's life along the Congo. But there is something more at issue here. The imperialist 'idea' seems to rest upon this 'pure', possibly voluntary, loss of individual will. Impractical, dangerous, taking white men deeper into alien country – the 'idea' of it is the mainspring animating not only this 'harlequin' but also Marlow and the man to be met at the end of the line, Kurtz himself. However, it is Kurtz who has taken the 'idea' to its most extreme limit. He is also the central puzzle to the aesthetic and political principles that have brought *Heart of Darkness* into being. Marlow's narrative may reject the foolhardiness of glamorized adventure but his story is nevertheless drawn into an equally hypnotic journey towards something that proves impossible to define, so strong is its pull.

It is upon Kurtz that most discussions of the novella turn. For perhaps three-quarters of the narrative, his presence is deferred. A characteristically impressionistic picture of him slowly builds up.

Rumours of his life, his work, and his ideals accumulate with a sonority such that when he is found, dying, surrounded by hoarded masses of ivory, he has assumed the magnitude of a deity on earth. The harlequin is besotted by him: 'He made me see things – things (p. 55), he says, telling Marlow that the inspirational Kurtz had won the adoration of the Africans around him too. Yet Marlow paves the way to his final destination with ominous, but carefully unrevealing, comments on Kurtz's ruinous 'methods'. Having sighted decapitated heads set upon poles on the fencing around Kurtz's house, Marlow is moved to declare: 'I want you to understand that there was nothing exactly profitable in these heads being there. They only showed that Mr Kurtz lacked restraint in the gratification of his various lusts, that there was something wanting in him' (p. 57). And the exordium that follows ranges over Kurtz's unwavering fascination for the 'solitude' to be found at the heart of darkness. It is never entirely clear what the 'things' are that have been seen, if not by Kurtz, then by his 'harlequin' acolyte.

There is, for a start, insufficient evidence to determine whether Kurtz has engaged in acts of cannibalism. In a sense, any approach to Marlow's story that attempts to settle matters along the lines of absolute values loses out. One persistent problem always returns to any interpretation of this narrative: 'What *did* Kurtz do?' Posing this question, Juliet McLauchlan demonstrates that the necessity of raising it drives at the metaphysical centre of the text.[35] Although atrocities of some kind have been committed at Kurtz's hands, Marlow's narrative does not take up anything like the moral high ground against this strangely alluring figure. Instead, Marlow seems drawn, just as the harlequin has been drawn, to engage in the interpretive puzzle that is, similarly, handed over to the reader. And the problem is precisely what has driven Kurtz to do whatever he has done. Michael Levenson argues that Kurtz signifies 'the *reductio* of imperialism'. By that, Levenson means that Kurtz's function in this story is to expose the unethical basis upon which imperialism rests: that the desire for more and more territory is mindlessly fixated on its targets, whatever the consequences. It follows, then, that 'rational acquisition becomes irrational hoarding . . . economic routine becomes primitive ritual, . . . a commodity becomes a fetish, [and] indirect violence becomes overt barbarism'.[36] The 'idea', therefore, has no rationale. It simply exists for itself.

Kurtz, then, embodies the unofficial version of the imperialist mind. Yet, to repeat, his actions are to be condemned only by implication. What prevails instead is Marlow's overwhelming sense of the powerful force of the 'idea' that can drive a man to this end. Although Kurtz's 'brutal instincts' (p. 65) are mentioned, Marlow later states that Kurtz struggled with his ruinously impassioned soul. It is at this point that the story offers a parable familiar to nineteenth-century realism: the battle between free will and determinism. However, that contest has a distinctly modern aspect here, forcing attention on a topic dear to traditional literary studies, that may well account for the deep respect paid by literary educators to this novella. The topic in question is the human condition. Kurtz ultimately represents the individual striving to come to terms with mortality. Kurtz's last words are 'The horror! The horror!' (p. 68). And their ghostly whisper haunts Marlow afterwards. The 'horror', like the 'idea', and, in some respects, like the equally magnificent 'Intended', forces home the giant proportions of the meaning or unmeaning of life.

Since this topic is a spectacularly large one, it is not altogether unpredictable that Marlow's encounter with it should prove irresistible to both him and the multitude of critics who have been struck by its lasting impression. None the less, even if this point is highly relevant to the overall outcome of the story, it may be seen to detract, finally, from the fact that there is a very specific kind of mortality at stake here. Only two men (apart from Marlow's predecessor) are dignified with proper names in this story: Marlow and Kurtz. Everyone else, from the women glimpsed in the trading company's headquarters in Belgium to the ironically named 'pilgrims' aboard the ship (as if the crew were participating in a civilizing mission) are, for the most part, undifferentiated and indefinable: indeed, they seem, in terms of the style adopted here, to be nothing more than vague impressionistic brushstrokes. And wherever individuals are mentioned, but not named, they seem reduced to functions: there is a 'manager', a 'helmsman', and, with more symbolic power than the others, the 'Intended' (although this figure, the fiancée, may appear to be subsumed within a higher order of things 'Intended' by or upon Kurtz).

Chinua Achebe, most controversially of all writers on *Heart of Darkness*, has pointed to Marlow's stereotypical depiction of African peoples, as in the following extract: 'They shouted, sang; their bodies streamed with perspiration; they had faces like grotesque masks – these chaps; but they had bone, muscle, a wild vitality, an intense energy of movement that was as natural and true as the surf along their coast' (p. 17). Achebe's abundant quotations bear out the consistently negative representation of Black people; and Achebe's attack on Conrad has caused an extraordinary offence to sections of the British literary establishment, as demonstrated in a recent review of his essays, and subsequent exchange of letters.[37] The trouble is, Achebe diagnoses Conrad's unremitting racism from these examples when, in fact, it is not an author but a narrator (who is himself narrated) who marks out these impressions. Possibly Achebe would like to collapse the distinction between author, text, and narrator, and see them as speaking in unison, free from irony. But it is, indeed, the case that *Heart of Darkness* mediates this predictable racism through a narrator twice removed. Moreover, the ascription of darkness applies to both London as well as Africa. Concepts of darkness and blackness strive to bring Europe and Africa within the same ambit. For example, when surveying, from a distance, the 'monstrous town . . . the brooding gloom in the sunshine, a lurid glare under the stars', the narrator reports that 'darkness was here yesterday' (p. 9), by which he means Roman times. Yet, as we read on, it is clear from his description that a different pall is hanging over this metropolis since this is, presumably, a 'civilized' place. In a sense, Africa's function in the narrative is to provide a *literal* darkness so that the *metaphoric* darkness of London (and Brussels) can be comprehended. In other words, without taking African darkness for granted, the gloomy monstrosity of London would fail to make sense. It would seem, then, that Marlow's African travels towards savagery are strategically designed to make an anti-imperialist comment on the heart of empire. To reiterate: the journey to Africa, and the 'darkness' encountered there, will, somehow, explain the 'monstrous' features of a town, now the capital of a country, that must, centuries ago, have been a source of horror to the Romans. England was once an Africa of kinds, and, it may well appear, it still is.

This is a contentious point since the analogy drawn up here, made in the name of a critique of empire, actually requires one of empire's key assumptions in order to proceed. Africa, inevitably, must remain the defining ground of darkness so that the machinations of imperialism can be exposed. Given the complexity of this narrative, it is perhaps worth pausing for a moment to consider how this story might have been written otherwise. Imperialism, after all, could have been interrogated from within the dark streets of London: the smoky city which provides the starting point for the narrative, and which *The Nellie* leaves abandoned in its wake. Instead, Africa becomes the first and only place that can mark out the 'horror' of life and death. Only in a 'primitive' world, it seems, can civilized *man* discover the primitive meaning or unmeaning of his birth, life, and death, and how and why his homeland is shrouded in political ignorance. Contact with savages provides the challenge to the civilized soul of man, and provides a context for 'forgotten and brutal instincts' (here Kurtz's; p. 65) that, awkwardly, seem to derive from the heart of the African interior only to commit violence against it. Figured in this way, Africa turns out to be both the source *and* the object of 'primitive' lusts. On hearing the 'wild and passionate uproar' of the African tribes, Marlow remarks: 'were you man enough you would admit to your self that there was in you just the faintest response to the terrible frankness in that noise' (p. 38). Africa, in its frankness, is being used here to articulate a universal truth about masculinity: an instinctual violence to which imperialism has given terrifying rein. This truth – of violence shared by all men, civilized or savage – is, then, to be located in Kurtz and the painted bodies and faces that depict the native Africans. Such a view may appear to give *Heart of Darkness* a radical and revisionary edge.

But it does not. It does not because the emphasis here inescapably falls upon the word *man* ('were you man enough'). *Heart of Darkness*, no matter how unorthodox its narrative methods, bears a fundamental allegiance to the adventure story whose shallowness and propagandist aims it implicitly condemns. Marlow's narrative is, at base, a story by a heroic man about a heroic man told to men – all in a seafaring context. However, in yet another textual reversal, this tale does not expand upon the waters of the ocean but narrows to a point. There, Marlow locates, and is horrified (if still awed) by his man. But, true to Conrad's habitual inversions of convention, Kurtz is not saved from the clutches of the jungle. Instead, Marlow witnesses this anti-hero die in transit on the return journey. The point is that the story remains within the generic frame of popular adventure writing. *Heart of Darkness* exposes, but never the less maintains, the presuppositions – of race and gender – of the genre it is ostensibly contesting.

Undoubtedly, Marlow's tale pitches the hard reality of empire against the 'glamour' of adventure. Dying, Kurtz voices 'primitive emotions' that leave their mark on Marlow's mind: 'My Intended, my station, my career, my ideas – these were the subjects for the occasional utterances of elevated sentiments' (p. 67). Kurtz has been reduced to a stark set of principles. Africa has not made him into a hero but into a man who comprehends what it is to be a 'man'. He then expires. And Marlow is left contemplating his own 'destiny' (p. 69). In Kurtz, it seems, Marlow discovers a truth about his own mortality. Kurtz had 'something to say' (p. 69). But its meaning remains undisclosed, nebulous, private. It is as if Marlow has been initiated into a masonic ritual which only those who have had the same spiritual experience can comprehend. In the horror-stricken moment of Kurtz's death, it appears that Marlow has discovered a secret too overwhelming to put into words. It would seem that Marlow had met with his alter ego or double. To come to terms with Kurtz, therefore, is, for Marlow, to know what manhood means. Heroism has not so much been eradicated but raised to a metaphysical power. The glamour of adventure has been exposed, and in its place there is altogether more resonant 'glamour' of the 'idea'. In other words, 'horror' becomes the gothic substitute for (and may well be the flipside of) adventurous 'glamour'.

The pre-eminence of masculinity (rather than just mortality) per- sists in the coda to the story. A year after Kurtz's death, Marlow meets with the Intended (the fiancée). In this encounter, she tells Marlow: 'I want – I want – something – something – to – to live with . . . His last word – to live with'. Here, Kurtz's fateful echo plays on Marlow's memory. But instead of telling the Intended of the twice repeated 'horror', he informs her: 'The last word he pronounced was – your name' (p. 75). At the moment that the truth might be revealed, Marlow decides not to release it. On numerous occasions, it has been pointed out that Marlow is acting charitably, preserving the young woman from the 'idea' that made Kurtz act in the way he did. However, this is only speculation. The point is, it is Marlow, not the Intended, who remains closest to Kurtz. The homosocial bond has greater value than the love between Kurtz and the unnamed woman in his life. Marlow retains the prerogative to know the truth about Kurtz from which everyone else, including the reader, is excluded. This is, definitely, a man's world. (It is perhaps not accidental that, at this time, women would, more actively than ever before, begin their campaign for suffrage.) Critical of the 'direct simplicity' of 'yarns', *Heart of Darkness* ultimately remains one. And of what does it essentially tell? It, too, is a familiar tale: of survival against the odds; of making a safe return from the 'horror' of the interior; and of knowing the compulsive need for such stories to be told. The only difference – but it is, of course, an astonishing one – is that this narrative has investigated what it is that unstoppably drives popular fictional heroes into the depths of the interior.

In one respect, *Heart of Darkness* marks the terminal point of imperialist adventure and witnesses the inception of literary Modernism. Much of its cultural value rests upon this fact. The authors of *The Empire Writes Back* stress how imperialism underwrites Modernism:

> Africa is the source for the most significant and catalytic images of the first two decades of the twentieth century. In one very significant way the 'discovery' of Africa was the dominant paradigm for the self-discovery of the twentieth-century European world in all its self-contradiction, self-doubt, and self-destruction, for the European journey out of the light of Reason into the Heart of Darkness. As such, the more extreme forms of the self-critical and anarchic models of twentieth-century culture which Modernism ushered in can be seen to depend on the existence of a post-colonial Other which provides its condition of formation.[38]

This is a view not frequently expressed in critiques of Modernism. But it is one enabled by post-colonial revisions of Conrad's narrative, such as Achebe's *Things Fall Apart* (1958) and V. S. Naipaul's *A Bend in the River* (1979). That said, it remains to be seen how Achebe and Naipaul, in revising the imperialist script, may have reinstated the masculinist one. The period we now live in is said not only to be post-colonial but also postmodern – after, beyond, and away from Modernism, yet not entirely dissociated from it. And the cultural effects of both terms will obviously be different wherever one is positioned on the globe.

Hegemonic masculinity of an imperialist kind has, indeed, been global. In a postmodern epoch, where rewriting can also mean the undoing of dominant narratives (fictional, political, economic), it is certainly a time for different masculinities to emerge – ones which do not demonise women (Haggard), or which make a boy into a man before his time (Henty), or which, finally, substitute one bogus heroism for a higher, metaphysical one (Conrad). Whether new kinds of men can be heroes or not, and whether there are discourses available to enable such men to come into being (whoever they are), is as yet unclear. But these men, coming from post-colonial and postmodern conditions, could do well to study the imperialist genealogy of hegemonic masculinity before putting it behind them. That is why, as a final moment in this analysis, a survivalist conception of manhood needs to be investigated here. This type of masculinity marks the apogee of the imperial ideal. The imperial male survivor has, not so surprisingly, outlived the empire in popular culture. He is the boy, and then the man, who builds on the strengths of the archetypal adventurers already identified in the preceding chapters. Close to the hearts of Baden-Powell and Kipling, this form of maleness would turn out to be the progenitor of a distinctly twentieth-century kind of hero. He was the man each and every boy reader that ideologues of empire thought he could and should become.

# Notes

1   H. Rider Haggard, *King Solomon's Mines, She, Allan Quatermain* ([1885, 1887, 1887,]; London: Octopus Books, 1979). All references to this edition are included in the text.

2   J. A. Hobson, *Imperialism: A Study*, third edition ([1938]; London: Unwin Hyman, 1988); V. I. Lenin, *Imperialism, the Highest Stage of Capitalism: A Popular Outline* ([1917]; London: Lawrence and Wishart, 1933); and Ronald Robinson and John Gallagher with Alice Denny, *Africa and the Victorians: The Official Mind of Imperialism*, second edition (London: Macmillan, 1984).

3   Patrick Brantlinger, *Rule of Darkness: British Literature and Imperialism, 1830–1914* (Ithaca, NY: Cornell University Press, 1988), pp. 174–5.

4   Charles Dickens, 'The Noble Savage', *Household Words*, 7 (1853), p. 337.

5   On Broca, Galton, anthropometry and craniometry, see Stephen Jay Gould, *The Mismeasure of Man* (New York: Norton, 1981), pp. 73–112.

6   Dorothy Hammond and Alta Jablow, *The Africa That Never Was: Four Centuries of British Writing* (New York: Twayne, 1970), p. 100.

7   General Booth, *In Darkest England and the Way Out* ([1890]; New York: Garrett Press, 1970), pp. 11–12.

8   Sigmund Freud, *The Interpretation of Dreams*, translated by James Strachey ([1900]; Harmondsworth: Penguin Books, 1976), pp. 585–8.

9   Sander L. Gilman, 'Black Bodies, White Bodies: Toward an Iconography of Female Sexuality in Late Nineteenth-Century Art, Medicine, and Literature', *Critical Inquiry*, 12 (1985), p. 237.

10  Haggard, 'About Fiction', *Contemporary Review*, 51 (1887), p. 176.

11  Brian V. Street, *The Savage in Literature: Representations of 'Primitive' Society in English Fiction, 1858–1920* (London: Routledge and Kegan Paul, 1975), p. 59.

12  Wendy R. Katz, *Rider Haggard and the Fiction of Empire: A Critical Study of the British Imperial Fiction* (Cambridge: Cambridge University Press, 1987), pp. 73–4.

13  Sandra M. Gilbert and Susan Gubar, *No Man's Land: The Place of the Woman Writer in the Twentieth Century*, Volume Two, *Sexchanges* (New Haven, Conn.: Yale University Press, 1989), pp. 19, 36. For their complete discussion, see pp. 3–46. For an informative and wide-ranging overview of representations of women in Victorian fiction, including the emergence of the *femme fatale*, see John Goode, 'Woman and the Literary Text' in Juliet Mitchell and Ann Oakley, eds, *The Rights and Wrongs of Women* (Harmondsworth: Penguin Books, 1976), pp. 217–55; Goode briefly discusses *She* (pp. 235–7). For a sophisticated materialist critique of Gilbert and Gubar's 'gynocentric' reading of Haggard's romance, see Laura Chrisman, 'The Imperial Unconscious? Representations of Imperial Discourse', *Critical Quarterly* 32:3 (1990), pp. 38–58. Chrisman argues that Ayesha embodies a hybrid orientalist fantasy that exposes 'imperialism's bad faith, or negative self-knowiedge' (p. 46). Haggard's fiction certainly bears the contradictory traces – or ideologemes – of imperialist discourse: eugenics; capitalist exploitation (mining for gold and diamonds); nationalist myth-making; misogyny; and so on.

14  Wayne Koestenbaum, *Double Talk: The Erotics of Male Literary Collaboration* (New York: Routledge, 1989), p. 153.

15  Anonymous, 'The Culture of the Horrible: Mr Haggard's Stories', *Church Quarterly Review*, 25 (1888), pp. 390, 402.

16  William Watson, 'The Fall of Fiction', *Fortnightly Review*, NS 44 (1888), p. 336.

17  Watson, 'Mr Haggard and his Henchmen', *Fortnightly Review*, NS 44 (1888), p. 684.

18   Andrew Lang, 'Realism and Romance', *Contemporary Review*, 52 (1887), p. 699.
19   Quoted in Morton Cohen, *Rider Haggard: His Life and Works* (London: Hutchinson, 1960), p. 117; and in Peter Beresford Ellis, *H. Rider Haggard: A Voice from the Infinite* (London: Routledge and Kegan Paul, 1978), p. 119. Additional biographical information may be found in D. S. Higgins, *Rider Haggard: The Great Storyteller* (London: Cassell, 1981).
20   Koestenbaum, *Double Talk: The Erotics of Male Literary Collaboration*, p. 154.
21   Augustus M. Moore, 'Rider Haggard and "The New School of Romance"', *Time*, 16 (1887), pp. 513–24 quoted in D. S. Higgins, *Rider Haggard: The Great Storyteller*, p. 114.
22   James Runciman, 'King Plagiarism and his Court', *Fortnightly Review*, NS 47 (1890), pp. 421–39.
23   Quoted in Guy Arnold, *Hold Fast for England: G. A. Henty, Imperialist Boys' Writer* (London: Hamish Hamilton, 1980), p. 63.
24   G. A. Henty, *With Kitchener in the Soudan: A Story of Atbara and Omdurman* (London: Blackie, n.d.). All references to this edition are given in the text.
25   H. F. Wyatt, 'The Ethics of Empire', *The Nineteenth Century*, 61 (1897), p. 521.
26   Edward W. Said, *Orientalism* ([1978]; Harmondsworth: Penguin Books, 1985), pp. 84–5.
27   *Parliamentary Debates*, fourth series, 42 (1899), col. 344.
28   ibid., col. 376.
29   Haggard, *Rural England*, two volumes (London, 1902), II, p. 575 quoted in David Trotter, 'Kipling's England: The Edwardian Years' in Philip Mallett, (ed.), *Kipling Considered* (London: Macmillan, 1989), p. 59.
30   Benita Parry, *Conrad and Imperialism: Ideological Boundaries and Visionary Frontiers* (London: Macmillan, 1983), pp. 1–2.
31   Joseph Conrad, *Heart of Darkness*, third edition, *An Authoritative Text, Backgrounds and Sources, Criticism*, (ed.) Robert Kimbrough (New York: W. W. Norton, 1988). All references to this edition are included in the text. Kimbrough has brought together an informative sample of some of the most provocative essays on this novella, including its links with popular culture, as in Francis Ford Coppola's film, *Apocalypse Now* (1977).
32   Ian Watt, *Conrad in the Nineteenth Century* (London: Chatto and Windus, 1979), p. 170. Extracts from this study are reprinted in Kimbrough, pp. 311–36.

33  Oscar Wilde, *The Complete Works of Oscar Wilde*, (ed.) J. B. Foreman (London: Collins, 1966), p. 17.

34  Anonymous, 'The Cry for Men', *Fortnightly Review*, NS 70 (1901), p. 190.

35  Juliet McLauchlan, 'The "Value" and "Significance" of Heart of Darkness', *Conradiana* 15 (1983), 3–21, reprinted in Kimbrough, p. 385.

36  Michael Levenson, 'The Value of Facts in the *Heart of Darkness*', *Nineteenth-Century Fiction* 40 (1985), 261–80, reprinted in Kimbrough, p. 399.

37  Achebe's essay, 'An Image of Africa: Racism in Conrad's *Heart of Darkness*', was first delivered as a lecture in 1974, and is now collected in *Hopes and Impediments: Selected Essays 1967–87* (London: Heinemann, 1989). A response from within the defensive institutions of criticism is to be found in Cedric Watts, '"A Bloody Racist": About Achebe's View of Conrad', *The Yearbook of English Studies*, 13 (1983), pp. 196–209. The controversy about Achebe's views on *Heart of Darkness* has been rekindled in the *London Review of Books*; see Craig Raine, 'Conrad and Prejudice', 22 June 1989, pp. 16–17; and letters, 27 July 1989, p. 4, and 14 September 1989, p. 4. These exchanges show only too clearly that imperialist struggles between those who teach 'English' in England, and support Conrad, and those, like Achebe, who acknowledge the components of imperialist identity within 'English' and doubt Conrad's authority, are still violently active.

38  Bill Ashcroft, Gareth Griffiths, and Helen Tiffin, *The Empire Writes Back: Theory and Practice in Post-Colonial Literatures* (London: Routledge, 1989), p. 160.

# 5

# Empire Boys

## Defending the Empire: *Scouting for Boys*

I suppose every British boy wants to help his country in some way
or other.

There is a way, by which he can do so easily, and that is by
becoming a scout.

A scout, as you know, is generally a soldier who is chosen for
his cleverness and pluck to go out in front of an army in war
to find out where the enemy are, and report to the commander
about them.

But, besides war scouts, there are also peace scouts, i.e. men
who in peace time carry out work which requires the same
kind of abilities. These are the frontiersmen of all parts of our
Empire. The 'trappers' of North America, hunters of Central
Africa, the British pioneers, explorers, and missionaries over Asia
and all the wild parts of the world, the bushmen and drovers of
Australia, the constabulary of North-West Canada and of South
Africa – all are peace scouts, real *men* in every sense of the
word, and thoroughly up in scoutcraft, i.e. they understand
living out in the jungles, and they can find their way anywhere, are able to read meaning from the smallest signs and
foot-tracks; they know how to look after their health when far
away from any doctors, are strong and plucky, and ready to
face any danger, and always keen to help each other. They
are accustomed to take their lives in their hands, and to fling
them down without hesitation if they can help their country by
doing so.

They give up everything, their personal comforts and desires
in order to get their work done. They do not do all this for

their own amusement, but because it is their duty to their King, fellow-countrymen, or employers.

The History of the Empire has been made by British adventurers and explorers, the scouts of the nation, for hundreds of years up to the present time.

The Knights of King Arthur, Richard Coeur de Lion, and the Crusaders, carried British chivalry into distant parts of the earth.

(Robert Baden-Powell, *Scouting for Boys*, 1908)[1]

No other document promulgates such a range of British imperialist ideals of boyhood than Baden-Powell's *Scouting for Boys*. Across 300 pages of camp yarns, drills, and countless points on good conduct, a strategic arrangement of liberal and conservative discourses promptly comes into action to guarantee that the Boy Scout will serve his country to the best of his ability. An idealizing Tory patriotism is the dominant force shaping this new model of organizing the leisure time of Britain's young men. Here Baden-Powell upholds a highly reactionary form of patriotism in an effort to defend a demoralized empire at a time of crisis after the pyrrhic victories of the second Anglo–Boer War (1899–1902).

It was during the course of this war – specifically, the renowned siege of Mafeking – that his plans for Scouting first went into practice. For the most part, Baden-Powell's patriotism draws on those chivalric myths of heroism first popularized in the 1830s and 1840s. (Medieval revivalism among Benjamin Disraeli's Young England coterie, which took as one of its touchstones Kenelm Digby's *The Broadstone of Honour*, published in 1822, provides the main context for Baden-Powell's interest in brave young knights performing noble deeds.) But this is not an exclusively chivalric vision of history. Nostalgic appeals to days gone by are interwoven with the altogether different concerns of several movements that first emerged in the nineteenth century, each of which was adopted by the Scout movement to strengthen the moral fibre and toughen the physique of the nation's growing population of male youth.

The patriotism that fires *Scouting for Boys* rests on a number of widely held beliefs about race, class, and gender at this time. Baden-Powell's manual, which has been in print ever since it was first published in 1908, is very much the culmination of imperial ideals of boyhood. This chapter opens with an analysis of an ideal that was the result of several decades which fashioned the lower middle-class boy into an acceptable vehicle of empire. He became, by 1908, a young man who could adequately emulate his public school peers, many of whom were graduating to administer the crown colonies.

Among the most important of the Victorian movements influencing Scouting was philathleticism, encouraged in the many recently opened public schoolss. Equally authoritative were the various manifestations of soocial Darwinism, which promoted the concept of 'race health' and which were often mobilized as scientific proof of Britain's natural dominance. It is important to note, however, that the earliest theorist of this doctrine, Francis Galton, did not take the sociological account of the surviival of the fittest to the racist extremes of the imperialist propagandists who drew on his work. Galton argued in the 1860s that besiides the 'endurance of steady labour, tameness of disposition, and prolonged development', there were no marked distinctions to be made between 'the nature of the lower classes of man from that of barbarians', adding that 'in the excitement of a pillaged town the English soldier is just as brutal as the savage'. Moreover, noting that the forces of civilization put a brake on the rigours of natural selection, Galton emphasized how modern society had the economic means to accommodate forms of mental and physical weakness that would have disposed of their victims in savage times. Yet even if Anglo–Saxons were, underneath the veneer of civilization, fundamentally savage, there was one decisive fact dividing the lower races from their European superiors, and that was education. Without an extended and carefully organized childhood, adult barbarians would, according to Galton, remain 'children in mind, with the passions of grown men'. It followed, therefore, that the 'highest minds in the highest race seem to be those who had the longest boyhood'.[2] Scouting would lengthen boyhood as no organization for young people had done before, and with every intention to improve the substance of a basically brutish race. Galton's eugenics movement, founded in 1904, indirectly gave Baden-Powell the momentum to arrest the much-debated 'degeneracy' inhibiting the development of the thousands of working-class boys who were both physically and morally wasting away in the larger towns and cities.

Finally, one Victorian principle supporting the ideology of Scouting is that propounded by Samuel Smiles in *Self-Help*. The numerous editions of Smiles's manual of advice for aspiring gentlemen elevated, as never before, a liberal ideal of independent citizenship. A strong adherent of the Puritan work ethic, Smiles fostered those dominant nineteenth-century bourgeois values of thrift and economy:

> National progress is the sum of individual industry, energy, and uprightness, as national decay is of individual idleness, selfishness and vice. What we are accustomed to decry as great social evils, will, for the most part, be found in but the outgrowth of man's own perverted life; and though we may endeavour to cut them down and extirpate them by means of Law, they will only spring up again with fresh luxuriance in some other form, unless the conditions of personal life and character are radically improved. If this view be correct, then it follows that the highest patriotism and philanthropy consist, not so much in altering laws and modifying institutions, as in helping and stimulating men to elevate and improve themselves by their own free and independent individual action.[3]

Taken together, then, philathleticism, social Darwinism, and self-help mark out the main coordinates of Baden-Powell's highly successful plan to ennoble the status of what it meant to be an Edwardian boy, one keen to rise up from the working and lower middle classes – particularly the latter. In 1910, Baden-Powell claimed that of 11,000 Scouts in the London area, over half had been recruited from the lower middle classes. Moreover, these boys were concentrated in greater numbers in the Home Counties, rather than the poorer north of England.[4] It was to this expanding class of potential middle managers that Scouting most directly had its appeal. 'Any number of poor boys have become rich men', Baden-Powell, following Smiles, reminds his readers in a section on 'How to Make Money' (p. 244). *Scouting for Boys* supplied as much advice and sound training as it saw fit to broaden the opportunities for all boys to make the most of their lives. And one of its central forms deployed to represent this particular set of ideas was the camp 'yarn', a story whose narrative elements explicitly drew upon the boys' own adventure story, and indeed recommended classic tales of heroic deeds to its thousands of young male readers.

The Scout Leader expanded upon these mid-Victorian precepts by transforming them into powerful metaphors of survival in a potentially hostile environment. In *Scouting for Boys*, a boy's education relies on a fundamental skill: learning how to survive out of doors unaided. Whatever his task, the Scout must be on the look-out for every imaginable danger. This programme of study proceeds on the assumption that unless the boy learns how to master the land (to use a compass, to identify footprints, and so on) he will be unable to make the transition into manhood. To this day, Boy Scouts are obliged to learn techniques that enable them to tame, as well as respect, the natural world. As one patriotic phrase follows another in *Scouting for Boys*, it becomes clear that the boy's physical and moral education is paramount in enabling the myths of empire to live on.

Baden-Powell comprehensively guides his boy readers towards mastering techniques to conquer and, importantly, to preserve a previously undiscovered world, one that is, paradoxically, unknown to the boy, but none the less his by virtue of being British. Scouting invited its members to live out a narrative in which the ideal protagonists were the trappers, hunters, and frontiersmen popularized in history textbooks and, more significantly, in the boys' weeklies that had been on the ascendant since the 1860s. In the popular representations of history to be found in these publications, the past unfolded as an adventure that began with the Crusades and led right up to the Victorians' exploits in all corners of the empire, including Baden-Powell's famous deeds in South Africa. It was a compelling story. But British history, as Baden-Powell failed to indicate in his opening words, is by no means a chronicle of continual heroic endeavour and fitness and survival. Were the empire as naturally strong and secure as he would have liked his growing numbers of Scouts to believe, there would have been no need for Scouting to take off on such a grand scale in 1908. Scouting enabled its boys to become the heroes imperialism expected them to be. However, as boys' bodies and minds all too clearly demonstrated, they were not born heroes. The empire, glorious though it was, had in many ways been failing them.

Baden-Powell's aim was to recruit Scouts from the much maligned East End and comparably degenerate working-class areas of the larger British cities. His main constituency, however, belonged to a slightly higher class fraction which traditionally sought to emulate those whom they knew to be their betters. As Michael Rosenthal states in his history of the phenomenal appeal of Scouting to the British boy:

> Locating the principles of admirable behaviour – patriotism, a sense of honour, self-sacrifice in an aristocratic, heroic (and highly mythologized) past far removed from the imaginative world of working-class lads, Baden-Powell conferred on Scouting an august tradition that emphasized the need for the lower classes to look to their betters for instruction and moral marching orders.[5]

There were, then, clearly demarcated standards of behaviour and types of endeavour to look up to. These aspirations were constantly reinforced by propaganda – whether in the popular press or in the elementary school curriculum – that, either implicitly or explicitly, placed the British at the top of a racial ladder and at the helm of all the world. In addition, the state was taking an exceptionally close interest in boys' health and fitness for the army. In response to these cultural imperatives, Scouting went to remarkable lengths to devise schemes whereby boys could be led towards some useful goal, and be duly rewarded for it.

Unfaltering attention to moral and physical improvement has never left the Scout movement. Since 1908 there has been an increasingly complex system of badges awarded for work done well by individual Scouts. The 1985 edition of the Scout Association's handbook, *Challenge and Adventure*, lists over seventy different activities deemed worthy of an award. As Scouting grew in size, with branches in most parts of the world, each boy could find at least some task he was capable of completing, whether it involved mastering the use of a compass or organizing a prayer reading. Some of the activities listed are strikingly recondite and ritualized. They would appear to owe much to procedures adopted by the Freemasons. In order to obtain the Patrol Activity Award, for example, the 1985 manual suggests that boys between the ages of ten and a half and fifteen and a half should attempt one or more of the following feats at an indoor Patrol Meeting: cooking an egg over a candle; building a Roman ballista from garden canes and elastic bands; making a contour model; and conducting part of a meeting blindfold or in total silence.[6] The first edition contains fewer incentives. A list of 'Badges of Merit' occupies only one page at the end of the book. But it sets out at great length the survivalist skills required of a Scout – tying knots, making camp beds, or undertaking some other useful activity.

Whatever the task, as long as it prrovided the boy with techniques to master a skill with due training and application, it took its place in an ascending hierarchy of adversarial challenges. Furthermore, with its special focus on the open-air life and nature – where time was to be spent identifying and tracking but never harming animals – Scouting ensured that its boys ranged across the green fields of Britain getting plenty of fresh air into their lungs. Apart from exercising his mind and body, the boy's life in the great outdoors of the homeland performed, in the main, three ideological functions. To excite patriotic nostalgia and to bring about spiritual renewal was one of them. Britain was there to be discovered, understood and assimilated as a place to be respected and, above all, protected. In one sense, Scouting took its boys out on to the land to broaden their comprehension of national identity. Like colonialists before them, they too could mark out this country as their own and learn to defend it. For the majority of Scouts, the British countryside was certainly uncharted territory since many of them had grown up in the cramped confines of large urban centres.

Second, Scouting combined this unstated wish to identify the boy with his country with its ostensible purpose: to ensure that its members travelled out of the smoky cities that troubled the late Victorian and Edwardian social conscience. In squalid urban areas, well-meaning Tories, like Baden-Powell, perceived appalling moral corruption running in parallel with stunted growth among children. As statistics were gathered that indicated deficiencies of diet among the poor, commissions on public health were eager to see physical recreation secured on the elementary school curriculum. That said, thousands of boys did not join the Scouts simply to develop their chests and learn to behave like their superiors. There was a third and final reason for their attraction to this system of challenges and rewards. They followed Baden-Powell because of the enormous cultural value staked upon them to lead the empire forward as *men*. *Scouting for Boys* follows the compass-bearings of a particular kind of independent adventurer who has to learn to look after himself, whatever natural forces appear to threaten him. He is the man who can fight off unknown dangers, who can cut a path through the jungle, and who can, for King and country, set forth on missions to change a backward and uncivilized world. These are the implied promises Baden-Powell makes to his young survivors in uniform.

It is, however, noticeable that the commandeering patriotism of *Scouting for Boys* immediately turns its attention away from the image of the soldier to that of the explorer or pioneer. Part of the massive success of the Boy Scouts was its apparent dissociation from explicit military principles. (By contrast, the Boys' Brigade, founded in 1883, closely resembled an adolescent army.) In Scouting, there were seemingly no enemies to fight, and no weapons to handle – except dummy guns. In 1908, Boy Scouts were learning, not the skills involved in managing real weapons, but the practical skills that were necessary to sustain successful manoeuvres against the foe (such as reconnoitring). This youth movement, therefore, could draw to some degree on the sympathies of those more liberal-minded (and, again, lower middle-class) families with misgivings about militarism. In Scouting, the stress was on masculinity as a harmless exercise of tracking into the wilds. There might be dangers. But no boy was put in fear for his life. It has to be said that the militaristic inflections of Scouting remain a central subject of debate among researchers. The extent to which the Scout movement was either overtly or covertly training its recruits as imperial cadets remains an open question. The central point here is that Baden-Powell was a former military hero, and his development of Scouting had, to a not insignificant degree, its origins in the controversial campaign he conducted during the infamous siege of Mafeking during the second Anglo–Boer War.

Mafeking became a symbol of something far broader than Baden-Powell's celebrated resistance against the Boers. It turned into a focal point of concern about unseemly behaviour among the lower classes. Several facts about the siege and the subsequent outbursts of national pride in Britain throw light on the immediate context of imperialism preceding the establishment of Scouting. The two wars against the Boers in South Africa (1881 and 1899–1902) had been marked by several humiliating defeats at the hands of Boer farmers wielding firearms. Jameson's Raid of 1895, four years before the second of these wars, was an outstanding instance of British military mismanagement. It was an attempt to win over the Uitlanders (a disenfranchised mobile labour force mining for gold and diamonds in the Transvaal) to the British side. The majority of Uitlanders were British, and they had for some time been organizing to consolidate their rights as citizens in the Boer republic. Cecil Rhodes, the Prime Minister of the Cape Colony, realized that the complicated and dishonourable plot he had put together to seize power from the Boers would backfire, largely because the Uitlanders were likely to be placated by promises of enfranchisement by the Transvaal government. (It was the question of the franchise for the Uitlanders that would precipitate the ensuing three year war, which led to the deaths of 25,000 women and children held in British concentration camps.) Rhodes ordered Jameson against the proposed raid. But Jameson ignored him. As he advanced with 500 mounted police towards Johannesburg, Jameson discovered that the Uitlanders had struck a deal with the Boer leader, Kruger. Consequently, no support was given to Jameson's men who had to surrender after a ferocious battle. The place Jameson set out from was Mafeking. It stood as a symbol of wounded national pride during the second war. In 1900, after 217 appalling days of siege, the garrison at Mafeking was relieved. The Commander-in-Chief there was Baden-Powell.

Baden-Powell's defence of Mafeking involved systematic rationing and a highly inventive adaptation of resources. Bombs of dynamite, for example, were fashioned out of meat tins. But these feats of survivalism were achieved at a cost. As commanding officer, Baden-Powell handled the siege in an explicitly racist manner. In order to conserve rations for the whites, he executed a 'leave-here-or-starve-here' policy towards the native population. 'Hunger had them in its grip, and many of them were black spectres and living skeletons', noted one journalist in the account of his experiences there. Rosenthal explains:

> As the native population starved . . . the white garrison survived the 217 days with essentially no diminution in its meat ration,

and with substantial amounts of bread and vegetables as well. Seldom has a siege been endured with less hardship – for those who weren't natives. When the relief columns finally arrived, they found to their surprise that the imperilled defenders were in fact far better supplied than they were themselves, and promptly turned to the town's provisions.[7]

In the most comprehensive of the many studies of the second Anglo–Boer War, Thomas Pakenham stresses that the relief of Mafeking was far from a victory. It was, after 217 days, a relief from humiliation, and above all the avoidance of defeat.[8] Scouting is intimately involved with the relief of Mafeking. The siege is described in the first of the camp yarns in *Scouting for Boys*. 'We had an example of how useful Boy Scouts can be on active service', writes Baden-Powell, 'when a corps of boys was formed in the defence of Mafeking, 1899–1900.' The boys took on jobs formerly done by men:

> Every man was of value, and as their numbers gradually got less, owing to men getting killed or wounded, the duties of fighting and keeping watch at night got harder for the rest. It was then that Lord Edward Cecil, the chief staff officer, got together the boys in the place and made them into a cadet corps, put them in uniform and drilled them; and a jolly smart and useful lot they were. We had till then used a large number of men for carrying orders and messages and keeping look-out, and acting as orderlies, and so on. These duties were now handed over to the boy cadets, and the men were released to go and strengthen the firing line. (p. 17)

Having expanded upon the exploits at Mafeking, Baden-Powell swiftly points out that he is referring to this military event only because it serves as a good 'yarn' (an enabling narrative device, which converts the problems of history into an innocuous and instructive story), and 'that you need not wait for war in order to be useful as a scout' (p. 18). However, if war is not essential to Scouting, why does Scouting draw so much on its military background?

This question, like many others provoked by Baden-Powell's manual, proves difficult to answer. Obviously, Mafeking has to be understood as an adventure which is presented here to persuade boys that they do not have to be men to do the work of soldiers. But Scouts are not, according to Baden-Powell, to be mistaken for members of the military. Here, the circumstances of an imperial war have awkwardly given rise to the conviction that military conflict is not the aim of Scouting. The boy is both prepared for war and yet, with the universal application of the Scout's manifold skills, he is not involved in fighting battles. Over the years, Baden-Powell reiterated that 'Scouting has nothing to do with soldiering', and that 'it is merely the practice of backwoodsmanship we do, not preach war and bloodshed to the lads'.[9] But even if war is not the avowed aim of the preparatory exercises that constitute Scouting, it is the potential scenario against which the movement is set. It should be noted that Baden-Powell conceived militarism in what now seem very restricted terms. His view of militarism was entirely consonant with that of other men of his class and education. For him, the Scouts were not part of the military because they did not handle firearms. Yet, as Rosenthal indicates, 'military ideals of service and behaviour inevitably constituted the basis of human excellence' in Baden-Powell's eyes; and he adds: 'Baden-Powell would have found difficult the notion that civic society might properly esteem values different from those cherished by the army.'[10] Scouting, then, was not explicit about the war for which it appears to have been making preparations. Rather, it mobilized its young recruits to 'Be prepared!' for anything which threatened to invade the empire. The Scouts were to be led forward with all the character-building exercises that should make them ready for service in the forces. At the same time, they were in combat against the moral and physical insufficiencies of the working classes. The example of Mafeking could, when placed within the complete scope of *Scouting for Boys*, serve a double function: to illustrate the skills required to prevent either germs or Germans from infecting Britain. Mafeking, in a sense, was being upheld as a preventative to the unruly excesses of the notorious crowds which erupted on to the streets after news of the relief reached Britain. A few historical details will show how and why this was the case.

On 19 May 1900, *The Times* carried a long report on the extraordinary public celebrations of the relief of Mafeking. The rowdy behaviour of the jubilant crowds became so renowned that a new word (a Cockneyism) entered the language – namely,

mafficking. At this time, working- and lower-middle-class support
for the empire was at its height. Members of the educated middle
classes deplored the noisy masses taking to songs and chanting out
of doors. Two years later, the liberal *Fortnightly Review* carried
an article revealing the deep impression left by the ostentatious
behaviour of the crowds on that day:

> We have always known that the worst part of the London mob could
> be a disgrace and a danger if it got out of hand. 'Mafficking' has
> simply shown with formidable clearness the force of that suggestion.
> We may be absolutely certain that in times of public excitement,
> with peril nearer home, the brutal side of this huge rowdyism,
> if it should once break out, will be as menacing as its levity is
> uncouth, unwholesome and repellent.[11]

Such distinctly middle-class and anti-imperialist loathing of jingoistic working people was by no means novel. Similar fears of
the indiscriminate mob recur time and again in earlier Victorian
writings. (One of the best-known examples is Matthew Arnold's distaste in *Culture and Anarchy* for the unruly crowds demonstrating in
Hyde Park.)[12] Although in 1900 the working classes were relishing
an imperial victory, in what was supposedly a moment of patriotic
high spirits, the idea of working-class men and women filling the
streets was viewed by educated moralists as not only out of order but
also as a profound source of anxiety. The Mafeking celebrations had
notoriously led to attacks on the premises of pro-Boer supporters.
However, as Richard Price argues, claims of violence among the
working-class mafficking crowd were subject to manipulation by
respectable liberals and considerably exaggerated at the time.[13]
Mafeking, and the 'mafficking' that followed, certainly marked a
flash point in class relations since the jubilant crowds comprised
working-class people and office workers – clerks who belonged to a
group that should, it was felt, behave in an appropriately restrained
manner. 'Mafficking', if supporting the cause of empire, seemed to
be dragging down moral standards to an unacceptably low level,
especially when Britain's international relations were entering a new
phase of potential conflict with other European imperial powers.
In the pages of the *Fortnightly Review*, untamed patriotic fervour
threatens to become a 'peril' in the future when victories are fought
'nearer home'. Such sentiments stem from the Edwardian fear of

invasion coupled with similarly commonplace concerns about the undisciplined energies of the mob rudely destabilizing the moral order from within.

In any case, not only was the mob noisy, and potentially uncontrollable, it was also physically unfit, as recruitment campaigns to the 1899–1902 war had shown. The Boy Scout was trained to function as a much more desirable young man than the majority of working-class volunteers who came forward to serve in the army. In 1899, 8,000 out of a total of 11,000 who came forward in Manchester were rejected as unfit. Even if this statistic cannot make much sense in the abstract, the percentage of unsuitable men certainly appears high. Earlier, reports of the Poor Law Board had produced some alarming figures indicating the extent of bad health among working-class boys. Gareth Stedman Jones has researched the scope of the problem:

> Commenting on the failure of 15-year-old London boys to reach the required standards of height and girth, the Metropolitan Poor Law Inspector considered in 1871 that, 'it is well established that no town bred boys of the poorer classes, especially those reared in London, ever except in the very rare instances, attain the above development (4'10½ inch & 29 inch chest) at the age of 15. A stunted growth is characteristic of the race.'[14]

Baden-Powell's movement was not, of course, the first to address this question. The 1860s and 1870s were decades when many charitable bodies established clubs for working-class young men. Summer camps were a special feature of these organizations. In 1870, Thomas John Barnardo opened his Labour Home for Destitute Youths in Stepney Causeway. Barnardo issued carefully treated postcards with impressive 'before' and 'after' photographs illustrating the transformation his homes were capable of achieving when boys were put into his care. One picture would be typically entitled 'Once a little vagrant', while next to it an accompanying portrait proudly displayed a model citizen: 'Now a little workman.' Later, in 1896, Arthur Pearson (who was both Baden-Powell's publisher and the editor of the popular Tory newspaper, the *Daily Express*) set up the Fresh Air Fund to provide country holidays for city children. Baden-Powell's first Boy Scout camp at Brownsea Island, Dorset, followed in the wake of all these developments in juvenile welfare, bringing together boys aged between thirteen and sixteen from the Poole and Bournemouth Boys' Brigade with ones from public schools (Eton, Harrow, Cheltenham, Repton, Wellington, Charterhouse; in other words, the finest establishments). At its most utopian, Scouting was supposed to dissolve class differences by placing each boy in the same uniform, learning the skills, and rehearsing the same camp-fire yarns.

Scouting succeeded as no other youth movement or welfare scheme preceding it had done, and that was largely because of its attraction for lower middle-class boys who were not having to make a living on the streets. The lower middle-class boy had time to be a Scout. He certainly had more time to devote to enjoying the popular culture of imperialism, especially in the juvenile weeklies designed for him. By stark contrast, the plight of working-class boys, particularly those involved in street trading, remained a persistent problem right up to the First World War. There was less time available for many working boys to turn into the respectable individuals who could absorb the imperialist ethos enshrined in Scouting's open air pursuits.

The conflict between children as learners and children as workers would come to a head with the institution of elementary education under the acts of 1870 and 1880. In the 1860s, the working-class boy was not so easy to reform as Barnardo's propaganda might have suggested. The charitable homes and boys' clubs, along with the organized youth movements (such as the YMCA, established in 1844, and the Boys' Brigade), could not clear the streets of the 'roughs' who terrorized passers-by. If working-class boys were not involved in exhausting or demeaning forms of labour, they seemed to be causing trouble. The question of violent crime and discord among young working-class men reached a climax at the turn of the century. The hot summer of 1898 produced notorious scenes of threatening behaviour among young men larking about with water taps. They were known from that time on as 'Hooligans'. Geoffrey Pearson suggests that the name may have come from a music hall song performed by the Irish comedians, O'Connor and Brady. In any case, it was, as Pearson notes, 'ingenious of late Victorian England to disown the British Hooligan by giving him an "Irish" name.'[15] The word became such common currency that it was applied in a celebrated article to one of the main champions of empire, Rudyard Kipling, in 1899, for his jingoistic posturings. Surprisingly, perhaps, in a speech delivered to the National Defence Association in 1910, Baden-Powell referred to the 'best class of boy – that is, the hooligan'.[16]

Although this connection may appear surprising, the link between the Scout and the hooligan was forged out of an unfailing belief in the inherent pluckiness of the British boy, a point vindicated by the extensive body of writing on 'boy labour' produced between 1900 and 1920. (In this context, boys stood for men in their mid- to late teens and early twenties.) Tracts of this sort set out to show that young working-class men possessed qualities which their public school peers had the privilege to develop to the full. According to the Rev. H. S. Pelham, working boys were said to possess an 'unceasing sense of *humour*'; he was 'supremely *confident in his powers*'; he was 'wonderfully *sharp*'; and he was 'above all things *loyal* to his friends.'[17] Yet it was difficult for some advocates of boys' clubs to guarantee an acceptable level of reform among young men:

> It should be the mission of boys' clubs to prevent the growth of the rough lad or the Hooligan gang, and this can best be done by subjecting the embryo Hooligan at an early age, with boys of other classes, to the discipline of the clubs. It is true that a working lads' club may become 'too respectable'; but is this a reason for excluding respectability? A club should be representative of the boys, not the roughs, of the district. It will not do the best work if it is confined to the lowest class.[18]

In this account by W. J. Braithwaite, with its emphasis on discipline and subjection, there is clearly a class of working boy which cannot be trained on its own. Conversely, there is a danger in raising working-class boys well above their station. This extract expresses a noticeable degree of caution about turning working-class boys into respectable young men. It was proving increasingly difficult to find what were thought to be good enough jobs for them. Like these social reformers, Baden-Powell believed Scouting could serve as a tool to lead its members into better employment.

The energies of the hooligan, therefore, were to be channelled into a different use of his leisure time outside the rote-learning he frequently militated against in school (an issue explored in chapter 1).

Baden-Powell was one of many who believed that elementary schooling failed to deliver 'the quality that counts, *character*' (p. 291). Schooling was thought to be deficient in another important respect. The closing pages of *Scouting for Boys* are fraught with worries about a generation of young men without a sound career ahead of them. The elementary school system was not tied to programmes for developing apprenticed forms of labour. Until the Education Act of 1902, elementary school education was dominated by the rigorous inculcation of the 3Rs: reading, writing, and arithmetic. Bearing these failings of elementary education in mind, Baden-Powell devotes several paragraphs to the growing employment opportunities offered by the industrial expansion of Canada and Australia – where, no doubt, basic skills in survival would be required. Scouting, then, could lead its boys, if not into more respectable and better paid work, then towards new and improved lives in the colonies, thereby saving 'the horde of unemployed leading miserable, wasted lives in all parts of the country' (p. 288). In his 1904 essay 'The Boy and his Work', J. G. Cloete writes in a similar vein, discovering one possible solution to the problem of obtaining valuable employment:

> If girls should succeed in supplanting boys as messengers to any appreciable extent, there can be little doubt that it would be a good thing for the boys in the long run. As messengers they are learning nothing useful beyond a certain amount of discipline, and the work itself to the boy mind is apt to be deceptive. It holds out an alluring prospect of easy and regular work, of good wages and good clothes, but the boy finds out too late that it leaves him empty-handed at the finish. In fact, this introduction of girl labour has been hailed by some as a possible solution to many of the difficulties relating to boys.[19]

Again, more skilled and dignified jobs will correspondingly make boys into better men. Girls, by taking what is thought to be appropriately menial employment, are expected to serve as a reserve army of labour, supporting the career prospects of their male peers. For Baden-Powell, the comprehensive skills a boy might gain from the Scouts would undoubtedly be squandered on being a messenger. Scouting existed within an ambiguous space where a boy's leisure aimed to define his labour. He was learning how to enjoy the skills that should, according to Baden-Powell, equip him for an appropriate job. In the meantime, many working-class boys had much more labour than leisure to deal with.

Juvenile labour remained a pressing question right up to the First World War. In 1901 a government committee was appointed to examine the employment of children outside school hours. The consequent Report of the Inter-Departmental Committee on the Employment of Schoolchildren confirmed the findings of the Report on Elementary Education (concerning the conditions and numbers of children working for wages) published in 1899. The 1901 Report recorded that at least 144,000 children who were in full-time education were earning money at other times: mornings, evenings, and, on occasions, whole weekends. About 40,000 worked over twenty hours a week, while 3,000 managed to fit a full school timetable into forty hours of paid work. A matter of great concern was the case of children working as street-traders. A further Report in 1910 noted that in some towns a considerable amount of street-trading was done by children under the age of eleven. Time and again, successive Inter-Departmental Reports of government committees observed that street-trading was unskilled work that would only lead to vagrancy and crime. To bring an end to this bad situation, societies for skilled labour were set up, mostly at the promptings of social workers, and there was a consequent revival of apprenticeships. In 1910 the National System of Labour Exchanges came into operation and coordinated, with the assistance of the Juvenile Advisory Committee in some towns, boy and girl labour with the intention of helping young people hold down what were considered to be good jobs. These advisory committees kept a check on the attendance of young men and women at Continuation Classes designed to improve their technical abilities.

All these developments need to be understood within a wider network of relations concerning state intervention in the welfare of British people. The policies adopted here were those of a Liberal administration. In 1909, for example, the state introduced Old Age Pensions at five shillings a week for those over seventy years of age with a weekly income of less than 10 shillings. National Insurance was also brought in for the first time. At the end of their 1912 history of juvenile labour, O. Jocelyn Dunlop and Richard D. Denham proposed four reforms to improve the lives of young people: 'the raising of the school age, the creation of compulsory Continuation Classes, the further regulation of employment out of school hours, and the appointment of Juvenile Advisory Committees.'[20] From 1900–14, no less than twenty-eight different acts of parliament were passed, on the one hand, to extend educational provisions, and, on the other, to restrict hours of paid work undertaken by children. Each government report and subsequent act redefined how boys and girls could most productively spend their time. The law took them out of work and put them into training, either at school or in apprenticeships or other kinds of technically applied labour.

Guiding these dramatic reforms was the intention to keep young men and women at a safe distance from an adult working-class world of unemployment, drinking, smoking, and jobs of no consequence. The lengthiest piece of legislation affecting boy and girl labour was the Children Act of 1908 – popularly known as the Children's Charter – which prohibited anyone under sixteen from entering public houses and buying tobacco. The 1904 Inter-Departmental Committee on Physical Deterioration, which had been spurred on to counter the problems of recruitment to the army in 1899–1902, had pressed for a ban on children's smoking on the streets. One Chief Inspector of Recruiting is reported to have said that 'perhaps a third of the rejects from the Army in Lancashire might be attributed to smokers' heart'.[21]

This Committee was the one that exerted most influence on the freedoms and restrictions of young people's lives during the Edwardian period. Out of it came the establishment of the Officers' Training Corps under the guidance of Richard Burdon Haldane in 1907; his Territorial and Reserve Forces Bill included a clause concerning the training of cadets. (Baden-Powell had been encouraged to set up the Boy Scouts on Haldane's advice.) Not by accident did the YMCA choose to designate 1907 as 'Boys' Year'. Similarly, the energies that the twelfth Earl of Meath put into the Lads' Drill Association in 1899, and his subsequent achievements in ensuring the mass observance of Empire Day in schools from 1904 onwards, demonstrate how imperialism sought to regulate every hour of a young person's life. Given this exceptional interest in the minds and bodies of young men, 1908 was a highly appropriate time for Scouting to begin.

Baden-Powell's thoughts about Scouting long preceded the events at Mafeking. In 1884 he had published *Reconnaissance and Scouting* which was taken up by progressive educationists. When the first experimental Boy Scout camp was set up at Brownsea Island, he had been working on his scheme of youth training for over twenty years. Rosenthal cites a telling passage from Baden-Powell's report of this exemplary encounter between public school and lower middle-class young men:

> The rougher boys were perceptibly levelled up in the manner of behaviour, cleanliness, etc.; they watched and imitated the others and improved to a remarkable degree in so short a time. And I am certain no harm was done to the other boys: indeed they gained a broader knowledge and sympathy with those whom probably they had had through ignorance formerly looked down upon.[22]

Baden-Powell was obviously worried about the level each party might have attained at such unaccustomedly close quarters. As 'rougher boys' improved, their betters risked coming to 'harm'. He believed, like many conservative social reformers, that the lower orders had a potentially contaminating effect. Yet, just as the law was taming the behaviour and rescheduling the lives of working-class boys, the Scouts took it upon themselves to abide by their own legal model in the name of discipline. The cherished idea of living by a law – the Scout law where each boy pledged his commitment to Scout's 'honour' – necessarily reinforced the need for patriotic duty. Scout law, like the many rulings on the statute books affecting the work and leisure of young people, is the law of conservative Edwardian citizenship in miniature. Scouting legislated on points of honour, loyalty, duty, comradeship, courtesy, obedience, and thrift. Added to these qualities, the Scout was expected to express cheerful readiness, whatever the task. Moreover, he was to act as a friend to animals. These were the ingredients that would uphold 'character' and give a boy the attributes of a proper man.

   This attentiveness to living by the law had wider implications for each Boy Scout. Tireless in its fascination for forensic evidence, Scouting equipped its members with the skills of detection – tracking and spying – which were closely connected with the activities of the army and the police. Not coincidentally, the spy and the detective were assuming new, more dignified roles in popular fiction. And this is a hardly insignificant development when – to take one example – the invincible technique of fingerprinting is borne in mind. (The police introduced this method of identification in 1907.) The state, therefore, had its subjects under much closer scrutiny than before. One figure who counts among Baden-Powell's recommended reading for Scouts is Sherlock Holmes, who presented a novel type of culturally powerful man who was able, from observing every detail, to find everything out. Like the spy who in later stories set about unearthing state secrets, Arthur Conan Doyle's celebrated detective enjoyed a supreme form of agency – he had the power to master the world from a privileged point of view. Like an omniscient God, spies and detectives of this kind can see everything around them, and yet they possess the skills to remain invisible from the interrogating gaze of anyone else. Like the state, they have methods to reproduce ideology so successfully that its workings remain almost imperceptible. In this context, the Scout is so much of his world that his powers of observation cannot themselves be observed. Instead, the Scout carefully notes every tell-tale detail, and then, if something is amiss, he is equipped to report it to the authorities. Trained to lead patrols and follow animals unseen, Scouts are, moreover, obliged to camouflage their feelings: 'A Scout Smiles and Whistles under all circumstances' (p. 49).

A Scout, therefore, can never be known for what he is other than a Scout. He works in the name of his King, his country, and the law as an instrument of the state. He is not supposed to have community or class allegiances. Above all, he must definitely not think of himself as a political subject:

> You will many of you be inclined to belong to Conservative or Liberal or radical or other parties, whichever your father or friends belong to. I should not, if I were you. I should hear what each party has to say. If you listen to one party you will certainly agree that this is the only right one, the rest must all be wrong. But if you go and listen to another you will find that one is quite right, and the first is wrong.
>
> The thing is to listen to them all, and don't be persuaded by any particular one. And then be a man, make up your mind and decide for yourself which you think is best for the country and the future of the Empire – not some twopenny-halfpenny little local question

– and vote for that one so long as it works the right way, for the
good of the country. (p. 283)

Be independent, advises Baden-Powell, make up your own mind.
But, at the same time, he draws up clear limits about what should
and should not be considered political. Politics is seen exclusively
in terms of imperial destiny, not in the here and now. Any
connection with family, friends, and home (the 'little local question')
is deemed irrelevant. Tory imperialism not uncommonly yearned for
a future time when the nation had been led above and beyond the
internal divisiveness of party politics, particularly when the socialist
parties were gaining more purchase on the working-class vote. The
compliant independence demanded by Baden-Powell requires the
boy to reject any interest in himself as an individual or as one who
belongs to a smaller (and thus divisive) grouping, such as a trade
union or a political party.

A few examples from *Scouting for Boys* will reveal how the Scout
must be a dutiful servant of empire. In his second camp yarn,
Baden-Powell provides an exemplary narrative that synthesizes
the following, neatly categorized skills: 'woodcraft', 'observation',
'concealment', 'deduction', 'chivalry', 'pluck and self-discipline',
'health and strength', 'kind-heartedness', 'saving life', and 'duty'
(p. 28). The story in question concerns a young farmer named
Robert Hindmarsh and a gypsy, Willie Winter. Hindmarsh was a
'strong, healthy hill-boy' (the ultimate child of nature). Winter, by
contrast, lived as a 'tramp'. It is a simple tale of how Hindmarsh
discovers clues that finally lead to the conviction of Winter for
murder. One day Hindmarsh passed Winter on the way home.
An especially observant boy, he noticed the 'peculiar nails in the
soles' of Winter's boots. On his arrival home, he heard about the
murder of a local woman. He went to her cottage only to find strange
footprints. With this information, the police caught Winter. 'He
was tried, found guilty, and hanged at Newcastle'. Other gypsies
'who were his accomplices . . . were also executed' for having
stolen property. Hindmarsh was congratulated by the judge for
'ridding the world of such a dangerous criminal'. The boy, then,
has done his 'duty'. But there is, awkwardly, an ethical question
that interrupts the narrative. Where do human sympathies enter
into this violent world? Hindmarsh has, after all, been instrumental

in seeing a murderer hanged. One death has, with his aid, led to another.

Under the section entitled 'Kind-Heartedness', Baden-Powell writes: 'when the boy saw the murderer's body hanging on the gibbet he was overcome with misery at having caused the death of a fellow-creature.' Clearly, this sentence aims to temper the horror of the event. Why should a gypsy be executed by means as terrible as those he himself has used upon a 'fellow-creature'? Baden-Powell tries to sort out the moral dilemma with this brief paragraph: 'Winter belonged to a notable family. He was not the only one who distinguished himself, for his father and his brother were also hanged for different offences. Another brother, feeling the disgrace of belonging to such a family, changed his name from Winter to Spring, and became – a prizefighter' (p. 29). Several moral messages are at issue here. First, the hanging can be justified because Winter came, in any case, from a predominantly bad family. (His background must take the blame.) Second, the outcome indicates that good men can and should dissociate themselves from their shameful origins. And, finally, society is cut down the middle between those who defy the law and those who abide by it. The gypsy community is depicted as a degenerate group of conspirators while the good citizens are independent and healthy. One lot murders and steals and the other wins prizes.

This schematic division of social types persists throughout *Scouting for Boys*. In Baden-Powell's section on 'Details of People', his crude social Darwinist ethics are more clearly in evidence here than anywhere else. This section – part of the fourth chapter, on 'Tracking' – opens with these instructions:

> When you are travelling by train or tram always notice every little thing about your fellow-travellers; notice their faces, dress, way of talking, and so on, so that you could describe them each pretty accurately afterwards; and also try and make out from their appearance and behaviour whether they are rich or poor (which you can generally tell from their boots), and what is their probable business, whether they are happy, or ill, or in want of help.
>
> But in doing this you must not let them see you are watching them, else it puts them on their guard. Remember the shepherd-boy who noticed the gypsy's boots, but did not look at him, and so did not make the gypsy suspicious of him. (p. 121)

The spirit of Sherlock Holmes obviously presides behind these imperatives to spy and classify. Features of clothing and countenance are itemized to draw distinctions between different classes and different character types. It involves the process of stereotyping. Bad types have innately bad looks and, it follows, bad forms of behaviour. Scouts are encouraged to 'practise observation' with the guide of the following illustrations (Fig. 1). Beneath this instructive arrangement of drawings, Baden-Powell rather disingenuously asks: 'Perhaps you can tell the characters of these gentlemen?' (p. 122). In this triptych, the unflattering profile of working-class oaf and the shortened brow of what is supposed to be a Black man are placed on either side of the altogether larger, more erect features of a bright-eyed public school boy. The one in the middle, of course, is the ideal type of Scout who has achieved the greatest state of physical robustness and mental agility. With similar illustrations in mind, Lord Rosebery had written to *The Times* in 1900: 'An Empire such as ours requires as its first condition an Imperial Race – a race vigorous and industrious and intrepid. Health of mind and body exalt a nation in the competition of the universe. The survival of the fittest is an absolute truth in the conditions of the world'.[23] By 1908 Baden-Powell, equipped with human images derived from anthropometric exercises, had a comprehensive blueprint for a higher race of man to maintain and extend imperial dominance.

Later editions of *Scouting for Boys* printed a table outlining the central problems affecting 'national efficiency', and outlined

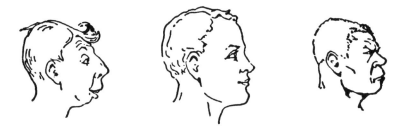

Figure 1   Notice the faces of people so that you will be able
to recognize them.

the preventative steps that Scout training could take to achieve better 'character' and physical well-being (Fig. 2). In this tabulated analysis of social evils, the abject poverty of the working classes – from the squalor of their homes to their want of patriotism – is comprehended in narrowly moral terms. In one column, infant mortality is connected with irreligion; cruelty is categorized with lunacy; and irresponsibility coexists with mental deficiency. All that is 'inefficient' is working-class by nature, although this table listing qualities of 'character' and physical health conspicuously makes no mention of class inequalities. What is more, the diagram claims that the causes of such 'national inefficiencies' can be traced to two main sources: 'want of self-discipline' and 'ignorance of sanitation'. That poverty could be located in 'drink' requires a considerable mental leap. Likewise blaming the high incidence of death among infants on parental 'ignorance' absolves the state of any 'responsibility' towards the poor. The fact that these 'inefficiencies' could not be related to economic conditions is hardly surprising. (As a substitute for these dubious 'causes', a list could be compiled that indicated 'lack of state welfare', 'low wages', and 'unemployment'.) In Baden-Powell's table, the role of the state has been rendered invisible. This is one of the familiar tropes of Conservative discourse whereby the working classes which fail to benefit from its political concerns are blamed for the social problems that befall them.

Baden-Powell was attempting, like Disraeli before him, to popularize conservatism within an apparently non-political realm that cut across all divisions of society. In an era when, after Disraeli's successful efforts to elevate the monarchy within the national consciousness, the Royal Family had become a model for all family relationships, so too had the Boy Scout become an ideal for all young men. Yet it should be noted that this type of boy was absorbed into imperialist ideology only when a number of political contradictions had been successfully overcome. The Scout may have been a model of compliance with the moral order but he was, in fact, a distinctly hybrid cultural product (as Baden-Powell's passing references to the boy-man and the hooligan-Scout bear witness). Scouting served a syncretic function to abolish those differences of class and race that tore at the roots of the guiding propositions of imperialism. The Boy Scout amalgamated the energies of the young mobster with the pieties of his public school peers; he traversed the division

| NATIONAL INEFFICIENCIES | CAUSES | ORIGIN | PREVENTIVE | SCOUT TRAINING AS REMEDY Additional to Scholastic Education— a systemised development of: |
|---|---|---|---|---|
| Irreligion<br>Indiscipline<br>Irresponsibility<br>Want of Patriotism<br>Selfishness<br>Corruption<br>Disregard of others<br>Cruelty | Indifference to Higher Conscience | Want of Self-discipline | Education in I. CHARACTER | I. CHARACTER through—<br><br>Good Environment<br>Sense of Honour<br>Sense of Duty<br>Self-discipline<br>Responsibility<br>Resourcefulness<br>Handicrafts<br>God through Nature study<br>Happiness<br>Religion in Practice<br>Fair Play<br>Helpfulness to Others<br>Personal Service for the Community |
| Crimes of Violence<br>Lunacy<br>Thriftlessness and Poverty | Drink | | | |
| Show off<br>Loafing and Shirking<br>Low Moral Standards<br>Gambling<br>Illegitimacy<br>Disease | Self-indulgence | | | |
| Ill-health<br>Squalor<br>Infant Mortality<br>Mental Deficiency<br>Physical Deficiency | Irresponsibility and Ignorance on part of Parents | Want of Hygienic and Physical Knowledge | II. PHYSICAL HEALTH | II. HEALTH through—<br><br>Outdoor Practices (not merely Drill)<br>Responsibility for own Physical Development up to Standard<br>Health and Hygiene in Practice |

Figure 2   Baden-Powell's table of National inefficiencies

between urban and rural geographies, learning to love and become responsible for his country, thus undermining any awareness of distinctions between landed wealth and city-based poverty; and, like the native whose techniques in tracking his skills were based on, he brought together the knowledge of the savage with that of a civilized citizen. It was the work of adventure fiction to do the same. But, as Rudyard Kipling's writing demonstrates, myths such as this one are not always able to maintain the ideological purity they subscribe to. This is especially the case in Kipling's work where complicated routes of negotiation are engineered to overcome cultural differences in a strenuous attempt to consolidate forms of imperialist identity. Like Baden-Powell, Kipling's celebrated championing of empire was in his popular appeal to the mythical status of the boy.

## Kipling's Boyhood Empire: *Kim*

Rudyard Kipling stands as one of the most controversial voices of empire. Critical opinion remains divided about his imperialism and his contradictory attachments to competing strains of Conservative and Liberal thought. Since the 1890s, his writings have been routinely upheld as examples of either aggressive right-wing polemic or aesthetically ennobled works that transcend political interests. Lionel Trilling shows this division of interests, in *The Liberal Imagination*: 'for liberals of a certain age he must be an interesting figure, for he had an effect upon us in that obscure and important part of our minds where literary feeling and political attitude meet, an effect so much the greater because it was so early experienced; and then for many of us our rejection of him was our first literary–political decision.'[24] In the analysis that follows, *Kim* is not to be understood as either an artless piece of imperialist propaganda or as a technically accomplished exercise in the picaresque. Its narrative complexity is shown to lie within a different frame of critical reference. Indeed, this novel brings into play a complex series of connections between class, race, and gender that, curiously, make the ideal boy adventurer the one who thrives at the furthest remove from what might be thought to be his proper place in the world. Here, the most able boy hero imaginable is the one who least fits into the imperial social and political order around him.

*Kim* concerns the richly detailed spiritual journey towards manhood of a young orphan, Kimball O'Hara, who ultimately spies on behalf of the British Secret Service. He is of Irish descent, and Indian by birth. The novel makes much of Kim's capacity to rise up from his extraordinary origins. *Scouting for Boys* provides an outline of *Kim* in one of Baden-Powell's many camp yarns. (Baden-Powell and Kipling thereafter developed a longstanding professional relationship. *The Wolf Cub's Handbook* [1917], for the junior section of the Scouts, was based in part on *The Jungle Books* [1894–95]. And, more famously, in 1913 Kipling wrote 'A Boy Scout's Patrol Song', which has as its watchword and chorus 'All Patrols look out!')[25] Kim is admirably plucky, self-sufficient, and observant. Moreover, the boy is so skilled in all these respects that his travels across India, that shape the sequence of narrative events, culminate in a courageous act of spying on behalf of the empire against the Russian enemy.

Kim's story, therefore, was clearly worth retelling in *Scouting for Boys*. It could be adapted to didactic ends. In many respects, it was a familiar tale – many of the presuppositions on which it was based were already naturalized by generic conventions. *Kim* has allegiances with a number of Victorian traditions in children's literature, notably the narrative of the lonely orphan which begins with Charlotte Bronte's *Jane Eyre* (1849) and extends to Frances Hodgson Burnett's *A Little Princess* (1905), and which has also been noted as a motif in earlier Anglo–Indian fictions.[26] *Kim* dwells on this powerful image of the abandoned child and brings together elements of the spy and adventure story to create a picaresque narrative of heroism and survivalism. This was an amalgam of traditions in popular fiction that would give birth to, among other tales, Edgar Rice Burroughs's *Tarzan of the Apes* (1914); (discussed below).

Kipling's novel looks out on one part of the empire, India, more extensively patrolled than any other under British rule (particularly after the Sepoy mutinies of 1857). Here, India is an enchantingly colourful, rather magical place with plenty of remarkable scenery along the Grand Trunk Road. This road was a strategic route for commercial traffic across northern India. This busy route, where 'all castes and kinds' make their way, opens out as 'a wonderful spectacle', a 'river of life as nowhere else exists in the world' (p. 105).[27] Here, within this passing procession of Indian people, Kim commits a host of sounds, colours, tastes, and smells to memory. To all appearances, he travels through a country that is not, strictly speaking, his own. For Kim does not entirely belong to India. Throughout the novel, the narrator emphasizes Kim's special powers of observation, which are far greater than those of the multitude of nameless faces passing along the Great Trunk Road:

> The diamond-bright dawn woke men and crows and bullocks together. Kim sat up and yawned, shook himself, and thrilled with delight. This was seeing the world in real truth; this was life as he would have it – bustling and shouting, the buckling of belts, and beating of bullocks and creaking of wheels, lighting fires and cooking of food, and new sights at every turn of the approving eye. The morning mist swept off in a whorl of silver, the parrots shot away to some distant river in shrieking green hosts; all the well-wheels within ear-shot went to work. India was awake, and Kim was in the middle of it, more awake and more excited than anyone. (p. 121)

S. P. Mohanty points out that the moral investment in the 'approving eye' that surveys this scene 'does not forcibly *organize* the "new sights" around it; it embodies, rather, a desire to pay attention, creatively discovering the world's "real truth", learning to participate consciously.'[28] But, as Mohanty goes on to suggest, something more than 'participation' is at stake here. Kim may be completely immersed in India, and may appear to be consummately *of* it, but his centrality to this nation is markedly *greater* than that of any Indian or English person since Kim is said to be 'more awake and more excited than anyone' around him. This passage discloses that Kim holds a preferential vision of India – 'life as he would have it'. But if this is the India he prefers to see, what might be the India he chooses not to? These words, then, imply that this panoramic outlook on India cannot be completely entrapped by Kim's gaze. As the story travels the length of the Grand Trunk Road, it becomes clear that across the mind and body of this young boy there lies a conflict between the outlook of white supremacism and the alienation of imperialism from everything it seeks to keep under surveillance. It could be said that here Kipling's narrative indicates how it is trying to suppress an alternative story of India. Such an alternative narrative – of, for example, an emergent Indian nationalism – would no doubt challenge the authority of Kim's 'approving eye'.

Assimilated into Indian culture in some respects, and yet alienated from it in others, Kim embodies hybrid qualities in an extraordinary imperial fantasy about a boy's rite of passage towards manhood: a dangerous world of sex, politics, and religion that increasingly threatens to do him harm but whose temptations he wisely learns to resist. On what is an often hazardous journey (which comprises his sentimental education), Kim very nearly grows up. However, he does not quite reach an adult state of knowledge. He is instead contained by a trajectory of growth which thematizes the youthful strength of what is supposed to be a still-maturing empire. *Kim* represents the spectacular procession of empire forever, longingly and innocently, developing. Yet the overall pattern of development is not unilinear. Instead, it splits along seemingly parallel lines. The story sets up two differing models of development – one of accelerated growth, which is the boy hero's; and another that has a long history which will take many more years to raise to an adequate standard, that of India itself. Not insignificantly, even this uneducated orphan is able to achieve much more, both morally and physically, than the native peoples who populate the margins of the novel.

Kim, then, may stand as a figure for an India that has yet to mature but he still, even as a child, is able to rise above it. His supremacy, in this respect, is emphasized at the very start of the novel when Kim defies municipal orders by sitting on the gun called 'Zam-Zammah'. '[H]e had kicked Lala Dinnath's boy off the trunions – since the English held the Punjab and Kim was English' (p. 49). (Yet he is not quite as English as the narrator suggests at this point. This slippage between his 'Englishness' and 'Irishness' indicates how Kim variously represents white superiority *and* white subordination.) Already, at a very early age, Kim demonstrates his superior status. But Kim's superior whiteness is made to coexist with an unusual amalgam of Eastern mysticism and Irish charm – both of which take on positive *and* negative attributes as the novel progresses. This boy hero, therefore, bears the traces of competing discourses of national identity (Irish, Indian, British). One of the main problems facing the narrative is how Kim's peculiar status might develop. The narrative does not really conform to a conventional pattern of maturation, since Kim exists almost wholly outside the white world from which he has inherited his moral and physical strength.

Imperialist notions of development largely extrude out of two dominant, and in many respects closely related, nineteenth-century social beliefs: the Whig version of history and social Darwinism. Both of these doctrines, promoting the improved destiny of the race, clearly shape much of Kipling's work. But it needs to be pointed out that Kipling's imperialism came under fire for upholding values that, in many respects, were contrary to bourgeois ideals of progress and propriety. As chapter 2 shows, Robert Buchanan was one of Kipling's fiercest critics, appalled by the outlandish behaviour of Stalky & Co. In 'The Voice of the Hooligan', Buchanan made a vituperative attack on Kipling's successful *Barrack-Room Ballads* (1892), a volume praising the sentiments of its tough-talking soldier hero, the Cockney Tommy Atkins. Buchanan spoke in the pompous tones of a middle-class prude when condemning the coarseness of Kipling's soldier. His argument was based on an implicit equation between the working classes and the uncivilized others of empire: 'From time to time . . . the momentum towards a higher and more spiritual Ideal seems suspended altogether, and we appear to be swept centuries back, by a great back-wave, as it were, in the direction of absolute Barbarism'.[29] Kipling frequently attempted to represent the popular voice of imperialism, and it was precisely this interest in working-class patriotism that led liberals such as Buchanan to categorize Kipling as a jingoist on the side of 'barbarism'. In *Kim*, however, Kipling's imperialism does not emerge as a form of loudmouthed populism howling the battle-cries so loathed by Buchanan. His attitudes to empire comprise instead a complex set of beliefs largely dependent on his ambiguous predicament as an Anglo–Indian.

Like Kim, Kipling did not enjoy the class allegiances a British-born subject would have had. Raised in India, educated for several years at a minor public school in Devon, employed for a brief time as a journalist in India, and finally working as a full-time writer in Britain, South Africa, and the United States, Kipling is contradictorily at home in both the imperial expansiveness of the subcontinent and the Anglo–Saxon history of Sussex (his long-term place of residence). An overview of his complete works demonstrates that he belonged, in cultural terms, not to Britain but to a larger conception of empire, one that made him both more intimate with and, paradoxically, more distant from, imperialist concerns. As a key proponent of imperialism, he was placed in an antagonistic relation to the beliefs he espoused. One of his short stories, 'The Enlightenments of Pagett M.P.' (first published in the *Contemporary Review* in 1890), is often invoked to indicate Kipling's distaste in particular for those Liberal politicians who were taking a belated interest in India, and who intended to improve the bureaucratic machinery of the country without learning to understand the different cultural conditions of the land they had to administer. Kipling spoke in defence of empire as an outsider to Britain and an insider to Anglo–Indian experience. He held views that were neither wholly averse to, nor slavishly uncritical of, British rule. In her detailed study, *Victorian Attitudes to Race*, Christine Bolt remarks that Kipling's position was typical of the late nineteenth-century Orientalist who 'believed that British principles should be applied to India, but so disguised as to coincide with, or become acceptable to Indian notions of what was proper . . . [W]e have here an explicit assumption that Indian civilization and character were to be easily understood, at least through the superior perceptions of the Anglo–Indian.'[30]

Kipling's poem 'The Islanders', published to some controversy in *The Times* in 1902, helps to explain this point. To illustrate Kipling's shifting attitudes towards empire, Samuel Hynes compares this poem with another one, 'Recessional', printed in the same newspaper five years earlier (at the time of the pomp and pageantry accompanying Queen Victoria's Diamond Jubilee).[31] In 'Recessional', Kipling avows that imperialism is God's law; the Almighty has decided to bring 'lesser breeds' under His rule. 'The Islanders', a longer work written in thumping trochees (reminiscent of Tennyson's militaristic 'Locksley Hall' [1842]), is by contrast a thoroughgoing critique of Britain's neglect of its imperial domains. The poem attacks British military incompetence during the second Anglo–Boer War. Kipling emphasizes the ruinous exploitation of those 'men who could shoot and ride' from 'the Younger Nations'. Kipling's chief objection was to those British 'flannelled fools at the wicket' who had the privilege of a public school education but not the competence to command armies waging war overseas. Kipling had spent six months during the war in South Africa working as a reporter for a soldier's paper, *The Friend*. He witnessed there a great loss of life. According to him, the introspective 'islanders', in their much-vaunted 'splendid isolation', turned their backs on their imperial subjects at a time of desperate need. His particular concept of imperialism, therefore, registers the ambiguous position of those loyal colonials who rightly serve, but do not necessarily benefit from, the aggrandizement of empire.

Kim, supposedly, is the ideal Anglo–Indian, the one who possesses the knowledge of the native *and* the superiority of the European. However, as one section from the novel has already demonstrated, the desired coincidence between Eastern and Western values could only be achieved by trying to erase cultural differences through the lens of an 'approving eye'. This is both the knowing eye of imperialism and the innocent eye of a child. The trouble here is that Kim is made to bear the burden of both suppressing and carrying the burden of too many things. He embodies differences between East and West; between British supremacism and Irish subordination; between innocence and experience; and, to take a final opposition, between Kipling's Anglo–Indian imperialism and British imperialism. These tensions clearly mark *Kim* as an exceedingly complex cultural document.

*Kim*, therefore, represents a number of unorthodox attitudes against British imperialism, if from an Anglo–Indian imperialist perspective. The novel was, importantly, written very much from within the empire – at the receiving-end of imperial rule. Kipling was busy with the manuscript of *Kim* between February and April of 1900, when he acted as a war correspondent on *The Friend*, and finished it in the summer of that year in Britain. The conditions in which *Kim* was produced embraced three corners of the empire – India (its content); South Africa (the context for much of its composition); and Britain (its place of publication). But to read *Kim* is to travel through a land that is, although in final conflict with the Russians, largely at peace. Only the final Russian plot threatens to disturb the harmony of the sub-continent. For most of his journey Kim acts as the *chela* (beggar) for a Tibetan lama who is wandering in search of a celestial river. Along the Grand Trunk Road, Kim's life is often in jeopardy. But there are no fights.

India remains, so to speak, a realm of *difference without difference*. In his powerful critique of Kipling's unique brand of imperialism, Edward W. Said consolidates these main points as follows:

> There is no resolution to the conflict between Kim's colonial service and loyalty to his Indian companions not because Kipling could not face it, but because for Kipling *there was no conflict* and, one should add immediately, one of the purposes of the novel was, in fact, to show the absence of conflict once Kim is cured of his doubts and the lama of his longing for the River, and India of a couple of upstarts and foreign agents. But that there *might have been a conflict* had Kipling considered India as unhappily subservient to imperialism, of this we can have no doubt. The fact is that he did not: for him it was India's best destiny to be ruled by England. ('Introduction' to *Kim*, p. 23)

The substance of Said's remarks is indisputable. But a couple of points warrant qualification. Benita Parry argues that the two paratactically organized (or coterminous) systems of belief in the narrative – the lama's and Kim's; Buddhism and imperialism – represent not the syncretic resolution of Eastern mysticism with Western politics but instead denote 'disjunctive goals'.[32] In other words, Kim's travels with the lama operate as a cover for a spying operation. Said's final sentence may also be queried. Kipling believed that the best imperial rulers of India were the Anglo–Indians – men who were, in his unconventional thinking, central to the margins of empire.

The main point here, however, is that Kipling imagines conflict to exist not within the empire but *outside* it. In Kim's idealized India there are protagonists representing several subject peoples, along with white colonialists. 'The only thing that remains consistent', writes Said, 'is the inferiority of the non-white' (p. 30). Kipling's multifarious cast of characters brings India together as a composite nation. Yet, because it is so intermixed, India remains a place whose identity lacks a singular racial or religious orientation. Caught between Hinduism, Buddhism, and Islam, India is an agglomeration of diverse cultures without a stable centre. It is this interest in miscegenation (rather than the lack of conflict which Said observes) that is structured into every aspect of the narrative. Kipling's representatives of each Indian constituency are subjects with distinctively hybrid identities and divided loyalties. To quote from Said again: 'Everyone in *Kim* is therefore equally an outsider to other groups and an insider in his' (p. 36). But Said's statement once more needs slight modification, since it does not hold entirely true for Kipling's most special case of hybridity, Kim himself. This is because Kim has no group, class, or caste of his own. Even though Kim is marked out as a special child of empire at the start of the novel when he takes pride of place on Zam-Zammah, he is nevertheless obliged to move between the different cultures of India's many constituent communities. Continually travelling from one place to another, Kim can find no place to rest.

Kim, then, has no readily defined community. He is not (as Said seems to think) English. Instead, Kipling provides Kim with an unusual colonial legacy that prevents the boy hero from being wholly attached to either occident or orient. He remains, once again, somewhere in between – in what might be called a liminal zone. The orphaned son of an Irish soldier, Kim's full name is Kimball O'Hara. But he is without any formative memories to confer a sense of Irish identity upon him. The only proof he has of who he is are the documents placed in a wallet attached to a string around his neck. These documents depict his father's regimental mascot – a red bull emblazoned on a green field. It is interesting to see how, in the earliest chapters, this Irish symbol is magicked into an Eastern talisman. (Kim's pseudo-oriental characteristics take care of that.) Brought up as a token Indian, Kim turns his quest for identity into a prophetic search for the red bull and the green field in all their mystically Eastern significance. Since he is supposedly unacquainted with Western rationality, his romantic involvement with the regimental talisman produces a childlike naiveté. The orient, on one level, serves to keep Kim curiously untainted from the explicitly propagandist aims of imperialism.

Information about Kim's remarkable origins is provided in the opening sections of the novel. Given the complexity of the issues of identity at stake, it is worth quoting from these passages at length:

> Though he was burned black as any native; though he spoke the vernacular by preference, and his mother-tongue in clipped uncertain

sing-song; though he consorted on terms of perfect equality with the small boys of the bazar; Kim was white – a poor white of the very poorest. The half-caste woman who looked after him (she smoked opium, and pretended to keep a second-hand furniture shop by the square where the cheap cabs wait) told the missionaries that she was Kim's mother's sister; but his mother had been a nurse-maid in a Colonel's family and had married Kimball O'Hara, a young colour-sergeant of the Mavericks, an Irish regiment. He afterwards took a post on the Sind, Punjab, and Delhi Railway, and his Regiment went home without him. The wife died of cholera in Ferozepore, and O'Hara fell to drink and loafing up and down the line with the keen-eyed three-year-old baby. Societies and chaplains, anxious for their child, tried to catch him, but O'Hara drifted away, till he came across the woman who took opium and learned the taste from her, and died as poor whites die in India. His estate at death consisted of three papers – one he called his '*ne varietur*' because these words were written below his signature thereon, and another his 'clearance-certificate'. The third was Kim's birth-certificate. These things, he was used to say, in his glorious opium-hours, would yet make little Kimball a man. On no account was Kim to part with them, for they belonged to a great piece of magic – such magic as men practised over yonder behind the Museum, in the big blue-and-white Jadoo-Gher – the Magic House, as we name the Masonic Lodge. It would, he said, all come right some day, and Kim's horn would be exalted between pillars – monstrous pillars – of beauty and strength. The Colonel himself, riding on a horse, at the head of the finest Regiment in the world, would attend to Kim – little Kim that should have been better off than his father. Nine hundred first-class devils, whose God was a Red Bull on a green field, would attend to Kim, if they had not forgotten O'Hara – poor O'Hara that was gang-foreman on the Ferozepore line. Then he would weep bitterly in the broken rush chair in the veranda. So it came about after his death that the woman sewed parchment, paper, and birth-certificate into a leather amulet-case which she strung round Kim's neck.

'And some day', she said, confusedly remembering O'Hara's prophecies, 'there will come for you a great Red Bull on a green field, and the Colonel riding in his tall horse, yes, and' – dropping into English 'nine hundred devils.'

'Ah', said Kim, 'I shall remember. A Red Bull and a Colonel on a horse will come, but first, my father said, will come the two men making ready the ground for these matters. That is how my father

said they always did; and it is always so when men work magic.'
(pp. 49–50)

Kim's unusual predicament as the 'burned black . . . poor white'
– the child of the West who has metaphorically been blackened
by poverty in the East – would seem to place him in a world of
contemptible interbreeding. The woman who looks after him is
'half-caste'. Her mixed race is interblended with her dubious conduct (opium-smoker, prostitute). But although such an upbringing
may seem to bode badly for Kim, Kipling makes it work to the
boy's advantage. And so here begins a pattern of reversals that
persist throughout the story. Kim, curiously, can only prove his
resilient physical and moral strength by virtue of having been
abandoned by his disreputable father. European in origin, Kim
is Indian in instinct, and the intermixing of the two apparently
creates an ideal formula for Kipling's imperial imagination. 'The
woman who looked after him insisted with tears that he should wear
European clothes – trousers, a shirt, and a battered hat. Kim found
it easier to slip into Hindi or Mohammedan garb when engaged on
certain business' (p. 51). Throughout the course of his adventures,
Kim can dress however he likes whenever he needs to. It is because
he is so displaced and deprived by these manipulated accidents of
empire that Kim can demonstrate his pluck, the quality most deeply
admired by Baden-Powell.

As *Scouting for Boys* amply illustrates, *Kim* is an exemplary
narrative:

> Then Kim travelled about the country a great deal with a fine old
> Afghan horse-dealer to whom he was much attached, who was also
> an agent of the Intelligence Department. On one occasion Kim was
> able to do him a good turn by carrying an important message for
> him secretly; and another time he saved his life by overhearing some
> natives planning to murder him when he came along. By pretending
> to be asleep and then having a nightmare which caused him to
> remove from his position, Kim got away from the neighbourhood
> of the would-be murderers, and was able to give warning to his
> friend in good-time. (p. 14)

Baden-Powell's Kim, of course, is a strategic adaptation, a story
foregrounding a multiplicity of features central to Scouting. Military

logistics and survivalist tactics are the particular attractions in Baden-Powell's heavily slanted version of Kipling's novel, presenting a scenario of carefully opposed friends and enemies: life and death; warnings and rescues; and near misses and final victories. 'These and other adventures of Kim are well worth reading, because they show what valuable work a boy scout could do for his country if he were sufficiently intelligent' (p. 15). But Baden-Powell's interpretation, making Kim a Scout before his time, shows how a particular image of boyhood could convert every disadvantage to a winning position. Kim's celebrated acts of mimicry are so outstanding that he can always play at being someone else – Muslim, Hindu, or European. Yet this quality, so admired in *Scouting for Boys*, leads to a complication in Kipling's narrative. *Kim cannot be himself.* Like the model Scout, Kim's identity does not emerge from his camouflage. Yet unlike the Scout, Kim is not securely British. In fact, the comparison with *Scouting for Boys* throws light on one issue in particular: Kim can only undertake the work so highly praised by Baden-Powell because Kim is anything but respectably middle–class. In one sense, Kim brings into focus all those hybrid elements that Baden-Powell's Scout was devised to obliterate. Juxtaposed in this manner, both figures, the Scout and Kim, show how the cultural value of boyhood during this period had to be raised above differences of class and race while actually being supported by those differences. Kim's pluckiness may be founded on his racial superiority but it actually needs inferior qualities (like the ability to impersonate native Indians) in order to survive.

Kipling went to exhaustive lengths to obtain the right balance of class and racial features to enable Kim to make the most of the boy's heroic life. Although Kim's whiteness stands over and above his apparent blackness, he is not white enough to resolve the tension between his racial origins and his Indian 'sing-song' English. Why should this be the case? There is a good reason. Kim is unable to rise out of his Indian habits because of his Irishness. His father, like practically all the other subordinated figures in the story, is described in stereotypical terms. Altogether remote from the image of the ideal British soldier, O'Hara senior was a loafer, a drinker, and an unfit father. Kim only knows of his father through the stories he has been told. No self-consciously Irish stigma is attached to Kim. The description of Kim's father follows on from a considerable body of anti-Irish writing that abounded in the nineteenth century. An article on 'The Irish Abroad' from the conservative *Edinburgh Review* in 1868 provides a representative example of hostile British attitudes towards a nation that, like India, was making moves towards securing self-government:

> The Irish are deficient in that unquiet energy, that talent for accumulation, those indefinite desires, which are the mainsprings of successful colonisation, and they are deficient, too, in that faculty of self-government without which free institutions can neither flourish nor be permanently maintained.

Here, the Irish are said to be incapable of 'settled civilized habits' when compared with the Anglo–Saxon who 'is everywhere the more successful pioneer and backwoodsman.'[33] In this account, Ireland is nothing more than a place where poor ignorant whites are clamouring for what they least deserve: Home Rule (this article was published when Fenianism was emerging as a political force). Kim, then, is the ultimate orphan of empire, with the worst of both East and West to contend with. But the novel strategically reconfigures these qualities to make this boy the ideal instrument of an unconventional imperialism.

Kim's upbringing causes him no problems. His father is not a source of resentment but remains part of a continuing magical story. In fact, everything about Kim's life is translated into the realms of make-believe. His father belongs to a myth (he interprets the regimental mascot as an Eastern symbol), and his own childhood and adolescence are plotted along the Grand Trunk Road as if they were the episodic adventure that represents them. In many ways, the narrative method and the content are very closely aligned. Kim, after all, is an eponymous hero. Adhering to the romantic conventions of Victorian children's literature, *Kim* often seems to be placed at a far remove from the psychological complications demanded by nineteenth-century realism.

But, on a number of occasions, the novel is troubled by Kim's sequence of exploits. Two questions keep returning. What is Kim's identity? And what will be his destiny? Both concern where Kim can, finally, be placed. One thing is certain: Ireland is not his home. No one suggests he should settle there. It is the task of the narrative to rehabilitate him, somehow and somewhere, within India. On the one hand, India may appear culturally diverse enough to accommodate Kim. Then again, Kim may seem versatile enough to accommodate all of India. But this confusion is never clarified. At one point, Kim is asked by the horse-trader, Mahbub Ali, 'who are thy people?' Kim replies: 'This great and beautiful land' (p. 184). The novel sets itself the complicated task of sealing that fracture between Kim's 'people' and his 'land'. Yet it proves impossible to find a place for Kim. Time and again, Kim is discovered alone trying to comprehend his dislocated sense of self:

> 'Now am I alone – alone', he thought. 'In all India is no one so alone as I! If I die today, who shall bring the news – and to whom? If I live and God is good, there will be a price upon my head, for I am a Son of the Charm – I, Kim.'
>     A very few white people, but many Asiatics, can throw themselves into a mazement as it were by repeating their own names over and over again to themselves, letting the mind go free upon speculation as to what is called personal identity. When one grows older, the power usually departs, but while it lasts it may descend upon a man at any moment. (p. 233)
>     'I am Kim. I am Kim. And what is Kim?' His soul repeated it again and again. (p. 331)

There is no definitive answer to Kim's repeated inquiries into what or who he really is. But why? The novel insists on focusing Kim's anxiety. And each time the boy is either moved to tears or reaches a mysterious Eastern state of mind: 'mazement', something inexplicable that lies beyond the bounds of narrative reason or containment.

Represented as both an outcast from his Irish origins and an inauthentic Indian, Kim can only find succour in a humanistic world of feelings where his distinctly modern perception of alienation can be reconciled. Kim certainly may elicit a very wide range of reader responses, from sorrow for his plight to great admiration for his fortitude. The novel encourages the reader to experience his struggle with 'personal identity', and so to value him as much worse off than, for example, the Bengali Hurree Babu who in the eyes of the Russian spy is a symbol of 'little India in transition – the monstrous hybridism of East and West' (p. 288). Kipling depicts Hurree Babu as a comic amalgamation of European and Indian attitudes: prayers to the gods of Hinduism, on the one hand, and enthusiasm for the positivism of Herbert Spencer, on the other. The novel insists on the ludicrous incompatibility of these differing systems of belief. In fact, this incongruity is supposed to provoke laughter. It has to be noted that, although Hurree Babu is often mocked, Kim – the most extraordinary hybrid of all – is never derided. And that is because Kim is white.

His whiteness is of a special kind. Kim may be confused about his identity; he may have been abandoned to the cultural deficiencies of Ireland and India; and he may seem to have no place within the social order; but Kim is never lost in India – since he can be all things to all people. The same cannot be said for the other characters in this imperialist romance. Hurree Babu, the Bengali; Mahbub Ali, the Afghan horse-dealer; and Colonel Creighton, the Anglo–Indian ethnologist (and Secret Service agent) – all these characters are shown to be more culturally displaced than Kim, whose whiteness can always incorporate his black identity at whim. The older male characters inhabit a colonized country where cultural difference is stranger to them than it is to the boy who can always change his identity. There is no mystery about these men. They are not at all special but fit into recognizable categories. What is more, they are all adult participants in a spying operation which Kim, as a boy, barely understands. They are the explicit exponents of empire. Kim, by contrast, manages to mask his imperial interests, not only through his rapid changes of clothes, but because he is a mere boy. Since he is young, he perceives his imperial exploits as nothing other than an adventure, while the reader has the ironic privilege of recognizing it as something far more dangerous. And, courageous and innocent at once, he wins everybody's admiration. The lama calls him 'Friend of all the World.' (Baden-Powell mentioned in his eighth point of Scout Law that Kim's title, 'Little friend to all the world', should serve as a model for every boy in the movement.) Commentators often agree that 'in Buddhism, with its castelessness, purity, and austerity, [Kipling] found the golden mean', and they often view the lama's role as one epitomizing 'moderation and tolerance.'[34] However, it is less frequently observed that the lama's role is manipulated to evoke sympathy for British imperialism. Kim is friend to both Buddhism *and* spying.

One episode in particular is designed to bear out Kim's captivating innocence and refreshingly childish spontaneity. When he comes across the encampment of his father's regiment, the following brief interview takes place between himself and the Roman Catholic chaplain:

> Father Victor stepped forward quickly and opened the front of Kim's upper garment. 'You see, Bennett, he's not very black. What's your name?'
> 'Kim.'
> 'Or Kimball?'
> 'Perhaps. Will you let me go away?'
> 'What else?'
> 'They call me Kim Rishti Ke. That is Kim of the Rishti.'
> 'What is that – "Rishti"?'
> '*Eye* – rishti – that was the Regiment – my father's.'
> 'Irish – oh, I see.' (p. 124)

Later, Father Victor enquires: 'Are there many more like you in India? . . . or are you by way o' being a *lusus naturae*' (p. 146) – a freak of nature, one who blends Irishness and Indianness together into a playful mixture of sounds. He is, then, both natural and a freak, special and tarnished in one. And so his bewilderment in India becomes the greatest source of his strength to work in the service of empire. Towards the end, before Kim's final heroic act, Kipling's narrator states:

> Then did Kim, aching in every fibre, dizzy with looking down, footsore with cramping desperate toes into inadequate crannies, take joy in the day's march – such joy as a boy of St. Xavier's [the school he briefly attends] who had won the quarter-mile on the flat might take in the praises of his friends. The hills sweated the *ghi* and sugar suet of his bones; the dry air, taken sobbingly at the head of cruel passes, firmed and built out his upper ribs; and the tilted levels put new hard muscles into calf and thigh. (p. 281)

Kim's experiences as a spy have made a public school athlete out of him. He possesses untiring physical strength. Although he has been able to develop such physical power and intimate knowledge of India, he has not benefited from a sustained public school education or a respectable Anglo–Indian upbringing. Moreover, his gains in physical strength and mental agility are matched by losses in social status. At one point, a drummer boy of Kim's own age insults him: 'You talk the same as a nigger, don't you?' (p. 150). Kim does, and yet he does not. Such an incident, once more, aims to manipulate sympathy for Kim's peculiar hybrid role. Kim is not to be slighted as a 'nigger', but it is none the less understandable why he should be the object of such abuse. Kim has to be seen as almost completely Black before he can be recognized as defensibly white. No one else is vilified as harshly as Kim is in this upsetting exchange of words, and no one can be blamed for how he looks and acts, like a native. Kipling's narrative, therefore, has succeeded in going to the extremes of blackening a white boy to show how it is perfectly possible for Kim to be more of a native (an object for insults) than the natives themselves. All of these contradictory points accentuate Kim's unique role as a boy who *looks worse* than but is in fact *far better* than those who belong to a seemingly more ordered universe.

Finally, Kim is something even more remarkable than this native raised to a higher and whiter power. He is a hybrid inhabitant of empire who is not contaminated by literal miscegenation. Patrick Williams examines a brief moment of dialogue when Kim, discussing strategy with Mahbub Ali, casually interjects his particular contempt for his former Eurasian schoolfellows at St. Xavier's (the Roman Catholic school where he stays briefly):

'Their eyes are blued and their nails are blackened with low-caste blood, many of them. Sons of *mehteranees* [sweeper women] – brothers-in-law to the *bhungi* [sweeper].'
We need not follow the rest of the pedigree, but Kim made his little point clearly and without heat, chewing a piece of sugar-cane the while. (p. 192)

Williams notes that Kim has already been told by Colonel Creighton, after the boy has made a slighting remark about 'half-caste' boys whose mothers were 'bazar-women', that 'not at any time [should Kim] be led to contemn the black men' (p. 167).[35] Creighton states that since Kim is a 'Sahib and the son of a Sahib' the boy should not tolerate 'ignorance' of this kind. But Kim can only manifest what are considered to be the finest abilities of the Sahib by virtue of not enjoying the privileges of being one.

*Kim*, then, is an ambitious fiction wherein the adventurous boy hero is equivocally situated to be able, as plausibly as possible, to 'go native' and yet uphold the standards of the empire. The latter point struck one of Kipling's reviewers, who read the novel partly in the manner of the Victorian moral tale:

> The character of Kim is from first to last a masterly conception. As a study of adolescence – of the progress from boyhood to youth, and from youth to early manhood – it is incomparably fresh and true: full of the delight of the artificer in the work of his hands, of the joy that comes from nothing so much as from the sense of successful achievement. The pride of the labourer in a task well performed had always been a congenial and favourite theme with Mr. Kipling; and we know of no other which, once duly appreciated, is likely to do so much for the maintenance of our Empire in all its manifold interests.[36]

Since its earliest reviews, *Kim* has maintained a powerful hold over even the most attentive critics of Kipling's imperialism. Artistic 'freshness' and 'truth' have prevailed over the politically motivated structure of his writing. Noting the sophisticated level at which Kipling accomplishes 'syncretic solutions to the manichean opposition of coloniser and colonized', Abdul R. JanMohammed finds in *Kim* 'a positive acceptance and celebration of difference'.[37] But as Williams shows, although this narrative is in no respect crudely racist, its orientalist and imperialist assumptions are deeply embedded in it: 'Indians are particularly [to use Creighton's word] "contemned" as incompetent apers of the English: students from the university smoke cigars to try to appear like the English, but their cigars are cheap and rank-smelling; groups of pretentious long-coated natives gather to discuss philosophy with [another English official] Lurgan; babus all speak English in order to show off (and do it badly).'[38] So although JanMohammed makes it sound as if the cultural differences in this novel were evenly sorted out, this is not the case. The same has to be said for the treatment of gender differences. Williams remarks that women, if not quite as marginal to the novel as many commentators have claimed, present a further threat of interbreeding.[39]

Like a law-abiding Scout, Kim remains entirely continent. (He does, after all, for the most part accompany a Buddhist monk.) Towards the close of the novel, the Woman of Shamlegh asks him if he would like to know 'how the Sahibs render thanks' to her, by which she means sexual favours (p. 314). Although he holds her close and kisses her briefly on the cheek, he resists temptation, and promptly passes into the mountains. It is the only moment in the novel that explicitly touches on sexuality. And it is, moreover, an Indian woman's not a British man's, desires that are expressed: 'My Sahib said he would return and wed me – yes, wed me . . . Thy face and thy walk and thy fashion of speech put me in mind of my Sahib' (p. 313). Kim is bound by the moral direction of his narrative to turn his back on her, and not be tainted by the sexual longing to be found in this the outmost reach and most politically contentious zone of India. But after *Kim* the story of male survival would, as it moved into the stronger sexual concerns of the twentieth century, take up this barely glimpsed encounter with woman and enhance her function. The boys' own story gradually transformed its interests in adventure to a more sexualized type of romance.

## Lord of the Jungle: *Tarzan of the Apes*

Endowed with a naturally inquiring mind, and a highly observant eye, Tarzan decides to enter 'the closed and silent cabin by the little land-locked harbour' that he and his fellow apes often passed by. Inside, he comes across an alphabet book, and one of the first entries he finds runs as follows:

BOY

And now he had discovered in the text the page in which these three were repeated many times in the same sequence.

Another fact he learned – that there were comparatively few individual bugs [bug standing for the letter B]; but these were repeated many times, occasionally alone, but more often in the company of others.

Slowly he turned the pages, scanning the pictures and the text for a repetition of the combination *b-o-y*. Presently he found it beneath a picture of another little ape and a strange animal which went upon four legs like the jackal and resembled him not a little. Beneath this picture the bugs appears as:

### A BOY AND A DOG

There they were, the three little bugs which always accompanied the little ape.

And so he progressed very, very slowly, for it was a hard and laborious task which he had set himself without knowing it – a task which might seem to you or me impossible – learning to read without having the slightest knowledge of letters or written language, or the faintest idea that such things existed. (p. 54)[40]

Although this passage advances an implausible model of language acquisition, it none the less marks a significant moment for all the narratives of boyhood survival discussed so far in this chapter. Here, Tarzan, reared by apes after his parents have died in the murderous heat of the jungle, discovers he is human. This truth steals upon him as he turns the pages of what, in fact, was his own childhood alphabet before he was left in the lap of fate, and then mercifully fostered by Kala, an ape with the power of 'universal motherhood' lying deep 'within her wild breast' (p. 35). Achieving an almost unmediated entry into language, he is, thereafter, increasingly separated from the apes, since the book he learns to read spells out his difference from those creatures he once thought he belonged to. In this well-known story, having become master of his language, Tarzan is finally confirmed (by way of the novel technique of fingerprinting) to be no one other than Lord Greystoke.

The enduring power of the Tarzan myth rests on incidents like this one, which enables him to resume his place within his rightful social order once he has been nourished by the dangerous warring forces of nature that have made him into the mightiest of men. He is, at one and the same time, lord of the jungle and lord of the manor. Neither identity can be separated from the other. There is, however, a fracture running between them. Tarzan is born a lord of the manor in order to act out his life as an ape. Conversely his experiences as an ape furnish him with the skills that enable his return to a place, his landed estate, where he has never actually been. The figure of Tarzan, then, has all the attributes of the noblest of savages. His double identity would seem to demonstrate that nobility rests on savagery, and that the savage has a nobility of his own. But both sides of this equation obtain their balance on the basis of a good many qualifications about heredity and race, and so the narrative involves detailing at length the cannibalistic practices of the African natives who seem as blood-thirsty as the lions prowling Tarzan's domain.

Like Kim, Tarzan is an alien in the land of his birth, and yet, in spite of his outsider status, he has the knowledge of a native inhabitant. But whereas Kim can play the role of not just one, but any, of the native cultures of India, Tarzan acts the part of an animal, and, to a carefully controlled degree, he behaves like one. In fact, he has been plunged into a life among those primates with which Darwin's *The Origin of Species* (1859), of course, had controversially linked human beings. His predicament obviously places him in very close proximity to nature. He possesses a privileged understanding of the animal world. Tarzan's extraordinary story moves between competing doctrines of experience and instinct. For the main part of the narrative, he stands as a figure battling between his sense of shame at his white and hairless skin, marking out his difference from the apes ('Tar-zan', in ape language, means white skin), and his death-defying powers as the most athletic, and, by heredity, most civilized of men, far superior in intelligence to the creatures around him. The narrator asks:

> How may we judge him, by what standards, the ape-man with the heart and head and body of an English gentleman, and the training of a wild beast?

> Did men eat men? Alas, he did not know. Why, then, this hesitancy! Once more he essayed the effort, but of a sudden a qualm of nausea overwhelmed him. He did not understand. (p. 78)

Like Kim, Tarzan's plight concerns the problem of his identity: '"What are you Tarzan?" he asked aloud [to himself]. "An ape or a man?"' (p. 206). It is the main function of the narrative to sort out for him exactly who he is, and the story achieves its resolution on the basis of systematic exclusions. Noting the 'swarthy, sun-tanned villainous-looking fellows' (p. 106) who lead a treacherous life on the high seas, Tarzan observes that they 'were evidently no different from the black men – no more civilized than the apes – no less cruel than Sabor [the ruthless lioness]' (p. 107). At the start, mutinous traitors are to be blamed for abandoning his parents, John and Alice Clayton, in the wilds of Africa. Later, similar unscrupulous types show the same lack of principle when they cast another generation of hapless scientific explorers on to the hazardous shores of the dark continent. Framed by these familiar plot devices from boys' adventure fiction, *Tarzan of the Apes* is self-consciously extending a well-worn tradition of 'jungle' narratives where working-class men bear striking resemblances to brutish Africans. On this occasion, however, chapters with titles such as 'Heredity' appeal to contemporary eugenics to confirm the prejudices of earlier juvenile literature.

Burroughs's novel has major antecedents in the stories comprising Kipling's *Jungle Books*. He wrote in 1939: 'I presume that I got the idea for Tarzan from the fable of Romulus and Remus who were suckled by a she-wolf, and who later founded Rome; and also from the works of Rudyard Kipling, which I greatly enjoyed as a young man.'[41] Kipling also acknowledged Burroughs as his rightful heir: 'My *Jungle Books* begat Zoos of them. But the genius of all the genii was one who wrote a series called *Tarzan of the Apes*. I read it, but regret I never saw it on the films, where it rages most successfully.'[42] Like Kipling's Mowgli, Tarzan knows the law of the jungle. But whereas in Kipling's stories Mowgli is forever being trained, like a Scout, in jungle law, Tarzan eventually rises above them. Victorious in killing one of his greatest enemies among the bull apes, he declares: 'I am Tarzan, King of the Apes, mighty hunter, mighty fighter' (p. 101). This show of power is soon confirmed by the narrator: 'A personification was Tarzan of the Apes of the primitive man, the hunter, the warrior' (p. 103).

Through this hybrid icon of hyper-masculinity – at once primitive in instinct *and* noble in mind and body – Burroughs is able to unleash a fantasy of invulnerable imperial potency. Yet not only could Tarzan inhabit a figurative space in which the white man's body might dominate the heart of darkness from within, he could also legitimate Tarzan's sexual urgency as a product of his animal upbringing. Once Tarzan's eyes have settled upon Jane Porter, seeking shelter on the beach, an all too understandable animal passion works within him. 'He knew that she was created to be protected, and that he was created to protect her' (p. 141). And finally their desires for each other are fulfilled: 'He did what no red-blooded man needs lessons in doing. He took his woman in his arms and smothered her upturned, panting lips with kisses' (p. 157). This piece of sexual plotting is so familiar in the twentieth century that it may seem hardly worth remarking on. But it is significant because it stands at the beginning of a popular tradition celebrating a distinctive type of modern manhood. Tarzan obviously bears the traces of earlier varieties of man – the gentleman of Victorian fiction; the imperial soldier at the battle-front; the Scout making himself at home out of doors – but he is, for all to see, a belatedly Darwinian being whose sexual passion knows no reason. The political imperative to survive has here transformed into a sexual imperative to be a man. No one is going to tell Tarzan how to obtain what he desires.

The image of Tarzan is the ancestor of many powerfully heterosexual popular heroes – Ian Fleming's James Bond is perhaps the most obvious one. Burroughs produced another twenty Tarzan stories which send their lordly protagonist on a series of missions that trace not so much the decline of British imperial rule but, as John Newsinger suggests, the rise of the United States as a superpower:

> Tarzan, of course, played his part in the defence of the British Empire against the various challenges that confronted it: first of all from German rivalry during the First World War, then from the activities of Communist agents between the wars and lastly from the Japanese in the Second World War. Burroughs could not resist the temptation to use the Tarzan stories as overt vehicles for his own commentary on international affairs, giving voice to his often paranoid hatred and warning against the dangers that threatened Western Civilization. Only his death in 1949 saved us from Tarzan's wholehearted involvement in the Cold War, fighting the Mau Mau in the forest of Kenya, the Vietcong in the paddy fields of Vietnam and the Sandinista in the jungles of Nicaragua.[43]

It almost goes without saying that Rambo, the jungle survivor of the Vietnam War, is Tarzan's most disturbing post-war heir. Fuelled by insuperable aggression, this hyper-combative type of male remains an enduring emblem in popular culture. Social and cultural conditions may have radically changed between the Edwardian era and the 1980s but the close ties connecting the survivalist skills of Kim, the Boy Scout, and Tarzan and their descendants are striking. Even if consensus affirms that imperialism is a dirty word, and that its ideals have been exposed as a sham, there is still an imperialist war being played out by 'boys' own' heroes against both real and imaginary enemies, whether in the Third World or in the film industry. Produced at the turn of the century, these icons of intrepid adventurousness were designed for survival. They belonged to a myth that would have both commercially and politically successful futures.

# Notes

1   Robert Baden-Powell, *Scouting for Boys*, second edition (London, 1908), pp. 1–2. All further references to this edition are included in the text. It has not been possible to consult the first edition.
2   Francis Galton, 'Hereditary Talent and Character', *Macmillan's Magazine*, 12 (1865), pp. 318–27 reprinted in Michael D. Biddiss, (ed.), *Images of Race*, The Victorian Library (Leicester: Leicester University Press, 1979), p. 69.
3   Samuel Smiles, *Self-Help with Illustrations of Conduct and Perserverance*, abridged by George Bull ([1859]; Harmondsworth: Penguin Books, 1986), p. 20.
4   Baden-Powell, 'The Boy Scouts', *National Defence*, 4:17 (1910), p. 447 cited in John Springhall, *Youth, Empire and Society: British Youth Movements, 1883–1940* (London: Croom Helm, 1977), p. 127. Springhall's study makes useful comparisons between the Boy Scouts, the Cadet Corps, the Boys' Brigade, and the Woodcraft Folk.
5   Michael Rosenthal, *The Character Factory: Baden-Powell and the Origins of the Boy Scout Movement* (London: Collins, 1986), p. 60. The following discussion is greatly indebted to Rosenthal's comprehensive study. The development of Scouting also needs to be appreciated in terms of the increasing popularity of the Volunteer Corps and the work of the National Service League (founded in 1901); on these movements, see Anne Summers, 'Edwardian Militarism' in Raphael Samuel, (ed.), *Patriotism: The Making and Unmaking of British National Identity*, Volume 1, *History and Politics* (London: Routledge, 1989), 236–56. The relations between elementary schooling, military youth organizations, and imperialist propaganda are discussed by Pamela Horn, 'English Elementary Education and the Growth of the

Imperial Ideal: 1880–1914' in J. A. Mangan, (ed.), *Benefits Bestowed? Education and British Imperialism* (Manchester: Manchester University Press, 1988), pp. 39–55.

6   Derek Capper, *Challenge and Adventure: The Handbook for the Scout for the Membership Badge, Explorer Award, Chief Scout's Award, Patrol Activity Award, Leadership Award and Chief Scout's Challenge* (London: the Scout Association, 1985), p. 118. For the Chief Scout's Award, it is worth noting, Scouts are invited to relate a short story concerning the history of the movement: 'Some ideas might be: B.-P. at school; B.-P. as a spy; the Zulu wars; the defence of Mafeking; Brownsea Island; *Scouting for Boys*; the first Jamboree; Scouts at war; the Gang Shows' (p. 102).

7   Rosenthal, *The Character Factory*, p. 43.

8   Thomas Pakenham, *The Boer War* (London: Weidenfeld and Nicolson, 1979), p. 400. It should be noted that Pakenham's charges against Baden-Powell's handling of the siege of Mafeking have been challenged by Tim Jeal, *Baden-Powell* (London: Hutchinson, 1989), pp. 260–77.

9   Cited in Geoffrey Pearson, *Hooligan: A History of Respectable Fears* (London: Macmillan, 1983), p. 75.

10  Rosenthal, *The Character Factory*, p. 192.

11  Anonymous, 'England after War', *Fortnightly Review*, NS 72 (1902), p. 4.

12  'The rough has not yet quite found his groove and settled down to work, and so he is just asserting his personal liberty a little, going where he likes, assembling where he likes, hustling as he likes. Just as the rest of us, – as the country squires in the aristocratic class, as the political dissenters in the middle class, – he has no idea of a *State*, of the nation in its collective and corporate character controlling, as government, the free swing of this or that one of its members in the name of the higher reason of all of them, his own as well as that of others. He sees the rich, the aristocratic class, in occupation of the executive government, and so if he is stopped from making Hyde Park a bear-garden or the streets impassable, he says he is being butchered by the aristocracy' (Matthew Arnold, *Culture and Anarchy*, (ed.) J. Dover Wilson [1869; Cambridge: Cambridge University Press, 1932], pp. 80–1). Arnold clearly would not tolerate working-class *ressentiment*, along with all types of anti-social behaviour. Wilson explains the context to the succession of public disturbances at Hyde Park during 1866–67: see pp. xxv–xxxii.

13  'The analysis of jingoism conducted by [J. A.] Hobson . . . in *The Psychology of Jingoism* [1901], was a moralistic comment coloured

by a failure to observe society at a deeper level than that of events like Mafeking Night. Furthermore, his analysis revealed nothing new or significant. His belief that jingoism was transmitted through the media of the public house and the music hall . . . was not only true but what it did describe was nothing peculiar to the imperialist age. It merely revealed Hobson's low opinion of the "brutal" and "credulous" working class . . . In fact, the mafficking crowd, vulgar though they may have been, was not a "mob", was not generally in a legal state of riot, neither, as one historian has suggested, was Mafeking Night itself an "orgy of rowdyism"': Richard Price, *An Imperial War and the British Working Class: Working-Class Attitudes and Reactions to the Boer War 1899–1902* (London: Routledge and Kegal Paul, 1972), pp. 175–6. On issues of class, imperialism, and jingoism, see also Price, 'Society, Status and Jingoism: The Social Roots of Lower Middle-Class Patriotism, 1870–1900' in Geoffrey Crossick (ed.), *The Lower Middle Class in Britain 1870–1914* (London: Croom Helm, 1977), pp. 89–112, and Gareth Stedman Jones, 'Working-Class Culture and Working-Class Politics in London, 1870–1900: Notes on the Remaking of a Working Class' in *Languages of Class: Studies in English Working Class History 1832–1982* (Cambridge: Cambridge University Press, 1983), pp. 179–238.

14   Stedman Jones, *Outcast London: A Study in the Relationship between the Classes* ([1971]; Harmondsworth: Penguin Books, 1984), p. 129.
15   Pearson, *Hooligan*, p. 75.
16   From a speech by Baden-Powell delivered to the National Defence Association in 1910, cited in Pearson, *Hooligan*, p. 51.
17   Rev. H. S. Pelham, *The Training of the Working Boy* (London: 1914), p. 3.
18   W. J. Braithwaite, 'Boys' Clubs' in E. J. Urwick, (ed.), *Studies of Boy Life in our Cities* (London: Dent, 1904), p. 191.
19   J. G. Cloete, 'The Boy and His Work' in Urwick, *Studies of Boy Life in Our Cities*, p. 114.
20   O. Jocelyn Dunlop and Richard D. Denham, *English Apprenticeship and Child Labour: A History with a Supplementary Section on the Modern Problem of Juvenile Labour* (London: T. Fisher Unwin, 1912), p. 350.
21   *Report of the Inter-Departmental Committee on Physical Deterioration*, *Parliamentary Papers*, 32 (1904), p. 76.
22   Cited in Rosenthal, *The Character Factory*, p. 86.
23   Cited in Bernard Porter, *The Lion's Share: A Short History of British Imperialism 1850–1983*, second edition (London: Longman, 1984), p. 130.

24  Lionel Trilling, *The Liberal Imagination: Essays on Literature and Society* ([1951]; Harmondsworth: Penguin Books, 1970), p. 126.

25  The friendship that developed between Kipling and Baden-Powell is outlined in Hugh Brogan, *Mowgli's Sons: Kipling and Baden-Powell's Scouts* (London: Jonathan Cape, 1987). 'Kipling's verse and prose had . . . been telling the British public what to expect of its modestly heroic regiments; at Mafeking Baden-Powell and his men vindicated a dream, the more beguilingly because of the failures of all the other imperial forces in South Africa. It is not really surprising that a wave of patriotic love washed over the brave and successful commander. This was the happy warrior that every boy in England [taught by Kipling] longed to be' (p. 20).

26  B. J. Moore-Gilbert notes that *Kim* follows in a tradition of Anglo–Indian fiction featuring abandoned British orphans, particularly John Lang's 'Who Was the Child?' (1859) and F. M. Crawford's *Mr. Isaacs* (1882): *Kipling and 'Orientalism'* (London: Croom Helm, 1986), pp. 23–4.

27  Rudyard Kipling, *Kim*, (ed.), Edward W. Said ([1901]; Harmondsworth: Penguin Books, 1987). All references to this edition are made in the text.

28  S. P. Mohanty, 'Kipling's Children and the Colour Line', *Race and Class*, 31 (1989), pp. 23–4.

29  Robert Buchanan, 'The Voice of the Hooligan', *Contemporary Review*, 76 (1899), p. 774.

30  Christine Bolt, *Victorian Attitudes to Race* (London: Routledge and Kegan Paul, 1971), p. 197.

31  Samuel Hynes, *The Edwardian Turn of Mind* (Princeton: Princeton University Press, 1968), pp. 19–21.

32  Benita Parry, 'The Content and Discontents of Kipling's Imperialism', *New Formations*, 6 (1988), p. 59.

33  Anonymous, 'The Irish Abroad', *Edinburgh Review*, 127 (1868), pp. 507, 509.

34  K. Bhaskara Rao, *Rudyard Kipling's India* (Norman, Oklahoma: University of Oklahoma Press, 1967), p. 32. In *Kipling and 'Orientalism'*, Moore-Gilbert writes: 'The Lama is the principal fount of Kim's moral awareness and thus crucial to Kim's quest for his own identity. His continual emphasis upon the middle way generates a practical sympathy with all degrees of humanity which Kim, too, comes to embody on their travels' (p. 129).

35  Patrick Williams, '*Kim* and Orientalism' in Philip Mallett, (ed.), *Kipling Considered* (London: Macmillan, 1989), p. 48.

36  J. H. Millar, 'Recent Fiction', *Blackwood's Magazine*, 170 (1901),

pp. 793–5 cited in Roger Lancelyn Greene, (ed.), *Rudyard Kipling: The Critical Heritage* (London: Routledge and Kegan Paul, 1971), p. 270.

37  Abdul R. JanMohammed, 'The Economy of Manichean Allegory: The Function of Racial Difference in Colonialist Literature', *Critical Inquiry* 12 (1985), pp. 66, 78. JanMohammed's theory of Manichean allegory, based on the writings of Frantz Fanon (in *Black Skins, White Masks* [1952] and *The Wretched of the Earth* [1961]), is dealt with at length in his *Manichean Aesthetics: The Politics of Literature in Colonial Africa* (Amherst: University of Massachusetts Press, 1983).

38  Williams, '*Kim* and Orientalism', p. 37.

39  Williams underlines his points by using extracts of correspondence between the then Viceroy of India, Lord Curzon, and Lord George Hamilton on the potentially contaminating effect of native women on British soldiers: '*Kim* and Orientalism', p. 49. Williams is citing Kenneth Ballhatchet, *Race, Sex and Class under the Raj* (London: Weidenfeld and Nicolson, 1981), pp. 119–20.

40  Edgar Rice Burroughs, *Tarzan of the Apes* ([1914]; London: Methuen, 1917), p. 54. All references to this edition are made in the text.

41  Letter to Donald Herne, 12 August 1939 in Irwin Porges, *Edgar Rice Burroughs: The Man Who Created Tarzan* (Provo, Utah: Brigham Young University Press, 1975), pp. 129–30.

42  Rudyard Kipling, *Something of Myself: For My Friends Known and Unknown*, (ed.) Robert Hampson ([1936]; Harmondsworth: Penguin Books, 1987), p. 162.

43  John Newsinger, 'Lord Greystoke and Darkest Africa: The Politics of the Tarzan Stories', *Race and Class*, 28: 2 (1986), pp. 65–6.

# Conclusion

The turn of the twentieth century supposedly marked the height of
the British empire. The military successes of the second Anglo–Boer
war were, it would seem, testimony to the undeniable superiority of
an imperial race. Britain had much to celebrate. Victoria's reign, for
imperialists, ended truly victorious. Yet even in the most patriotic
declarations of imperial prowess, declarations that grew louder and
louder in the year of Jubilee (1897), it often appeared that British
supremacy was an ideal that did not necessarily enjoy the support
of its worthy subjects. One extreme example of Tory propaganda
points to the conspicuous fracture opening up within the concept
of empire. In his preface to C. de Thierry's *Imperialism* (1898), a
book dedicated to the Primrose League, W. E. Henley approvingly
quotes from Kipling's rousing poem, 'The Native-Born' (1894):

> 'We've drunk to the Queen – God bless her!
>     We've drunk to our mother's land,
> *We've drunk to our English brother*
>     *(But he does not understand)*.*[1]

Since Kipling maintained an ambiguous colonial position (as both
a supporter of the empire and, as an Anglo–Indian, an outsider to
Britain), he was always quick to note the considerable inconsistencies in British national identity. It was his lifetime labour to devise
narrative strategies both to observe and resolve these differences in
order to create a strong imperial culture. He, perhaps more than
any other writer, was troubled by the internal divisions of empire.
Yet, given his political outlook, his manifest disturbance with these
noticeable ruptures within empire never turned into a critique.

These divisions within empire were marked along several lines.
One of these was nationality itself which, as *Kim* demonstrates,
often equivocated in Kipling's work. This equivocation concerns the

peculiar relation between the meanings of 'Britain' and 'England'. The uneven connections between the two terms persist to the present day. 'Britain' was to incorporate Irish, Scottish, Welsh, and English identities, on the understanding that the latter would subsume all of the others. Britain and England, however, could not mean quite the same thing (if they did, there would be no discrimination between them). Examined closely, these two national terms – Britain and England – mutually supported and contradicted one another. Britain was apparently the totality of which England was its major part, while England was the superior culture which incorporated inferior kingdoms. Depending on context, Britain was greater than England because it signalled the unification of Ireland, Scotland, and Wales, while England was greater than Britain because it could be placed over and above the Celtic nations it had annexed. There was the British empire, on the one hand, and the English language, on the other. The fact that both Britain and England existed side by side in this manner suggested that the lack of homogeneity was a political problem.

Henley is quoting from Kipling's poem because he is concerned that the empire is in danger of falling to pieces. He is articulating the characteristic fears of empire at this time. Here, the empire may all too easily degenerate in the face of an overwhelming mass of ill-educated and physically unfit working people. Although many members of the working classes have had patriotism instilled in them, they threaten to weaken the fibre of the nation to such a degree that the Germans will have no difficulty invading Britain. Kipling's narrator reveals that although the spoils of the British empire have been celebrated by the masses there is still something of a problem with the 'English brother' who does not fully understand what imperialism means. By implication, this 'English brother' may betray the empire by giving priority to either class loyalties (in the form of socialism) of self-seeking business interests (in the form of liberalism). At a time when the Queen ('God bless her!') represented the stability and purpose of empire, it was men who seemed to be her weakest supports. Victoria, then, was fulfilling her symbolic function as the maternal nation – caring and constant in one. She was the mother in whom all her children could place their respect and trust. Yet, although her femininity provided the empire with an assuring image of continuity, her gender was a sign of imperial vulnerability. As a female monarch, Victoria commanded the love of her people but she could not lead them into battle. Only through an appeal to a potent masculinity could the future of the empire be secured. A special figurehead is needed, in Henley's words, 'to make the "English brother" understand . . . that it is for him to divine and formulate the spell which is to make our vast and scattered empire one', and that is 'a great man'. But this man of the moment was proving hard to find. Henley looked forward to the arrival of the 'Great Man' in a truly messianic spirit:

> Even among us Anglo–Normans, empire-builders, masters of the earth, as we are, the Great Man is none too common. Let him come now, and he will find his materials ready to his hand. We are not one of the 'dying nations', we! Our tradition is alive once more; our capacities are infinite. Meanwhile, though the processes of uniting have begun, we are not yet a united Empire. But, come the Great Man or not, it is certain that the four corners of the world would rise to arms at the report of an assault upon England. Such an assault is always well within the bounds of probability. In the end it is uncertainty; for it is written, or so it seems, that the world is for one of two races, and of these the English is one. Let us English, then, consolidate – consolidate – and still consolidate.[2]

The contradictions of this passage are obvious. Although the English are 'masters of the earth', great men are hard to identify within the race. Although the English have conquered the world, they are potentially subject to assault. Although there is no 'Great Man' to lead the English forward, all 'four corners of the globe' would rise up to protect the mother country from attack. Although the empire has always had a great 'tradition', it has still to 'consolidate' its interests. A nation of 'great men' above all needs a saviour. An empire with 'infinite capacities' appears to be in the throes of imminent death. There are dangers to be confronted everywhere. The enemy is both without and within.

*Empire Boys* has attempted to show how and why imperialism staked such a high claim on a specific kind of masculinity to perpetuate its aims. British culture invested so much energy in glamorizing male heroes because they represented, as Henley's words disclose, a tremendous lack: they were not to be found in the empire. Henley suggests that even an imperial race had not managed to produce those very beings upon which the empire was supposed to subsist: 'great men'. So where had these men been all along? They were located in the pages of story books which pieced together a myth that could absorb boy readers for hours. It was within the compulsions of these boys' own narratives that all the problematic elements of male identity could, momentarily, cohere. Henley was one among many who desperately wanted to believe these stories to be true.

Each chapter of this book has tried to demonstrate how 'great men' – whether the heroes of the *Boy's Own Paper*, public school stories, or adventure fiction – had far too many incompatible demands placed upon their minds and bodies for them to conform to one prevailing type who could surmount each and every obstacle set before him. Yet these fictions devised extraordinary techniques to cover over their many inconsistencies. It was the duty of boys' narratives to suture those discrete elements that, for example, made the hero an agent of moral restraint, on the one hand, and the embodiment of intrepid exploration, on the other. By way of tracing aspects of a history of modern masculinity, the analyses of popular narratives offered here should indicate that male identity is something that can never be fully gained. Somewhat in spite of himself, Henley half recognizes that this is so, as do many of the writers of juvenile fiction in those moments of hesitation where disjunctions between opposing systems of value have to be concealed. Late twentieth-century men certainly need to acknowledge this point, and so dismantle unitary ideas of maleness. There are new male identities to be discovered and examined. Let us hope that these innovative masculinities will not be upheld as ideal heroic models but, rather, celebrated for their ability to accept change and difference – in the name of a more democratic future.

## Notes

1   Rudyard Kipling, 'The Native Born' cited by W. E. Henley, 'Introduction' to C. de Thierry, *Imperialism* (London: Duckworth, 1898), p. xiv.
2   Henley, ibid., pp. xiv–xv.

# Further Reading

Bailey, Peter, *Leisure and Class in Victorian England: Rational Recreation and the Contest for Control, 1830–1885*, second edition (London: Methuen, 1987). Includes a useful discussion of the rise of athleticism in Victorian Britain.

Bolt, Christine, *Victorian Attitudes to Race* (London: Routledge and Kegan Paul, 1971). A thoroughly documented introduction to the main debates conducted by Victorians about America and slavery, the Morant Bay rebellion, Africa, and India.

Brantlinger, Patrick, *Rule of Darkness: British Literature and Imperialism, 1830–1914* (Ithaca, NY: Cornell University Press, 1988). Covers a great deal of material including the genealogy of the myth of the dark continent, and the rise of imperial gothic in fiction.

Drotner, Kirsten, *English Children and Their Magazines 1751–1945* (New Haven, Conn.: Yale University Press, 1988). Several chapters include a comprehensive discussion of magazines for Victorian boys and girls.

Eby, Cecil Degrotte, *The Road to Armageddon: The Martial Spirit in English Literature 1870–1914* (Durham, NC: Duke University Press, 1988). Analyses a number of topics related to the present study, including Scouting and invasion narratives.

Girouard, Mark, *The Return to Camelot: Chivalry and the English Gentleman* (New Haven, Conn.: Yale University Press, 1981). Lavishly illustrated account of the chivalric ideal in Victorian Britain. Includes chapters on Disraeli and the Young England coterie, and on Baden-Powell's Boy Scouts.

Haley, Bruce, *The Healthy Body and Victorian Culture* (Cambridge, Mass.: Harvard University Press, 1978). A highly readable and detailed account of the Victorians' developing interest in physical well-being, especially through public school philathleticism.

Koebner, Richard and Helmut Dan Schmidt, *Imperialism: The Story and Significance of a Political Word, 1840–1960* (Cambridge: Cambridge University Press, 1965). Provides a very helpful analysis of the genealogy of the concept of imperialism, particularly during the last quarter of the nineteenth century.

Parry, Benita, *Conrad and Imperialism: Ideological Boundaries and Visionary Frontiers* (London: Macmillan, 1983. One of the few studies to investigate how imperialist and aesthetic considerations are woven together in the work of a writer whose political affiliations are often strategically ignored by literary criticism. Examines six novels including *Heart of Darkness* and *Lord Jim*.

Porter, Bernard, *The Lion's Share: A Short History of British Imperialism 1850–1983*, second edition (London: Longman, 1984). The most accessible and detailed of the many introductory textbooks on this vast area of inquiry.

Richards, Jeffrey, (ed.) *Imperialism and Juvenile Literature*, (Manchester: Manchester University Press, 1989). Contains, among other things, essays on publishers of juvenile fiction, the Robinsonade, Ballantyne, and Henty.

Rose, Jacqueline, *The Case of Peter Pan or The Impossibility of Peter Pan or the Impossibility of Children's Fiction* (London: Macmillan, 1984). A significant work of cultural history on the political implications of what it means to write for children.

Said, Edward W., *Orientalism* (London: Routledge and Kegan Paul, 1978). A Foucauldian study of how the West produced knowledge of the East through practices such as philology, travel writing, and literary representation.

Street, Brian V., *The Savage in Literature: Representations of 'Primitive' Society in English Fiction 1858–1920* (London: Routledge and Kegan Paul, 1975). Examines the anthropological contexts shaping the assumptions of adventure fiction by Buchan, Burroughs, Haggard, and other popular writers.

# Index

Printed in Great Britain
by Amazon

16560546R00138